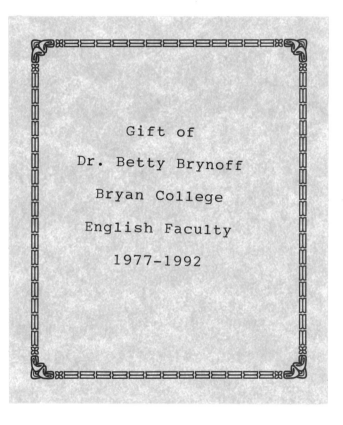

The Sea and Prisons

The Sea and Prisons

A Commentary on the
Life and Thought of Albert Camus

Roger Quilliot

Translated
by
Emmett Parker

The University of Alabama Press
University, Alabama

The original French edition of this book was extensively revised and augmented by the author for this, the first English language edition.

Table of Contents

Translator's Preface

I have long thought Roger Quilliot's *La Mer et les Prisons* to be one of the most perceptive of the many studies devoted to Albert Camus and his work. The original version of M. Quilliot's book appeared in France in 1956 and could not take into account the last phase of Camus's work: *La Chute* [The Fall], *Exil et le royaume* [Exile and the Kingdom], and *Actuelles III,* and certain of Camus's adaptations for the theater, such as *Les Possédés* [The Possessed], all of which appeared in 1955 or afterwards. In this revised and considerably enlarged version of *La Mer et les prisons,* prepared at the suggestion of the University of Alabama Press, M. Quilliot has amply filled this lacuna. Moreover, since writing the earlier version, M. Quilliot, as director of the two-volume *Pléiade* edition of Camus's works, has had access to a wealth of information concerning Camus's life and works—manuscripts, correspondence, previously unpublished material, etc.—to which he did not have access before, and which have provided him with the invaluable special insights that have been brought to bear in the revised study. I am very pleased to have had some role in making available to readers unacquainted with the French language this significant assessment of one of the most important writers of our time.

I have tried to remain as faithful to the French original as the inexact art of translation will permit. However, I have made a few technical changes: chapter titles from the various collections of essays have been set in quotation marks rather than in italics as in the French version, page references have been added for a number of citations from Camus's works, and a brief bibliographical listing has been provided as a convenience to the reader.

Since M. Quilliot used a great many brief citations to Camus's works for which page references often were not given, I have translated all of these myself. Thus, all such citations for which page references are given are from the French *Pléiade* editions: *Théâtre, récits, nouvelles* (Paris, 1963) and *Essais* (Paris, 1965); the only exception to this rule is quoted material from the *Carnets* [notebooks] that is not included in the *Pléiade* edition.

UNIVERSITY, ALABAMA   EMMETT PARKER

May, 1970

Biographical Chronology

The more significant dates in Camus's life are here listed in conjunction with the dates of certain political events and literary works in terms of which he had to define himself. By its very brevity such a portrait seeks to avoid any fictitious construction or interpretation of the facts.

1913

November 7: Albert Camus is born at Mondovi, Département of Constantine, Algeria. His father, Lucien Camus, a warehouse worker at a wine-making establishment, belongs to an Alsatian family that had settled in Algeria in 1871. (See the "Avant-Propos" to *Actuelles III.*) The mother, Catherine Sintès, is the second of nine children in a family of Majorcan origin. (Camus will name his daughter Catherine; Sintès is the surname of Meursault's friend Raymond in *L'Étranger.*)

1914

August 3: Imperial Germany declares war on France.

"I grew up, along with all the men of my age, to the sound of the drums of the first war, and our history since has not ceased to be one of murder, injustice, and violence" (*L'Été*).

Camus's father, mobilized in the First Zouaves, is wounded in the Battle of the Marne, dies in a hospital at Saint-Brieuc, and is buried there.

The mother moves to Algiers, where Camus grows up amid poverty in a two-room apartment in the lower-class Belcourt quarter (93, Rue de Lyon). He lives there with his mother, who works first in a cartridge factory and later as a housecleaner—almost deaf, she speaks very little (see "Entre Oui et Non" in *L'Envers et l'endroit*); his older brother, Lucien; his grandmother, Catherine Cardona (the same surname as Marie in *L'Etranger*), who is authoritarian and dramatic by nature (see "L'Ironie" in *L'Envers et l'endroit*); and a sickly uncle, Etienne, a cooper (evoked in *Les Muets*): "I did not learn about freedom in Marx. It is true: I learned about it in the midst of misery" (*Actuelles I*).

1918–1923

Louis Germain, a teacher at the *école communale* (primary school) in the Rue Aumerat, taking an interest in the child, has him do extra work outside class and enters him in the competition for secondary school scholarships. Many years later, Camus will dedicate the *Discours de Suède,* his Nobel Prize speeches, to M. Germain.

1923–1930

As a scholarship pupil at the Lycée Bugeaud, Camus is a day-boarder in the "Letters and Sciences" division.

1926

André Gide's *Les Faux-Monnayeurs* [The Counterfeiters], Henry de Montherlant's *Les Bestiaires,* and André Malraux's *La Tentation de l'occident* [The Temptation of the West] are published.

1928

Malraux's *Les Conquérants* [The Conquerors] is published.

1928–1930

Camus is goal keeper for the football team of the Racing-Universitaire d'Alger: "After all, it is for this that I so liked my team, for the joy of victories, so wonderful when associated with the fatigue which follows effort, but also for that stupid urge to weep in the evening after a defeat" (*Hedomadaire du R.U.A.*).

1929–1930

"I was sixteen years old when I encountered Gide for the first time. An uncle who had taken charge of a part of my education sometimes gave me books. A butcher with a large clientèle, his real passion was only for reading and ideas. He devoted his mornings to the meat business and the rest of the day to his library, to gazettes, and to interminable discussion in the *cafés* of his neighborhood.

"One day he handed me a little book with a parchment-paper cover, assuring me that 'this would interest' me. I read everything indiscriminately at that time; I must have opened *Les Nourritures terrestres* after having finished the *Lettres des femmes* or a volume of *Les Pardaillan.*

"To me those invocations seemed obscure. I faltered before the hymn to the riches of Nature. In Algiers, at sixteen, I was saturated with those riches; I wished for others, no doubt. And then 'Blida, little rose . . .'; I was well acquainted, alas! with Blida. I gave the book back to my uncle and told him that it had in fact interested me. Then I returned to the beaches, to distracted studies and leisurely reading, to the difficult life that mine was. The rendezvous had not come off" (*Hommage à Gide*).

The same uncle also has him read Anatole France.

1930

Malraux's *La Voie royale* [The Royal Way] is published.

In his "philosophy year" at the lycée, Camus is the pupil of Jean Grenier. (See Grenier, *Albert Camus* [Paris, 1968], Chapter I.)

At the first signs of his tuberculosis, Camus leaves the family apartment, which is unsuited for the kind of care he needs. He moves first to the "Boucherie Franco-Britannique," the home of his uncle, Gustave Acault, a man of Voltairian and anarchist tradition. Later, Camus will be hospitalized for a pneumothorax treatment (see "L'Hôpital du quartier pauvre"); and still later, after 1932, he will lead a very independent life, living successively in the four corners of Algiers, sometimes alone, sometimes in a communal arrangement.

1932

Camus pursues his studies in "Lettres Supérieures." His classmates include André Belamich (to whom he will later entrust the translation of García Lorca) and Claude de Fréminville. His professors are Paul Mathieu and Jean Grenier, the latter a philosopher and essayist with whom he will form a lasting friendship, and to whom he will dedicate both "La Mort dans l'âme" in *L'Envers et l'endroit* and *L'Homme révolté:*
". . . I was to meet Jean Grenier. He gave me, among other things, a book. It was a novel by André de Richaud entitled *La Douleur.* I do not know André de Richaud. But I have never forgotten this beautiful book, which was the first to speak to me of what I knew: a mother, poverty, beautiful evenings in the heavens . . . I read it in one night, according to the custom, and upon awakening, endowed with a strange and new freedom, I advanced, hesitating, upon an unknown land. I had just learned

that books poured forth something besides escape and pleasant distraction. My stubborn silences, those vague and sovereign sufferings, the extraordinary world, the nobility of these close to me, their misery, my secrets, in sum, all that could be put into words. . . . *La Douleur* permitted me to see into the world of creation into which Gide was to guide me further" (*Hommage à Gide*).

1931–1932

Camus frequents, among others, Miquel, a future architect; Bénisti, the future sculptor; Jean de Maisonseul; and Max-Pol Fouchet, a writer and critic.

1932

Camus publishes four articles in *Sud,* an Algerian periodical review.

1933

January 30: Adolf Hitler rises to power.

Camus will soon play a militant role in the anti-Fascist Amsterdam-Pleyel Movement founded by Henri Barbusse and Romain Rolland.

Malraux's *La Condition humaine* [Man's Fate] is published.

Camus reads Proust at Grenier's suggestion. (See "Roman et révolte" in *L'Homme révolté.*)

Grenier's *Les Îles* is published. This brief series of essays, which takes up the problems of existence in a simultaneously ironic and poetic mode and in a mood of grave skepticism, shows Grenier to have been one of Camus's philosophic masters—a debt that Camus will never fail to acknowledge. *Les Îles* will influence *L'Envers et l'endroit* and *Noces,* and in the 1950's Camus will write a preface for a new printing of the Grenier work.

1934

Camus marries Simone Hié; their union will end two years later.

Toward the end of the year, Camus joins the Communist Party and is entrusted with propaganda activities among the Moslem populations.*

* In a letter of June 8, 1955, Camus affirmed to the author that he had left the Communist Party in 1935 after Pierre Laval's trip to Moscow (May, 1935) brought about a reduction in the Party's pro-Moslem activities. It would seem that

1935

Malraux's *Le Temps du mépris* [The Time of Scorn] and Montherlant's *Service inutile* are published.

Camus voyages to Majorca (see "Amor de vivre" in *L'Envers et
l'endroit*): "For me, I know that my wellspring is in *L'Envers et l'endroit*,
in that world of poverty and light in which I long lived and whose
memory still preserves me from two opposing dangers that threaten
every artist, bitterness and self-satisfaction. . . . But about life itself, I
know nothing more of it than what is said, awkwardly, in *L'Envers et
l'endroit*."

During this entire period, 1930–1936, Camus is pursuing his
philosophy studies at the University of Algiers, financed in part by a
number of interest-free loans that were granted him. Even so, he has to
take on a certain number of jobs in order to make ends meet. During this
particular year, for example, he works regularly in the Meteorological
Service of the University and furnishes a report on the pressure systems
of the southern territories. At other times, he is a salesman of auto accessories, an employee in a maritime brokerage firm (like Meursault),
and an employee of the Algiers prefectural administration. (Grand, in
La Peste, will be a city administration employee.)

1936

Camus prepares for a "Diplôme d'Études Supérieures" in philosophy.
His thesis, *Métaphysique chrétienne et néoplatonisme*, deals with the relationships between Hellenism and Christianity as expressed in Plotinus
and Saint Augustine: "I felt I was Greek living in a Christian world."

His reading includes Epictetus, Pascal, Kierkegaard, Malraux, and
Gide.

Camus experienced an inner crisis at about this time, and a reading of the *Carnets*
confirms this surmise. In any case, Camus's friends are of the opinion that he
probably continued to hold his Party card through the year 1937. Indeed, his position as the head of the Maison de la Culture, which the Communist Party controlled, cannot be explained otherwise. In the view of Camus's friends, the break
—and Camus's exclusion—came about as a result of incidents between the Communist Party and Messali Hadj's Parti du Peuple Algérien, which maintained the
Communists were the instigators of repressions inflicted upon it.

Several articles have spoken of Camus's having become a Freemason. This
claim remains, up to the present time, wholly unsubstantiated.

March 7: Nazi Germany reoccupies the Rhineland.

May: The "Popular Front" is victorious in France.

June–July: Camus travels in Central Europe (see *Carnets I* and "La Mort dans l'âme"); his first marriage breaks up once and for all during the trip.

July 17: There is civil war in Spain.

In the course of the years 1935 and 1936, Camus takes charge, along with a few friends, of the Maison de la Culture and founds the Théâtre du Travail. It is for the latter that he writes, in collaboration with three comrades, *Révolte dans les Asturies;* the performance is banned, but the play appears under the imprint of an Algiers publisher, Charlot. Around Gabriel Audisio and Charlot there develops a Mediterranean literary movement with the motto "Les Vraies Richesses" [True Riches].

1936–1937

Camus is taken on as an actor by the theatrical troupe of Radio Algiers, with which he spends two weeks a month traveling about the cities and villages of Algeria.

1937

Camus becomes a journalist for *Alger-Républicain,* which is under the editorship of Pascal Pia (to whom Camus will dedicate *Le Mythe de Sisyphe*). He takes on, successively, a wide variety of editorial tasks, from editing the *fait-divers* column to editorial writing, from covering local meetings to writing literary reviews. He has a special interest in shedding light on major Algerian political trials. He is also known to sell advertising space for the paper, on occasion.

February: At the Maison de la Culture, Camus lectures on the "new Mediterranean culture."

May: With other Algerian intellectuals, Camus signs a manifesto favoring the Blum-Violette Project, which the group considers a "minimum" step toward correcting colonial Algeria's social ills.

For reasons of health, Camus is unable to present himself as a candidate for the Agrégation degree in philosophy.

May 10: *L'Envers et l'endroit* is published.

August–September: Camus projects an essay on Malraux. He stays for a time in Embrun, France, where he has gone for a mandatory rest, and then journeys to Florence, Italy (see "Le Désert" in *Noces*), passing through Marseilles, Genoa, and Pisa along the way.

This is a period of lucid and bitter exaltation, of which *Noces* will be the fruit. He prepares *La Mort heureuse,* a novel that will remain unpublished during his lifetime.

Camus turns down a position in the private secondary school of Sidi-Bel-Abbès; he fears the possibility of becoming bogged down in school routines.

October–December: His reading includes Sorel, Nietzsche, and Spengler (*The Decline of the West*).

The Théâtre du Travail disbands and is replaced by the Théâtre de l'Équipe.

Camus considers leaving Algiers for Metropolitan France.*

* From a letter to Gabriel Audisio.

1938

Malraux's *L'Espoir* [Man's Hope] and Sartre's *La Nausée* are published.

Even at this time, Camus, who admires Sartre's book very much, is nevertheless opposed to Sartre's esthetic, and he reproaches Sartre for insisting upon the ugliness of human life as a basis for the tragic nature of existence: "And M. Sartre's hero has not perhaps furnished the true meaning of his anguish when he insists on what repels him in man, instead of founding on certain of man's grandeurs reasons for despairing" (*Alger-Républicain,* October 20, 1938).

Camus writes *Caligula,* considers writing an essay on the Absurd, and gathers notes that he will use for *L'Étranger.* He reads Nietzsche's *Ecce Homo* and *The Twilight of the Gods,* and Kierkegaard's *Fear and Trembling* and *Sickness unto Death.*

September 30: the Munich agreements are concluded.

1939

March: Czechoslovakia is annexed by the Third Reich.

Camus is reading Epicurus and the Stoics.

A review, *Rivages,* is founded by Camus, Audisio, Emmanuel Roblès, and others.

Sartre's *Le Mur* appears: "A great writer always carries with him his world and his message. M. Sartre's message converts one to nothingness but also to lucidity" (*Alger-Républicain,* March 12, 1939).

Rachel Bespaloff's *Cheminements et carrefours* is published.

May: Charlot publishes Camus's *Noces.*

June: Camus reports on the Kabylian famine: "There is no more hopeless spectacle than this destitution in the midst of the most beautiful land in the world."

International tensions force Camus to abandon plans for travel in Greece: "The year of the war, I was to set sail in order to repeat Ulysses' voyage. At that period, even an impecunious young man could conceive the sumptuous project of crossing the sea to an encounter with the light." (*L'Été*).

September 3: World War II begins: "The first thing is not to despair. Let us not listen too much to those who cry out the end of the world" ("Les Amandiers" in *L'Été*). "Swear to achieve in the least noble of tasks only the most noble of acts" (*Carnets*).

Out of a sense of solidarity, Camus will attempt to enlist: "One must struggle to avoid war for his country. When it is there, he must be one with his country" (a reply to Carl Viggiani). He is turned down for reasons of health.

Camus visits Oran. (See "Le Minotaure" in *L'Été*.)

1940

Distribution problems having led to the conversion of *Alger-Républicain* into *Soir-Républicain* (at the end of a few weeks of coexistence, the former disappeared on October 28, 1939, while the latter had first appeared on September 15), the new paper's refusal to bend to demands of the censor leads to its demise on January 10. Under pressure from official quarters, Camus finds himself deprived of a promised job and soon he leaves Algeria, determined to write nothing for the controlled press. Thanks to a recommendation from Pascal Pia, he is able to go to work as a layout man for *Paris-Soir,* dealing only with the physical aspects of the paper's publication: "Feel at *Paris-Soir* the entire heart of Paris and her abject shopgirl's spirit" (*Carnets*). During this period he lives in a hotel on the Rue Ravignan.

May: *L'Étranger* is completed.

May 10: The Germans invade France. With the staff of *Paris-Soir,* Camus falls back to Clermont-Ferrand.

September: Camus works on the first part of *Le Mythe de Sisyphe.*

October: He takes up temporary residence in Lyons.

December 3: In Lyons, Camus marries Francine Faure, an Oranaise teacher of mathematics. In the course of the month he leaves the staff of *Paris-Soir.*

1941

January: Camus returns to Oran, where for a time he teaches "French Studies" in a private school attended by a number of Jewish children.

February: He completes *Le Mythe de Sisyphe.*

Under the influence of *Moby Dick,* he prepares *La Peste:* "One of the most overwhelming myths that has ever been imagined surrounding man's battle against evil and the irresistible logic which ends by raising up the just man first against creation and the creator, and then against his fellowman and himself" (article on Herman Melville in *Les Écrivains célèbres,* III [Paris, 1953]).

He reads Tolstoi, Marcus Aurelius, Vigny's *Grandeur et servitude militaires,* Sade, and Pierre de Larivey's *Les Esprits.* Thirteen years later, he will adapt *Les Esprits* for the Festival of Angers.

December 19: Gabriel Péri is executed: ". . . You ask me for what reason I placed myself on the side of the Resistance. That is a question without meaning for a certain number of men, of whom I am one. It seemed to me, and it still seems to me, that one cannot be on the side of concentration camps. I understood then that I detested violence less than the institutions of violence. And to be completely precise, I remember very well the day on which the wave of revolt within me reached its summit. It was a morning in Lyons, and I was reading in the newspaper of the execution of Gabriel Péri" (*Actuelles I*).*

---

* Camus was never talkative about his life as a member of the Resistance; he cared little for the "former combatant's" style—doubtless out of a sense of modesty and nostalgia. However, it seems that in 1943 he joined the "Combat" network of the Mouvement National de Libération, through the intermediary of

1942

Camus is again spitting up blood (Winter, 1941–1942) and is obliged to go for a rest at Chambon-sur-Lignon, where he stays from the end of the winter to the following autumn.

November 8: The Allied landing takes him by surprise just as he is about to return to North Africa; he turns back, then, and takes up residence at the home of Madame Oettly in Le Panlier, near Chambon. Because communications are difficult and he detests the train, he travels the sixty kilometers of hilly terrain from Saint-Étienne to Le Panelier by bicycle—despite his weak lungs. He will remain separated from his wife, who is in North Africa, until the Liberation.

It is at this period that he comes to know Francis Ponge (see the "Lettre sur le 'Parti Pris' ").

His reading includes Melville, DeFoe, Cervantes (see *La Peste*), Balzac, and Madame de la Fayette (see "L'Intelligence et l'échafaud"), Kierkegaard, and Spinoza.

July: *L'Étranger* is published.

1943

Le Mythe de Sisyphe is published. Some critics will see the work as lending support to the legend of Camus as a philosopher and voice of despair.

The first version of *Le Malentendu* and the first *Lettre à un ami allemand* completed.

For some months Camus divides his time between the Lyons and Saint-Étienne regions: "In my opinion, if hell existed, it would have to resemble these endless gray streets where everyone was dressed in black" (Preface to Leynaud's *Poésies postumes*. "French workingmen—the only people with whom I feel at ease, whom I desire to know and 'to live.' They are like me" (*Carnets*).

With the merger of the three Resistance movements (Franc-Tireur, Combat, and Libération), those involved in publishing the clandestine newssheet *Combat* move to Paris. Camus, at this time, becomes a reader

Pascal Pia and René Leynaud. (Camus dedicated the *Lettres à un ami allemand* to Leynaud, and wrote the preface to his *Poésies posthumes* [Paris, 1947].) Camus's role in the network was one of information-gathering and clandestine journalism. He was soon to make the acquaintance of Claude Bourdet.

for Gallimard and lives in André Gide's apartment in the Rue Vanneau.
He meets Aragon for the second time.

1944

Camus meets Sartre for the first time. "No, I am not an existentialist.
Both Sartre and I are always astonished to see our two names associated.
We even think of publishing one day a classified announcement in which
the two undersigned will affirm having nothing in common and will
refuse to be responsible for the debts they may respectively contract. For,
after all, it is a joke. Sartre and I published all our books, without exception, before knowing one another. When we met, it was to confirm
the differences between us. Sartre is an existentialist and the only book of
ideas that I have published, *Le Mythe de Sisyphe,* was directed against
the philosophers called existentialists" (November 15, 1945).

The second *Lettre à un ami allemand* is completed.

August 24: "Paris opens fire with all its ammunition in the August
night" (from the first openly distributed issue of *Combat*).

Camus, along with Pascal Pia, assumes the direction of *Combat.*
Among his associates are Georges Altschuler, Marcel Gimont, Albert
Ollivier, Roger Grenier, J. B. Vivet, and J. Lemarchand.

Le Malentendu is staged at the Théâtre des Mathurins, with Maria
Casarès and Marcel Herrand in the principal roles. The critical reception
is mixed.

1945

May 8: Camus, in the company of Gide in the Rue Vanneau, hears
that the war in Europe is at an end. He soon moves into the Rue Séguier
(see "Jonas").

May 16: There are massacres at Sétif, Algeria, and ensuing repressions by the colonial government. Camus will go to Algeria to see the
situation for himself and to set forth his conclusions in *Combat:* "A great
national policy for an impoverished nation can only be an exemplary
policy. I have only one thing to say in that regard: that France really
implant democracy in Arab countries . . . Democracy is a new idea in
Arab countries. For us, it would be worth a hundred armies and a thousand oil wells" (interview in *Servir,* December 20, 1945).

August 6 and 9: Atomic bombs are dropped on Hiroshima and

Nagasaki: "Mechanistic civilization has just attained its final degree of savagery. We are going to have to choose in the more-or-less near future between collective suicide and intelligent utilization of scientific conquests" (*Combat,* August 8, 1945).

September 5: Camus becomes the father of twins, Jean and Catherine.

A presentation of *Caligula* at the Théâtre Herbetot introduces Gérard Philipe to the public. The critic Robert Kemp sees the play, which enjoys a great success, as "a manual of those in despair."

Camus's essay "Remarque sur la révolte" is published in *Existence* (Paris, 1945). It will serve as the point of departure for *L'Homme révolté.*

1946

Early in the year, Camus goes to the United States, where he is received badly by the various "security agencies" and welcomed warmly by the youth of the universities. At Harvard, he lectures on the theatre; in New York, on the crisis of civilization ("The Human Crisis," the French text of which has disappeared). He completes *La Peste* with difficulty.

He discovers the works of Simone Weil, of which several will be published by Gallimard under his editorship.

Camus abandons the editorship of *Combat* for several months. A controversy with Mauriac in 1944–1945 has led him to question systematically his own views on the problem of violence: "We were in hell and we never got out of it! For six long years we have been trying to accommodate ourselves to it" (*L'Été*).

René Char's *Feuillets d'Hypnos* is published. Camus forms a deep friendship with Char.

October: Camus engages in political discussions with Sartre, Malraux, Koestler, and Sperber.

1947

A revolt breaks out in Madagascar and Camus energetically protests against its repression by the French: ". . . The fact is there, clear and truly hideous: we are doing in these cases what we reproached the Germans for doing" (*Combat*).

The Communist Party withdraws from the Government. The

Gaullist Rassemblement du Peuple Français is founded. Financial and political difficulties combine to break up the *Combat* team: Ollivier, Pia, and Raymond Aron support the R.P.F.; Jean Texier returns to the Socialist press; Camus resigns and turns over the editorship to Claude Bourdet; and Henri Smadja acquires ownership of the paper.

Sartre's Rassemblement Démocratique et Révolutionnaire is created. Camus, though sharing its general point of view, will never belong to the movement.

June: *La Peste* is an immediate success. A number of critics elaborate a legend of a virtuous Camus's "laic Sainthood."

August: He travels in Brittany in the company of Grenier. They visit Tréguier, with the novelist Louis Guilloux as their guide.

Summers of 1947 and 1948: Camus vacations in the Lourmarin area, where he had spent several days in 1946.

It is apparently in 1947 that Camus breaks with Merleau-Ponty, following a political discussion.

1948

February: Czech Communists stage a coup d'état in Prague.
Camus visits Algeria (see *L'Été*).
June: Yugoslavia is expelled from the Cominform.
Camus's reading includes Agrippa d'Aubigné, on whom he will write a kind of preface.

October 27: *L'État de siège,* a play written in collaboration with Jean-Louis Barrault, is staged unsuccessfully.

October: "Ni victimes ni bourreaux," first published in *Combat* in 1946, is reprinted in a periodical, *Caliban,* and gives rise to a polemical exchange between Camus and Emmanuel d'Astier de la Vigerie.

1949

March: Camus makes an appeal in behalf of some Greek Communists who have been condemned to death. He will make a similar appeal for other condemned men in December 1950.

June–August: He travels to South America. (See "La mer au plus près" in *L'Été* and "La Pierre qui pousse" in *L'Exil et le royaume.*) The trip aggravates Camus's already poor state of health, and for the next two years he will be barely able to continue work on *L'Homme révolté.*

Much of this period of semi-idleness will be devoted to reflection upon his work in general.

September: The Rajk and Kostov trials in Hungary and Bulgaria, respectively.

December 15: Camus leaves his bed to attend the première of *Les Justes,* with Serge Reggiani and Maria Casarès in the leading roles. The play is a critical success.

1950

Actuelles I is published.

Camus goes for a brief rest to Cabris, near Grasse, and then spends the summer in the Vosges mountains. Soon he will move into an apartment in Paris (29, Rue Madame).

1951

There is war in Korea.

October: *L'Homme révolté* is published, giving rise to a year of polemical controversy.

December: Camus testifies, by written deposition, in the trial of members of the Algerian nationalist movement (M.T.L.D.), at Blida, Algeria.

1952

He visits Algeria again. (See "Retour à Tipasa" in *L'Été.*)

August: He breaks with Sartre.

November: Camus presents himself as a candidate for the direction of the state-subsidized Théâtre Récamier. He resigns from UNESCO when Franco's Spain is admitted to membership.

He is at work on several projects: a novel, *Le Premier Homme; Nouvelles de l'exil et le royaume;* a play, *Don Juan;* and an adaptation of Dostoevski's *The Possessed.*

1953

June 7: There are riots in East Berlin: "When a worker somewhere in the world raises his bare fists in front of a tank and cries out that he is not a slave, what are we, then, if we remain indifferent?" (speech given in Paris in defense of the East Berlin workers).

Actuelles II is published.

June: Camus replaces Marcel Herrand, who has become ill, as director of the Festival of Angers. He stages his own adaptations of Calderon's *La Dévotion à la croix* and Larivey's *Les Esprits.*

1954

Camus writes nothing during the entire year, and except for his intervention in behalf of seven Tunisians who have been condemned to death he seems withdrawn from all political and literary activities: "My *Possédés* [his adaptation of *The Possessed*] has broken down, with all the rest, moreover; I do not know when I shall resume writing" (letter to Gillibert).

L'Été, a collection of texts dating from 1939 through 1953, is published.

November: He travels in Italy.

1955

March: Camus's adaptation of Dino Buzzati's *Uno caso clinico* (*Un cas intéressant*) is presented.

May: He travels in Greece, where he has planned to restage *L'État de siège* as an outdoor production. He delivers a lecture on the theatre.

June: Camus returns to journalism as a contributor to *L'Express,* giving particular attention to the Algerian problem.

A preface by Camus is included in a new printing of Grenier's *Les Îles.*

1956

Back in Algeria on January 23, Camus launches an appeal for a truce but is very rudely received by a number of his compatriots: "I have returned from Algeria quite in despair. What is happening confirms my conviction. For me, it is a personal misfortune. But one must hold on, not everything can be compromised" (letter to Gillibert).

February: Camus ceases to write for *L'Express* after riots in Algiers (February 6) sound the death-knell for his hopes. Later, he will intervene in favor of Jean de Maisonseul (May 28) and a number of other liberals and Algerian nationalists who have been put under arrest.

September 20: His *Requieum pour une nonne* (adapted from Faulkner), with Catherine Sellers, is a success.

Camus participates in a meeting protesting the brutal suppression of the revolt in Budapest.

La Chute is published.

Camus considers writing a sequel to *L'Été*, to be entitled *La Fête*.

1957

March: *L'Exil et le royaume* is published.

June: The Festival of Angers includes a performance of his adaptation of Lope de Vega's *Chevalier d'Olmédo*. Camus's "Réflexions sur la guillotine" appears in *Réflexions sur la peine capitale,* in collaboration with Arthur Koestler and Jean Bloch-Michel. *Caligula* is revived.

October 17: Camus is awarded the Nobel Prize. He is the ninth Frenchman, and the youngest, ever to receive it.

1958

Camus's health will be very poor throughout this year and the one following.

February: *Discours de Suède* is published.

March: *L'Envers et l'endroit* is republished with a new preface (prepared in 1954).

June: *Actuelles III: Chroniques algériennes* is published. It offers an analysis of the conflict and proposes some solutions. It is ignored by newspapers and academic journals alike.

June 9: He travels in Greece.

November: He buys a house in Lourmarin.

1959

January 30: *Les Possédés,* adapted from Dostoevski, is staged under Camus's personal direction. He envisages taking over the direction of a state theatre; Malraux offers him the Théâtre Français, but Camus prefers to do something new.

During most of the year Camus works a great deal but only with difficulty. By November, however, at Lourmarin, he seems to have regained his full capacities and is able to work with ease on a partial sketch of *Le Premier Homme.*

1960

January 4: Albert Camus is killed suddenly in an automobile accident at Villeblevin near Montereau, in a place known as "Le Grand Frossard," while riding in Michel Gallimard's car.

Abbreviations

The following abbreviations are used in parenthetical textual notes to refer to the various works:

A,I; A,II; A,III	*Actuelles I, II,* and *III*
CN,I; CN,II	*Carnets* [Notebooks]
EE	*L'Envers et l'endroit* [The Wrong Side and Right Side]
ER	*Exil et le royaume* [Exile and the Kingdom]
ET	*L'Étranger* [The Stranger]
HR	*L'Homme révolté* [The Rebel]
LA	*Lettres à un ami allemand* [Letters to a German Friend]
LP	*La Peste* [The Plague]
LC	*La Chute* [The Fall]
MS	*Le Mythe de Sisyphe* [The Myth of Sisyphus]
N	*Noces* [Nuptials]

PL,I; PL,II refer to the *Pléiade* volumes: *Théâtre, récits, nouvelles;* and *Essais,* respectively.

The Sea and Prisons

Introduction

"But in his obstinate search
only those can help the artist
who love him."—A. CAMUS

"You have been for us . . . the admirable conjunction of a person, an action, and a work . . . You summed up in yourself the conflicts of the age and you surpassed them through your ardor to live." These lines, which Jean-Paul Sartre, in 1952, wanted to ring out like a death knell, summarize still today "the Camus phenomenon." And Sartre's final homage to Camus, written in January 1960, bears out this fact: "This man in motion questioned us and was himself a question which sought its answer."

It was a torn epoch among all epochs into which Albert Camus was born in November 1913, on the threshold of World War I, on Algerian soil. A year later, his father died at Saint-Brieuc, leaving two "wards" to the nation. Camus was twenty when Nazism seized power in Germany. He was twenty-three when the sinister farce of the Moscow trials was played out and when Franco, on the other side of the Pyrenees, unleashed a civil war—Camus, who felt bound to Spain by way of his entire maternal line of forebears, was never to pardon him.

In 1944, Hitler, though dead, lived on. He survived in the Siberian work camps whose scandal Khruschev was to reveal to us twelve years later. International wars were followed by revolutions and colonial wars, the Sétif massacres in Algeria in 1945, the massacres in Madagascar in 1947: "The fact, clear and hideous, is there; we are in truth doing in these cases what we reproached Germany for doing." The cancer of the Indo-Chinese involvement was to gnaw at us for seven years running. In the meanwhile, there was coming into being a counterbalance, the atomic terror, the last degree of mechanistic barbarism.

This strife-torn age imposed action: social, political, and deliberately anticolonialist action in which Camus, the Algerian, the son of poor and needy working-class people, was to be involved by way of the Communist Party and anti-Fascist movements; journalistic action exercised successively in the Algerian dailies *Alger-Républicain* and *Soir-Républicain,* before reaching its peak—begun during the Resistance period—in *Combat* with editorials of rare nobility. Camus, for years, was to take a position at the outposts of peace. Resolutely opposed to the two great power blocs, a Don Quixote to the "world federalism" of Garry Davis, a speaker at numberless meetings for the defense of various freedoms, he welcomed refugees from the East, supported the Spanish Republicans, testified in court in favor of Algerian nationalists.

Everything seemed simple to him then—until the day when Algeria, in its turn, became the central concern. He fought for Moslem emancipation, brought widespread public attention to the propositions of Ferhat Abbas in 1945, supported Pierre Mendès-France in 1956, defended Algerian autonomy within a federal framework. Then came the time of armed combat, terrorism and military "sweeping" operations, torture and mutilations. When one suffers from "sickness for Algeria," what can one say that will not be either hollow or deadly. His death has left us uncertain as to what his reactions might have been at the hour of Algerian independence.

This passionate attachment to justice, as well as to peace and freedom, he doubtless owed as much to his hard daily struggle for existence as to his love of life. While he was pursuing his philosophy studies at the University of Algiers, he worked at numerous jobs in the way American students do: selling automobile accessories, working in the prefectural secretariat, and as a meteorologist, and in a shipbroker's office. As ardent to live with his body as with his mind, he combined, in the manner of the Ancients, the passion for sports with the passion for the theatre. The former goalkeeper for the Racing Universitaire d'Alger soccer team would later be a regular visitor to the grandstand of the Parc des Princes in Paris, and the actor of the Théâtre de l'Équipe in Algiers was to become the director of *Réquiem pour une nonne* and *Les Possédés*. Such activities could easily make us forget the sickness that gnawed at him from his seventeenth year on, the pain which slyly reappeared in 1941 and in 1948, and which explains many silences.

His work could not possibly be detached from so rich and varied an experience. Writing is a manner of being that gathers in and dissolves within it all others. Camus liked to say that he wrote only from experience; the limits of his imagination as well as his scorn for dialectical subtleties are well known. Nothing seemed to him more imperative than perfect accord between words and acts. And his costliest torment was to translate into words precisely what words could not but distort. In this sense, his entire work is nothing but an endlessly renewed struggle against the mystifications of language in the name of language itself.

Such a loftiness of view does not go without pride, pride as solitary as the work itself. Few books were more expectantly awaited, more closely watched than his. After the dazzling success of *L'Étranger,* people lay in wait for him, out of impatience to christen him or to roast him. I know, however, of scarcely any work as directly linear, as constant, as profoundly one as his. *L'Étranger* does not stand in contradiction to *La Peste* nor *Le Mythe de Sisyphe* to *L'Homme révolté.* From one to the other there is no leap from debauchery to virtue or from selfishness to charity. And *La Chute,* which disoriented the critics, clearly showed this. I see in his various works only a difference in lighting or in dominant elements, and often a wavering, interior to the man himself, as a result of the events that agitated his life or his world. Each book is only a phase of that patient description of the universe which Camus made the principle of his work and which he pursued with method and tenacity. A description that is, however, only a kind of stubborn, exemplary, and tragic tête-à-tête in which each of the world's faces reveals to us a new face of the man without there ever being a question either of another man or of another world.

Such a figure was bound to attract all those who mean to deny nothing of themselves or of their times and who consent to live in the midst of perpetual contradictions. In the days following the Liberation in 1944, literary renown—and the critics—seized upon this still new name. After *La Peste,* and the Prix des Critiques which it was awarded, came renown. Then it was by the hundreds that one soon counted the studies that weekly and daily periodicals in every language devoted to him; articles in journals and reviews numbered in the dozens. Already, he was assuming a place in the small gallery of internationally known contemporary writers.

Until about 1954, however, no overall study of Camus had been published, if one excepts the limpid work of Robert de Luppé. Such an undertaking, it is true, ran into the obstacle of our ignorance of the most important events of his life and of the genesis of his work. With *Caligula* alone how many errors of judgment might have been avoided if people had known the date of its conception! They might have been more careful of discerning in it the influence of Sartre, whom Camus had not yet read at that time, or of seeing in it the flowering of a dramatic talent of which *Le Malentendu* might just as well have been the first manifestation.

For a long time, *L'Étranger* constituted the limit beyond which criticism scarcely ventured, *Noces* and the hard to find *L'Envers et l'endroit*—which had been published in a limited edition in Algiers in 1937—being cited only as secondary evidence. Today the entire work, plunging its roots into the period between the two wars, is being gradually reunited with its past. And we know from experience that if initial works often sin against form, they are only the more important for their content.

For too long a time, partial and spotty studies of his work falsified our perspectives. It is not a matter of indifference, in fact, that the author of *Noces* should also be, within the space of less than one year, the author of an impassioned newspaper commentary on the famine-stricken Kabylia and its suffering; that *Le Malentendu* should have come forth at the time when the first *Lettre à un ami allemand* was being elaborated; that, finally, *L'Été* and the second volume of *Actuelles* are co-related in the same way as poetry and logical affirmation. It was a risky business, in the early stage at least, to set apart the dramatist from the man of action and the journalist from the poet and novelist.

Such was my concern in 1954, when Camus, having become aware of a study of mine on the sense of the Absurd, proposed that I expand the chapters devoted to him into a comprehensive study of his work. Already, in 1948, he had very kindly taken an interest in an article I had written that attempted to analyze the controversy surrounding "Ni victimes ni bourreaux" which had opposed him to Emanuel d'Astier de la Vigerie. A few years later, following the appearance of *L'Homme révolté,* I sent him the draft of a since published work in which I evoked the figure of Saint-Just in terms similar to his. He was good enough to take an interest in that work; and from that time on we kept up regular relations, in which the already celebrated author generously accepted as an equal the beginning essayist.

In 1954, he was in the valley of despair. Fragile health, family and personal difficulties, a crisis of confidence after so many broken friendships (Merleau-Ponty, then Sartre . . .), everything pointed toward a taking stock of himself and his position. Where did he come from? He tried to rediscover his past in his preface to *L'Envers et l'endroit.* Where had he arrived? He had the feeling of having reached a final point with the second cycle of his quest: after the Absurd, revolt. He kindly placed at my disposal his notebooks (*Les Carnets*), unpublished at that time— and I can attest to the fact that nothing in them was held back—answered my questions, reacted to my manuscript. He found my judgment of *Le Malentendu* and *L'État de siège* severe, but attempted in no way whatsoever to alter it. Better still, in subsequent editions of *Le Malentendu* he took into account certain of my criticisms. For nearly two years I had the pleasure of meeting regularly with him and of questioning him. His only restriction was the wish that my study treat only the finished work and say nothing about the future; thereby, he mischievously abandoned me to the risks of prognostication.

In the years that followed I saw him now and then. The theatre had reclaimed him; he spoke freely of his hopes and of his torment at no longer being able to create. Algeria especially caused him anguish, as did the twists and turns of French political life, which he despaired of ever seeing set straight. He remained discreet on the subject of the Nobel Prize, which overwhelmed him. Some cried academicism, others buried him beneath bouquets. He suffered in consequence, uncertain about his literary future. He seemed to have regained his stride with *Le Premier Homme,* which he had just barely begun when tragedy struck . . .

The esteem that he bore for my works merited for me the responsibility of editing his work for the *Pléiade* edition. This was a difficult undertaking, but one rich in discoveries. It was necessary to review a biography falsified by lapses in memory. The reading of manuscripts, and access to certain bodies of correspondence (with Francis Ponge, Guy Dumur, and René Char, especially) modified many perspectives. In the process of conversations with so many friends and acquaintances, I was able to add nuances to the image I had of the man no longer among us. I found him more vulnerable than I had imagined, and also more cyclical: obstinately generous, determinedly committed to his age, hungry for life as well as inclined toward asceticism. A player, a comedian, a Don Juan, capable of wild gaiety, and impassioned all at the same time, hiding in the deepest part of himself his old dream of unity. He was ironic but tender, and brutal sometimes. Quick to form bonds, he was also quick to break away from them.

The work has made its way. *La Peste, L'Étranger* have been printed in a total of millions of copies in most of the countries of the world (the U.S.S.R. excepted). His plays have been revived with unequal success. Scholarly criticism has taken the texts and is submitting them to an attentive examination which the distance of time and ever broader information is rendering more serene and more effective.

Earlier, my only objective was to help the author to take stock before new departures. At that time, all the bets were not yet down. Today his last word has been said and his work is living its own life. Perhaps after a number of years in which, to the general surprise, it has remained at the height of its reputation, his work will come upon one of those periods of purgatory that do not spare even the greatest. This amounts to saying that all commentary is of a provisional order. Has there ever been a body of work which, if it did not die, ceased to be ambivalent?

Let the critics persuade themselves, in the name of thematic, structural, or some other unity, that the work is most often only a once-removed mime of reality. Happy event, only too happy, if from the evocation of a universe, its colors and its characters, a meaning arises which the author in question might have admitted and which can touch from year to year his new and "sufficient readership."

It was still necessary to reconcile the indifference necessary for lucidity and the sympathy indispensable for any kind of comprehension. It is this I have striven to achieve over the past fifteen years, with the clear knowledge of having only too rarely succeeded. If I had had the patience of Sisyphus, I would have pushed my rock upward a hundred times over. But along with patience, Sisyphus teaches us modesty . . .

Paris, France   Roger Quilliot
October, 1969

1

The Universe of Poverty

"These eyes are wells
filled with a million tears."
—BAUDELAIRE (*Little Old
Women*)

Albert Camus contested in a friendly way the admiring interest that the critic Brice Parain expressed in his first work. It is true that its style is disparate and sometimes awkward. However, *L'Envers et l'endroit* seems to me to be without any doubt the most directly moving book Camus wrote.

In saying this, I do not mean to yield in any way to that "first work" kind of snobbery which, as if dealing with old stones, automatically accords unpublished and little-known writings a luster granted stingily to recognized masterpieces. It is true, however, that a given sketch by Rubens or Holbein is infinitely richer in movement and life than the finished work it foreshadows. But in the present case it is less the hesitations or the spontaneity of movement that touch us than the revelation of an adolescence lived in a world of poverty.

There are few works in which Camus so reveals himself and in which he was so led to confide directly in the reader. The introduction to Louis Guilloux's *La Maison du peuple*, like the preface to the 1954 edition of *L'Envers et l'endroit*, curiously returns to that past, as one tends to go back to one's own origins: "If despite so many efforts to construct a mode of expression and to give life to myths, I do not succeed one day in rewriting *L'Envers et l'endroit*, I shall never have succeeded at anything; there is my obscurely felt conviction." Such was undoubtedly his objective in *Le Premier Homme*, the unfinished novel on which he was working when he died.

Camus, according to Carl Viggiani,[1] retained from his childhood the memory of only two books: Roland Dorgelès' novel of the 1914–18 war, *Les Croix de bois,* and *Les Enfants de la mer.* "To the sea! To the sea!" Camus was later to have the chorus of *L'État de siège* [The State of Siege] utter this cry that he thought he had found in *Les Enfants de la mer. Les Croix de bois,* through the voice of the first of Camus's spiritual fathers,[2] his teacher Louis Germain, who read this book out loud, doubtless evoked for him the father he had not known, killed on the banks of the Marne in defense of a homeland he himself did not know. These two titles alone suggest a whole program. With them, we already have two myths: the purifying sea and the prisons of hatred and violence.

But Camus's literary vocation was not to come until later. Gide's *Les Nourritures terrestres,* read at the age of sixteen, was unable to turn him away from "the beaches, distracted studies, and idle reading." Jean Grenier gave him André de Richaud's *La Douleur*[3] to read. In it Camus found that everything could be said: poverty, the beauty of evening times, a mother. *"La Douleur* opened to me the world of creation into which Gide was to lead me."

Camus had made his first literary attempt in the high school review of his classmate George Didier.[4] Entitled *Le Monde vu de ma chambre* [The World Seen From My Room], it celebrated the glory of aviators.[5] His first real attempts date from 1932. His comrade Robert Pfister had founded a little review, *Sud.* One after another Camus published in it *Un Nouveau Verlaine* [A New Verlaine], *Un Essai sur la musique* [An Essay on Music], reworked from a philosophy theme, *La Philosophie du siècle* [The Philosophy of the Century], a consideration of Bergson, whom Jean Grenier was studying at the time, and a study of *Jehan Rictus, le poète de la misère* [Jehan Rictus, The Poet of Poverty[6]].

---

[1] Professor Carl Viggiani interviewed Camus in the process of preparing an as yet unpublished biography [trans. note].

[2] Jean Grenier was to be the second of these substitute fathers.

[3] Paris: Grasset, 1931.

[4] Didier became a priest and died in an auto accident in 1957.

[5] Already the taste for high altitudes, Clamence might say.

[6] Jehan Rictus, pseudonym of Gabriel Randon de St.-Amand (1867–1938), a lyric poet, novelist and dramatist. He was best known for his often brutal depictions of poverty, written in the argot of the poor. His poetic works are

These are the first weapons of truth, in which Camus's true worth does not yet show through. In any case, these sketches are indicative of his philosophical preoccupations—a philosophy that serves as a religion of the irrational; his conception of art—expression of the soul; a certain Hellenism; and his revolt in reaction to suffering and life. Closed up within himself by illness (see biographical sketch, p. xi), Camus dreamed, like Rictus, of giving form to "that thirst for tenderness which seizes man in the midst of his misfortune." Already he questioned the meaning of life: "I don't know why I'm on earth," Rictus had said, and Camus commented: "He wants to be happy. He wants it with all his strength. He wants to live, even if it were to be the life of a beast."

Art, then, he expected to be "the key opening the doors of the world, inaccessible by other means, where everything will be beautiful and perfect." Philosophy, he dreamed, might teach the truth, might provide "the answer" to "the question."

It is odd to note how much this young man, indifferent to Christianity, having only a mythological notion of gods or God, speaks so easily of fervor and of faith. In a series of poetic meditations in prose (*Intuitions, Souhait, Retour sur moi-même, Délires*), influenced by Rimbaud, Nietzsche, or Gide, are found simultaneously an ardent love of life and a fear of loving life too much, the desire for truth and the conviction that all inquiry is vain, the obsession with the meaning of existence and indifference, the dream of being God and the will to remain man. We sense an adolescent, his élan broken by illness, always ready to live instinctively at his own extreme limits, yet condemned to prudence. One feels that he is at one and the same time of this world and of elsewhere, royal and exiled, unique and ordinary, weary and fervid.

He maintained the same ambiguous relationship with people. He entered into marriage with Simone Hié, fascinated by this young woman's dazzling youth given over to the artificial paradise of narcotics. These two very young people were united by the same ardent love of play-acting,[7] by the same intuition of the ineluctable, by the same futile hope of being cured. Each was for the other a living example of the Absurd. Together they visited Palma, traveled across Czechoslovakia until their

---

collected under the titles: *Les Soliloques du pauvre* (1897), *Doléances* (1900), and *Cantilènes du malheur* (1902) [trans. note].

[7] See Max-Pol Fouchet, "Un jour je m'en souviens . . . ."

love found its death—a near victim of suicide—in the Prague Hotel of "La Mort dans l'âme" [Death in the Soul].

From this moment Camus discovered what the essay was to be for him: an intermediary between philosophy, conceived as the vital search for unity, and the tragic poetry born naturally out of that impossible quest. Already he divorced himself from all easy forms of literary expression as well as from mere realism. Writing could not be a game, nor a recording of appearances; it contests, makes claims, conquers, and reconciles in words that which cannot be conquered and reconciled in things.

"To give form to secret despair and love of life." These words, taken from a schoolboy's notebook, sound the tone of *L'Envers et l'endroit*. Camus was twenty at this time. We think of him given over entirely to the pleasure of living, still drunk with excitement from the athletic struggles enjoined under the colors of the *Racing Universitaire d'Alger*. We know that he was passionately devoted to the theatre, and was preparing a solid thesis in philosophy for the *Diplôme d'Études Superieures* in which Hellenism and Christianity confront each other through the severe countenances of Plotinus and Saint Augustine. He had not yet reached the stage of great hope for social renewal raised by the nascent Popular Front, which did not yet attract him. All this is true. And yet, at the end of a friendly meal, the time having come to leave for an evening at the movies and to let himself be carried away by the interplay of images, it took no more than a sickly, illiterate, and credulous little old woman to arouse in him a strange malaise. Later, at Palma, where he watched a buxom dancer with Dionysian hips in a modest cabaret whose entranced spectators cried out their love of life, it was "the ignoble and exalting image of life" that he discovered in the empty stare of the dance-hall idol.

"In the midst of ladies and amusements, this or that one thought me occupied at chewing over all to myself some jealousy or the uncertainty of some aspiration, while in fact I was thinking to myself of I know not whom, taken by surprise in the preceding days by a fever, and of his end, upon leaving a similar festivity, his head full of idleness, love, and happy times, and that the same fate dogged my own footsteps."[8] Singer of life, Montaigne was also a singer of death. The man who proclaimed "all is

[8] Montaigne, *Essais*, I (Paris: Garnier, 1948), 88–89.

good," the nonchalant and subtle pleasure lover, in his youth already hid within himself the torment of growing old. Endowed like him for a life of the senses and for fulfillment, Camus, with the aid of his illness, very soon discovered that "there is no love of life without despair of life" (*EE*, p. 44).

For years on end, childhood and old age go hand in hand, sharing the same amusements. The one obsessed by the past, the other turned toward the future, they meet each other at the limits of existence, bartering a few tatters of knowledge against a few scraps of impatience to live. The time comes when the young go to seek their illusions elsewhere than in old peoples' tales. For the old, it is the time of solitude and silence. "L'Ironie" [Irony] gives us an admirable account of this drama of incomprehension. There is much that could be said about the psychological finesse of these accounts: the despair of the old woman who takes refuge in God the way she would in pouting; the maladroit, if not morbid, curiosity of the narrator for that being imprisoned in her own body, condemned to the closed room of her memories; the irritated pity she inspires in him; the grudge-filled fraternity that impels life, vigor, and freshness toward immobility, wrinkles, and deterioration; the ebb and flow of gratitude, hope, and despair in the eyes of the invalid; and, at the end, the silent pathos of the farewell which the adolescent, snatched away by life, throws, not without repugnance, to the old woman who will return, still living, to her tomb. All this is told us briefly, with a few gestures, and a few exchanged looks, always in the same even tone. At no instant do the lines of the sketch grow heavy and dark; the whole is drawn in the grey tint which, despite the African sunlight, forms the unity of this world of poverty.

The poverty of the setting—whether the café in Palma, the restaurant in Prague, rich only in sad prostitutes, the apartments into which the narrator leads us, the few rooms in the poor quarter of Algiers where Camus spent his childhood, between a grandmother, always an actress whether the circumstances be good or bad, and a strangely silent mother, —everything in this book breathes acridity, sweat, and sorrow. Chateaubriand, an aristocrat to his fingertips, took infinite care to mask, under the pretext of esthetics, his few months of squalor in England; Camus, on the other hand, gives poverty its full emphasis: no effort at display, no appeal to pity. Beyond this, if the work is worthy of pity, it is so less for its poverty than for its emptiness.

What matter the rusted balcony, the worn-out chairs, and all those nameless objects! What matter the plaster Saint Joseph and the lead Christ! Poverty is also in peoples' hearts and in their thoughts. Must one condemn these men and women who seem scarcely moved by the mute despair of their invalid mother and who unthinkingly abandon her to go to the movies? Must we blame these young people, too impatient to lend an ear to the ramblings of an old man who is a bit "touched in the head"? As if it were natural for adolescents to prefer memories to life! As if the others, at the end of a week's work, did not feel the imperious need to enjoy themselves! To each his own misery. Back-to-back solidarity in the midst of sudden misfortune is one thing. That, the poor understand. But there are subtle forms of compassion that are a luxury: good works are the affair of the bourgeoisie, moral comprehension the affair of intellectuals. Neither good works nor moral comprehension commits one to anything, and neither, in the final analysis, mitigates loneliness.

Doubtless if our old woman had known how to read . . . but she did not know how, so who was going to waste time distracting her? Intellectuals can cope with aging as long as they maintain a sound mind; politicians, as outmoded as they may become, retain reserves of influence; industrialists have money—they grow old amid respect and power. But all those whose sole wealth resides in their arms and legs have nothing left but the ruminations of the humble, once the body grows numb.

Or flight—the aimless flight of the aged, on certain evenings full of spleen and internal ramblings, into a misty past; or flight into the future, into faith. It was a poor religion that Camus knew among his acquaintances, entirely associated as it was with the fear of death. The young and adults in their prime had scarcely any belief: they lived, they had the present and the future: "I worshipped the sky, the sea and the night."[9] Undoubtedly the sick old woman had once thought likewise. Faith is the affair of the sick, of the old, of widows—something one would see to later. Then came the time of belief. As the rift that imperceptibly separates the quick and the aged grew deeper, she gave herself up to God. Camus was

[9] From Carl Viggiani's notes.

aware of all the derisive, as well as the moving, implications in such a faith. He discovered in it an admission of impotence, an ultimate attempt to save oneself from loneliness; the banal plaster Christ takes on a magic value. God, under the circumstances, is only the agonized consciousness of approaching death, the painful consciousness that finds simultaneously its solace and its stimulus in faith. "She did not want to leave the world of human beings" (*EE,* p. 17) but human beings were leaving her. If they were to make some gesture of consent, if only they were to hold out their hand, she would come back to them at once, setting aside her Saint Joseph and holding him in reserve for future moments of anguish.

It was in such an atmosphere of spiritual poverty that Camus discovered the fundamental nature of faith. He was aware of all its natural, human qualities. Thus he was never to have for religion that intellectual hatred or that spirit of bitter rivalry that haunts a man like Sartre. "What were Christ and Christianity for you at that period?" Viggiani asked. Camus replied, "Nothing. But there was no hostility." But at the same time he experienced a sort of physical repugnance for a belief that was more superstitious than religious, filled with anguish and linked to the ebb and flow of life. Inversely proportionate to the ardor of life, it compensated and consoled. In vain, he understood it; it irritated him and drew his pity. It was only a phase of human existence that followed sports and flirtations, that followed love. A person was a Christian out of impotence or impatience. One person consoles himself for the loss of existence and another for having to bear it. In any case, one's back was turned on the present. This is without doubt the meaning of the book's final apologue in which the woman spends her Sundays at the graveside.

Camus thus did not concern himself with the problem of God's existence; it is not a game for the poor. From his childhood and from his reading of Nietzsche he retained the memory of a religion of invalids, women, and the aged. Other examples were to prove to him that it might sometimes be other than a remedy for loneliness. Can faith help us to live this life of the flesh more fully? This was the only question that made any sense to Camus: "In this moment, all my kingdom is of this world" (*EE,* p. 49). Impoverished kingdom, dominated by the frail shadow of a mother! She was an ordinary woman, less blessed by nature than others; a woman who did "housework" all day long, and who returned in the evening, tired, to a spiritless home. She was a passive woman, molded over the years by an authoritarian mother. "Her life, her interests, her children, were limited to being there, their presence too natural to be felt" (*EE,* p. 25). That manner of absence, of thick transparency which is exactly the same as Meursault's strangeness, we find already in that strangely silent mother. And yet from that quasi-animal poverty of spirit emanated a love that was both primitive and sure.

"My mother doubtless showed us tenderness, but less, doubtless, than we expected. Later, I understood . . . In reality, she lived only for us."[10] The manuscript enlightens us concerning this dissonance: Camus wondered about the seeming indifference of his mother at the time of his illness: she simply was unable to think of him as mortal. "She doubted that anything would ever separate them . . . She did not think of it . . . It seemed that between these two beings existed this feeling that comprises all the profoundness of death. And not all the outward trappings of tenderness, of emotion and of the past that one too often takes for love . . . A feeling so powerful that no silence in the world could diminish it."[11] Rieux's mother is marked by the same silences, the same discreet, faint presence, so faint that she could easily be forgotten. She too understands without saying anything: what use, moreover, in saying more? What use to understand? At her side, in the sphere of her silence itself, Camus discovered—lived—this disconnected language that made *L'Étranger* a success and in which some have occasionally tried to see a sort of genial fraud. "She is thinking about nothing. Outside, the light, the noise: here the silence of the night. The child will grow up, will learn . . . His mother will always have her silences. He will grow up in the midst of pain. To be a man, that is what counts. The grandmother will die, then his mother, then he" (*EE,* p. 26). An entire existence, the chains of existence linked end-to-end, unreeling over this emptiness. When the mother and the son exchange a word, "it is to say something" (*EE,* p. 29). In any case, the content has no importance: the essential thing is to touch each other with their voices, to render to the monotonous silence its thickness and its value.

A cantankerous grandmother's nagging or the muteness of a resigned mother, this is the very language of poverty, that of Caldwell's Southern "poor whites," of Faulkner's blacks, that also of our miners

[10] From Viggiani's notes.
[11] From a manuscript fragment for "Entre oui et non" (*Essais,* p. 1215).

squatting beside the walls of their "company houses" in small silent groups (a few rare, brief words, "to say something") waiting for the next shift. There is no place for distinctions or for vulgarity. This is life at its flattest, limited to work, fatigue, sleep: "life was hard, my mother worn out."[12] Language here has taken on anew its true proportions: an instrument of necessary intercourse or the gratuitous murmur let slip out of tenderness.

"Fifteen thousand francs a month, and Tristan has nothing more to say to Iseult. Love, too is a luxury . . ."[13] Poverty and work diminish the distinction between the sexes; and femininity, this bauble so dear to the "Beautiful People," has no place here. Peasants and working-class women fast reach motherly middle age. Of women, then, Camus was for a long time to know only the humble maternal tenderness that obsessed him—as though he had the sense of having discovered it only to lose it—or lips tasting of salt and the fragile splendor of bodies in full bloom. Marie Cardona in *L'Étranger* is a beautiful girl, sufficiently simple to be taken in by the purple prose of confessional magazines. But, in the final analysis, for a girl of the people like her, love is not so complicated: desire, a dab of friendship, an indefinable tenderness. One day, Meursault will be cut down on the scaffold as Camus's father had fallen at the front; and Marie, returned to the claims of work and everyday living, will cease to suffer and will forget as Camus's mother had ended by forgetting. Amorous passion was only to appear much later in the fundamentally virile Camusian universe.

Undoubtedly it would have burst forth sooner if the flame of love that united him for a brief period to Simone Hié had not seemed to him like an unfortunate parenthesis. That soon degraded experience confirmed for Camus that love could not be other than maternal silence or the burning of desire. Don Juan was to surge forth from this failure, renouncing unity for quantity, committing himself to a quest without illusions. Fascinated for a moment by the romanesque passion that a daughter of the bourgeoisie offered him,[14] he let himself be reclaimed by the rhythm and emotional climate of Belcourt. When he evoked a youthful love in *La Peste,* it was a poor young girl, Grand's wife, that he would depict. After

[12] From Viggiani's notes.

[13] Preface to Louis Guilloux, *La Maison du peuple* (Paris, 1953).

[14] Simone Hié was the daughter of a physician [trans. note].

the dazzlement of love's beginnings, weariness had also carried her off: "a man who works, poverty, the slowly closed-off future, there is no place for passion in such a universe" (*LP*, p. 1284). And Jeanne went away, weary, dreaming of some kind of rebirth.

There are hardly any feelings that poverty does not temper with indifference. Camus was near enough to sickness so that all at once he was able to grasp all the depth of its suffering, but detached enough, finally, from a solitude that he knew it was impossible to break. In friendship, the young Camus would demand much of himself and of others. And yet . . . "I had a friend, a hairy guy, who used to go swimming with me in the harbor . . . at that period, my hairy friend had disappeared from my life. We were not angry with each other. Only, he now went to swim at Padovani . . . Then, the hairy guy and I had only promised to see each other again"[15]—and they never saw each other again. His own mother, he approached with some "tender and non-human quality" (*EE*, p. 23). As if in spite of his desire to enter into direct contact with other beings, there subsisted between him and them a sort of screen, "that profound indifference that is in me like a natural infirmity."[16] Doubtless he owed it as much to his maternal ancestry as to poverty itself. The Spain that haunted him is the Spain of *Nada*, of resignation to nothingness, as well as the Spain of *La Révolte dans les Asturies* [Rebellion in Asturia], the play written in 1936 for the Théâtre de l'Équipe.

The simplicity of affection similar to that of objects and of beings: the quasi-linear simplicity of days without continuity. In this poor quarter with its narrow streets, in that cramped banal apartment was enclosed "all the *absurd* simplicity of the world" (*EE*, p. 30). From the height of the rusted balcony where, staring vaguely, a strange mother dreamed, life responds to nothing. However, that absurdity is like a close relative. Between the author and the world, as between the author and his mother, there was established a sort of secret correspondence. After all, that poverty, that emptiness, that silence, did it not encompass his entire childhood? Here, imagination, the poetry of dreams would be forms of denial. Renunciation of the Absurd, in the form of suicide or faith, would

[15] *R.U.A.:* the monthly newsletter of the Racing Universitaire d'Alger (April 15, 1953).
[16] From an unpublished manuscript.

have an aura of betrayal. One does not abandon so many memories whose entire wealth is composed of poverty.

Complications were scarcely possible either, with the Algerian sky directly overhead. The sky at least could not be snatched from the humble: "one drank in it the pure night itself." This contrast between the splendor of evenings and the bareness of Belcourt is the "right side and the wrong side" of Albert Camus's work. Sunlight and poverty reciprocally valorize one another there. The sun shines all the more intensely in that the lives there are dull; but existence is all the more empty in that the sun scours it and underlines its vanity. Thus light was to be both profusion and aridity, a promise of life and a sign of death, lifegiving warmth and cruel fire, consoling caress of evening, and implacable violence of noontimes.

The noontimes of the poor, in the truthfulness of bodies finally stripped of deceitful trappings. Noontimes on the beach, where force and cunning triumph. Noontimes of love and naked beauty. The sky overturns! And there are the evenings of the poor, when the day dies in the equility of reconquered night, when desire, having reached its own limits, makes an effort to survive on the other side of sleep. Ugliness vanishes, the world closes in upon itself; at that moment each one in the night rejoins his solitude.

Poverty, solitude, death—as many solitudes and deaths as there are living—tomorrow like today "since doing one's duty and accepting to be a man, all that leads to being old"[17]—the sun, the sea, tenderness and desire, it takes all that to make a world. Can one make a choice against the immense crowd of the humble? The right side and the wrong side of the world? One must accept everything. Between yes and no, "I cannot resolve myself to choose."[18] With Camus, equilibrium lies at the very beginning.

"Between Yes and No," this could also be the fundamental principle of Camus's esthetic. If solidarity constitutes one of the truths of the poor, evasion is a dupery. One does not with impunity cut art off from everyday

[17] "L'Artiste en prison" [The Artist in Prison], Camus's preface to a French edition of *The Ballad of Reading Gaol*.

[18] "Barrès ou la querelle des héritiers," *La Lumière*, No. 674 (April 5, 1940), p. 5.

life and it is useless to oppose the unique character of the former to the banality of the latter. Camus sought to disregard Oscar Wilde's refinements[19] or the eminent estheticism of Barrès in *Le Jardin de Bérénice*.[20] The life of the humble, who out of necessity dispense with a certain facade, seemed to him purer in its very bareness.

His first concern was less to distinguish himself from the ordinary than to resituate himself in it. "I have to write the way I have to swim, because my body demands it."[21] To swim is to commune physically with the sea; but also, since swimming is not completely natural to us, it is to master the sea. Mingled with it in a kind of act of possession, the swimmer remains a stranger to it. That simultaneous familiarity and exile are the lot of the faithful artist. Camus could not then—and this was a physical impossibility as well—resolve himself to copy reality. A certain kind of realism, burdening the artist under the weight of his own milieu, would have been, in his eyes, a betrayal of mankind. His lucidity was dynamic, and in no way passive. It only reflected the image of the world and of beings in order to discover their profound truth. I could imagine very easily that, like the Baudelaire of *La Danse macabre,* Camus uncovers at a glance behind a beautiful girl's laughter the mask of her final years, or the grimace of the corpse. "The great problems are in the street." That propensity—which sometimes manifests itself as a kind of infirmity—for QUESTIONING appearances, the corrosive lucidity that singles out for attack a weakness of the flesh that time marks imperceptibly, gives his work its "ironic" character.[22]

Irony tracks down falsifications, whether the sophisticated lies denounced by Pirandello or the fundamental "trickeries" so dear to Pascal. It fixes us again before the image of our becoming. One need only think of Goya's "Old Women." Its image would be meaningless cruelty if "The Young Women" were not also before our eyes or, in short, if the first picture were not the punishment of the second. The rancor of the painter is transfigured into the evocation of a destiny. In the same way, Baudelaire, in his *Tableaux parisiens,* slaved so tenderly over his old men be-

[19] "L'Artiste en prison."

[20] The third novel (1891) in M. Barrès' (1862–1923) trilogy *Le Culte du moi* [The Cult of the Self]; See Camus's 1939 article on Barrès in *La Lumière.*

[21] *Carnets.*

[22] "All my work is ironic," *Carnets.*

cause he rediscovered in them his obsession with the degradation of the flesh and inevitable death.

The interest that Camus brought to old age is ALSO attention to death; in sum, it is ESSENTIALLY this. The first glance was directed toward the sick woman in a pure movement of mingled curiosity and generosity, of one man to another, if we may say so. If that had been the extent of it, the encounter would have remained without a literary future. But just as Don Juan with a glance undresses the object of his desire, the suddenly awakened inquietude like some distant memory discerns, in the very heart of the old woman, mankind's fundamental suffering.

From that point, the persona is effaced behind the situation. We must be careful here to avoid a misconception; we are far removed from existential situations deeply implanted in the historical moment. The old man in face of death, the adolescent in face of his own strangeness, the poor in face of the monotony of existence, represent so many eternal situations. Everything unfolds as though there finally existed a prototype —not of man and his universe—but of the human condition in its progression from the cradle to the grave. From this moment, one can foresee that the notion of human nature will, for Camus, take on a certain consistency in the discovery of the limits that time and flesh impose upon us.

To continue with this analysis, Albert Camus possessed both intuition and metaphysical curiosity. He departs from a concrete detail, from a little scene, a brief emotion, sometimes without apparent consequence, and this detail soon permits a more general reality to pierce through. A given notation relegates the stage props to the background or, more precisely, with a quick sounding of the depths, supplies us with its full meaning. Lost in Prague, projected out of his daily habits, tossed about in a state of pure existence through a voyage to a foreign land, Camus became for himself a summary of his own life. Near his gravely ill mother, fear and a sort of disgust liberated him from his habitual preoccupations. "Nothing any longer existed, studies or ambitions, preferences in food or favorite colors, nothing but the sickness and death into which he felt himself plunged" (*EE,* p. 27). Anguish and being out of his element led him to the surface of himself and "gave to each object its miraculous value . . . each image becomes a symbol (*EE,* p. 43). Truth appears in that flash which precedes habit rediscovered.

"There is not," Oscar Wilde wrote from the depth of his prison cell, "a single unhappy being shut up with me in this miserable place who has no symbolic relationship with life."[23] The art of prisons, whether they be material or moral, individual or collective, is an art of the symbol. Prisoner of a certain solitude, as he had been a prisoner of poverty and was to be tomorrow a prisoner of illness, Camus attempted to pluck from each of the images sent to him by the world a significance that transcended it; he demanded a key, even if it should open the door upon the void.

But there is hardly any idea more equivocal than that of the symbol. Vigny, who was deceived with regard to his own art, said of the imagination that "it gives body to ideas and creates for them living types and symbols that are the palpable form and proof of an abstract theory."[24] For Baudelaire, on the other hand, it was for the artist to clarify the confused words of nature and to acceed, as by magic, to the familiarity of symbols. Thus, at times the idea emerges from the image; at times, it covers itself with the image as with a cloak. The first essays in *L'Envers et l'endroit* derive from the first formula. By contrast, in the woman's graveside apologue that ends the work, the story is no longer any more than a framework over which the meditation is constructed. The lesson detaches itself from real life and only imparts a "proof" to it.

Gauguin, speaking of Puvis de Chavannes who, according to him, sought to impart life to an abstract idea by way of a plastic representation, called this process Greek.[25] It is true that Greek lucidity reduced the world to clear images. It used myth to explain as well as to teach. This was the only poetry that Plato would allow to ornament his metaphysics and his ethics. But the Greece of shadows also had its symbols in which Empedocles, for example, condensed the entire mystery of the world. These symbols speak less of discovery than of an uneasy searching, less of the truth than the disturbing resistance of things. Depending on whether Camus insists on the one or the other, he passes from the shadow to the light, from the Dionysian myth to the Socratic myth, and what the symbol loses in depth it gains in effectiveness. He balances thus between abstract demonstration in which the words become allegorical (he was to

[23] "L'Artiste en prison."
[24] *Journal d'un poète.*
[25] *Lettres de Gauguin,* pp. 293, 300.

take part willingly in surveys of the kind that ask: "What are your ten
favorite words?") and the obscure myth that takes root in the unseen,
the instinctive, and the ambiguous. In any case, irony that overemphasizes
details and conjures away the essential establishes between the author and
his book—and in the other direction, between both of them and the
reader—a kind of distance that subdues emotion and transfigures it to
resemble indifference. With *L'Envers et l'endroit,* an impossible search
for man begins: Camus closes his hand upon individual beings; but,
through the magic of his obsession and his incurable irony, he opens it
again to reveal existence. A sort of incessant back-and-forth movement is
established between the universe, objects, and beings and their meaning
—or lack of it—without anything ever being held for certain or definitively.

One can arbitrarily class writers in two groups: Those who, like
Voltaire, adapt easily to all genres and to all periods, using their intelligence as a sharp tool, reacting to events with tireless curiosity. For these
the passions are secondary and have hardly any past. Others, like Rousseau
—and Camus is among these—come to literary life with their own
admiration and mistrusts, bearing with them "two or three great and
simple images upon which their hearts had opened for the first time."[26]
All of Rousseau—and Diderot's shabby tale cannot belie an entire body
of work[27]—is already there in the first *Discours.* Camus was unable to say
everything that was potentially contained in *L'Envers et l'endroit,* but the
essential part of his work derived from it, following the logic of his heart.

Those of his characters who are most alive—I do not say the most
fully developed—the most alive and the most effective, come straight out

---

[26] From an unpublished preface written for *L'Envers et l'endroit.*

[27] Diderot, as Rousseau himself points out in his *Confessions,* counseled
Jean-Jacques concerning various aspects of both the style and content of the
Discours sur les sciences et les arts (1750). The two men quarreled in 1757,
after which Diderot supposedly claimed to have been responsible for Rousseau's
having taken the negative rather than the affirmative side of the proposition
proposed by the Académie de Dijon, which inspired the first *Discours,* and for
having contributed heavily to its composition. However, this information is based
primarily on various remarks made in their Memoirs by Marmontel and Morellet,
friends of Diderot. For a fuller discussion of this question, see: George R.
Havens, "Diderot and the Composition of Rousseau's First Discourse," *Romantic
Review,* XXX (December, 1939), pp. 369–381 [trans. note].

of these early pages. They are the little withered old men who, seated in the form of a tribunal, muttering a few prayers, judge Meursault's attitude during the wake preceding his mother's funeral. On the day of the burial we meet old Perez, so pathetic in his stubborn insistence on following the lonely hearse; further on, there is Salamano, bound to his dog by a hate-filled friendship, and in *La Peste* the old man who spits on cats and the old asthmatic Spaniard, a paragon of total indifference. Each of these has his own way of playing slyly with age and of pathetically surviving himself. I will confess that any particular lofty dialogue between Rieux and Tarrou tells me less about the Absurd and about love[28] than old Salamano and Rieux's mother. Rieux's mother, Meursault's and Jan's . . . strange source of irretrievable life, the dim hearthfire that broods beneath the ashes, the mother remains for Camus more than a memory; she is the unalterable sign of a destroyed childhood.

Without any other artifice than that "mania for nudity,"[29] with which he already reproached himself in 1937, or that dry humor he scattered throughout his reflections, Camus attempted to say by preterition how much death and pain frustrated within him the ambition to live. "Is it not admirable, Jean," he wrote to his friend Jean de Maisonseul, "that life should be so passionate and so painful a thing?" At that moment Camus decided to be a writer in order to express that tragic fragility. The letter continues: "I want to live for that, and this is what matters . . . The rest will be a race from myself to myself."

Stationed like islands on the edge of society, the workers' enclaves hold on to their children's hearts: solitude and fraternity, two unforgettable lessons. "Of life itself, I know no more than what is said in formless fashion in *L'Envers et l'endroit*."[30] That should suffice to prove that the sentiment of the Absurd is something other than a romantic neurosis or a case of Baudelairean spleen; something other, too, than the literary translation of a physical illness. Events or illness might have sometimes

[28] "There is more of true love in these awkward pages than all that I have written since." From an unpublished preface, written for *L'Envers et l'endroit*.

[29] Letter to Jean de Maisonseul (July 8, 1937).

[30] Preface to the 1954 edition of *L'Envers et l'endroit*. It should be noted that at a distance of seventeen years Camus retains the same point of view, the same modest tenderness with regard to this first work, the same reserve with regard to his creative possibilities.

sharpened the anguish and the appetite to love; nothing is less contestable. But it is significant that such a point of view upon the world—could there be one less literary in its basic principle?—should have been presented us by a child of the people, at the threshold of maturity, and under the sky of Algiers.

2

Moderation and Excess of the Flesh

"Our table groans under hawthorn flowers that remind us that the springtime we had dreamed of has no equal but in the death that frightens us."[1] These aspirations toward unity, which we have already discerned in the first writings of the young Camus as early as 1933, now veer toward pantheism: "Who am I to speak of all that, of all that absorbing mystery, who am I but he who believes? But it is not in what is behind the odors and the flowers that I believe; it is in the odors and the flowers. And that means in appearances . . ." After a time of full innocence, Camus took hold upon the earth, the sensual world, upon objects and beings, the present and appearances. Not that all the mystery had disappeared, but it seems that the tragic aspect of the world came to reside less in the silence of the heavens than in the frailty of odors and of loves.

Camus read Valéry: "In the seaside cemeteries there is only eternity . . . Light! Light! In it man accomplishes himself."[2]

For that work of art of which he dreamed, after the bareness of *L'Envers et l'endroit,* the Mediterranean and the Algerian landscape offered him their natural splendor. Already, from the Hydra's hill, he swooped down upon the sea. Separated from his wife, he came to live in the cooperative home La Maison Fichu, which looked out over the city of Algiers, its roadstead, its harbor, and from which, through the olive trees and the caroubiers, the distant mountains of Kabylia could be seen.

> I had some comrades,
> A house before the world

---

[1] Letter to Simone Hié: late 1933 or early 1934.
[2] *Poème sur la Mediterranée.*

Life is a wandering smile
Miracle of loving that which dies.[3]

Little by little—the preparation of his thesis being a contributing
factor—he discovered in Algeria, a Mediterranean land, the heart of a
new culture. "It is not the love of reasoning and of abstraction that we
advocate in the Mediterranean world, but its life—the *cours,* the cypresses,
the rosaries of red peppers—the landscapes upon which the sun bears
down!" The Mediterranean had formed the Christianity of a Saint Francis
of Assisi; it must now bring to light a human collectivism—"all that lives
is ours"—and cause a literature to burst forth (*PL, II,* p. 1321ff.).

There were several engaged in this task at that time. Among them
Max-Pol Fouchet and Claude de Fréminville, Camus's co-disciples:
Fouchet launched the literary review *Mithra,* to which Camus contrib-
uted "Le vent à Djemila"; Fréminville followed in the footsteps of the
Algiers publisher Charlot, bringing out *Les Editions Cafre* (for Camus-
Fréminville), under whose imprint five or six titles were published.
Other than students, there were also two professors from the University
of Algiers, Jacques Heurgon and Jean Hytier. All followed with interest
the efforts of Guibert and Bosco, who were publishing the *Cahiers de
Barbarie* and a review, *Agedal,* in Morocco; and those of Jules Roy and
Jean Amrouche, who collaborated on another review, *La Tunisie fran-
çaise.* Soon Emmanuel Roblès would appear. The two masters of thought
and style were consistently the poet Gabriel Audisio and Jean Grenier.

Most of these names are found on the editorial board of the review
Rivages, the "first fruit of a still unruly vitality." The "Presentation" of
Rivages, written by Camus, defines the geographical limits of "Mediterranean inspiration": "From Florence to Barcelona, from Marseilles to Algiers, an entire people, teeming and fraternal, gives us our lives' essential
lessons." Its spirit he borrowed from Xenophon's ten thousand who,
finally seeing the sea again, danced on the shore that dance "which
consecrates beauty and living poetry as the only truths of a human life."

The same names and the same spirit reappear in the critical articles
Camus contributed to *Alger-Républicain.* I will cite, from the bulk of
them, Hytier's *Gide,* Armand Brua's *Les Fables bônoises, Littérature*

---

[3] A "song" from *La Maison devant le monde:* late 1936 or early 1937. This
cooperative house was to be evoked at some length in *La Mort heureuse.*

nord-africain (contributions from Audisio, Berthaut, Robert), Armand Guibert's *Périple des îles tunisiennes* and *Oiseau privé,* A. Breugnot's "Coplas populares andalouses" and *Keboul,* and Ignazio Silone's *Bread and Wine.*[4] "Men for whose contentment the earth suffices must know how to pay for their joy with their lucidity and, fleeing the illusory happiness of angels, accept to love only that which must die."[5]

These lines devoted to Guibert's *Oiseau Privé,* two months after the publication of *Noces,* could be applied perfectly to this poetic essay elaborated during the course of the two preceding years. From his childhood, Camus had run upon the beaches of Algiers; he went frequently to Tipasa, with Simone Hié at first, with his comrades from the "Maison devant le monde" later on. He visited Florence and other parts of Italy in 1936 and 1937. With Marie Viton, the scene designer for the Théâtre de l'Équipe, he took an airplane trip to Djemila. Following the example of Jean Grenier, who had celebrated Oran, Tipasa, and Djemila in his works, he lent landscapes a quasi-philosophical significance. It was not only the title, *Noces,* that he took from his teacher: "The marriage feast indeed is ready . . . ; go therefore to the crossroads, and invite to the marriage feast whomever you shall find."[6] Louis Faucon has quite rightly pointed out Grenier's direct influence, as well as that of Nietzsche—"a day will break over you . . . in which man and nature will celebrate their nuptials"—of Montherlant (*Service inutile* and *Il y a encore des paradis*), or of Valéry ("Inspirations méditerranéennes," in *Variété,* Vol. III [1936]).

Hence that style, at once classical in form and vibrating with barely restrained passion, at the limits of poetry and meditation. *Noces* in fact is but a long cry of love, a poem of intoxication and of "the fury to love."[7] A poem rich in colors and sensations, borne by that prose, at once sensual, shimmering and yet as though disincarnated, due to the effort of mastery, which identifies in Camus the French Classical element as defined by Gide: "the work of art tells of the triumph of order and moderation over

---

[4] Camus was later to establish friendly relations with Silone.

[5] *Alger-Republicain* (July 15, 1939).

[6] Matthew 22:1–14; this passage was used by Grenier in "Sagesse de Lourmarin," *Les Cahiers du sud* (May, 1936). (One better understands the attraction exercised over Camus by Lourmarin, a region dear to Grenier as well as to Camus's close friend, the poet René Char.)

[7] Victor Hugo, *Mugistusque Boum.*

internal romanticism. The work is all the more beautiful, the more rebellious the form that is dominated."[8]

At the end of a period of disarray into which an accumulation of conjugal, political, and scholastic disappointments had plunged him, at Fiesole during the summer of 1937 to be precise, Camus felt himself "free at last" with regard to his past and what he had lost. "I was to stop there, to find, finally, the end of a frenetic and overworked year of life . . . Today is not like a halt between yes and no. But it is yes and it is no. *No and revolt* in face of everything that is not tears and sunlight. Yes to my life whose future promise I feel for the first time . . . It is as though I was beginning the game all over again . . . But with . . . that lucid fever that urges me on in face of my destiny" (*CN, I,* pp. 76–78). The conquest of a moral and material independence, the exercise of a writer's vocation, the methodical adoption of a vision of the world conferring upon the simplest of joys and landscapes an exemplary power of regeneration—abundance or penury, the ways are many that lead to fulfillment in the awareness of life's precariousness.

One is tempted, in dealing with a book of which at least half was written in such a feverish state, to evoke the term romanticism. Neither the external evidence nor the author's state of mind authorizes such an imposition. Chateaubriand analyzed the romantic *mal du siècle* attitude in these terms: "One is undeceived without having tasted pleasure: desires remain, and one no longer has any illusions. The imagination is rich, abundant, full of marvels; existence is paltry and disenchanted. One lives with a full heart in an empty world; and without having exhausted anything, one is disabused of everything."[9] The nostalgia for the *Ancien Régime,* the terrified admiration the aristocrats gave to the Revolution and especially to the Empire, in their eyes, emphasizes the banality of the era. The world lacked charm, prestige, and panache. Those young men detested prose.

Let us reverse the terms of that analysis. In Camus there is no nostalgia for a brilliant society, no complacency in dreaming. He devours the savory fruit of existence. The Romantics turned with disgust from the present; Camus clings to it with all his power of love. There, everything

---

[8] André Gide, *Incidences.*
[9] *Génie du Christianisme.*

was only dereliction and disenchantment; here, we grasp the earth with all our roots. But the flower must fade and the enchantment vanish.

All things considered, we are infinitely closer to the French sixteenth century than to the nineteenth. The Renaissance took up anew the hymn to life, life of the body and the mind, which swelled the breasts of the shepherds of the Hellades. Human happiness had recaptured the keys to the terrestrial city. But it was mingled with precipitousness if not immoderation. A kind of fever, inherited from the Christian centuries and from the fifteenth century's *danses macabres,* frustrated desires and heightened worldly pleasures through consciousness of their fragility. Never were love and death more closely coupled.

Rarely had France loved the sunlight and life so much as in 1936. She was mistaken to expect so much from them—indeed she had it pointed out to her. But could the threat do other than sharpen desire and add to the disarray? If we pressed hard upon life, it was because the end loomed near and we had not so short a memory . . . More than any other, Camus had reason to fear the bitter tomorrows and to protest with all his being.

The insurrection of the flesh against destiny has always been poetic material. Foreign to the spirit of carefully planned intrigue and diversion, the poetry of *Noces* is entirely spontaneous. In its determination to ignore them, it launches a passionate protest against history and time. There is something defiant in that exaltation of nature and sensuality to which contemporary artists have scarcely accustomed us.

Noces recounts Camus's wild love of the Algerian land, warm, heavy with light, drenched with colors and aromas: "pinkish bouganvilleas," pale red hibiscus, "tea roses thick as cream," long blue iris, without mentioning "the gray wool of absinthes." But more than nuances, there is the fermentation of the plant world, the tumult and interplay of light, the vehemence of odors and the piercing colors that he excels in capturing: "the heavens white . . . or gorged with light," "the cymbals of the sunlight," "the blood of the geraniums," strike us in the face. The yellow, the blue, the red, and the green, laid on in thick splotches without shading or blending, clash with one another. And the imperious and virile sea tirelessly looses upon us its "white hounds" (*N,* p. 57). On the other hand, sounds and outlines have an humble and familiar quality that reassures us by their contrast. "The muted sound of the three-holed flute, the trotting of goats, vague noises come from the sky" (*N*, p. 60) revive the gentleness of ancient pastorals. The massive Chenoua Mountain range, without grace but without pride, opposes to so much violence the patience of its friendly curves. The weary flesh takes root there. Content with the limits at last recaptured, the surfeited eyes caress the tranquil hills.

The romantic who flees seeks unknown lands, virgin forests, infinite spaces—escape from the familiar, in short. He loves exotic colors; he finds satisfaction also in the diaphanous haze which, through its transparency, reveals a corner of the sky. Camus's sensual universe, on the contrary, is limited, thick, and fleshly. It is like a ripe fruit in our hand. Here, there is no other transparency than that of multicolored beads of water in a ray of sunlight. Adventure is being sought after in the violence of the sensations, in intoxication rather than in enchantment. Camus approaches the sensual world with an insolent and naive gourmandism.

However, this appetite of the senses envelops an internal drama hinted at in the constant gravity of tone. Such application to sensual enjoyment, such a tension in the midst of play, reveals anguish. The young Camus stands aside from himself and follows his own revels with anxious attentiveness; he has for his own youth the avid and anxious watchfulness that the poet Ronsard had for the distant and beautiful Cassandre Salviati. Never is sensuality entirely unadulterated by an underlying concern with eternity. The storm is in the heart of desire.

"If I try to find my true self, it is at the very depths of that light. And if I try to understand and to savor that delicate flavor that reveals the secret of the world, it is myself that I find at the depth of the universe" (*CN*, p. 21). The landscape is a source of revelation. In contact with it, the most secret passions manifest themselves in their innocence. What Baudelaire asked of a woman's hair or of a cat,[10] Camus borrows from various landscapes. Each wonderment of the senses corresponds to an attitude toward existence. In Camus's eyes, Algerian sites appear "like personae that one describes to signify indirectly a point of view toward the world" (*N*, p. 59).

[10] See in *Les Fleurs du mal:* "La Chevelure" [Head of Hair], and three poems on the subject of cats: "Le Chat" (XXXIV), "Le Chat" (LI), and "Les Chats" (LXVI) [trans. note].

Among the very first, Rousseau had conferred a meaning upon the natural landscape. The mountain revealed purity to him, just as the sea and the plains professed the infinite for Chateaubriand. With them, however, meditation was a comment upon human feeling and reduced it to clear ideas. With Camus, as with Jean Grenier, meditation forms a tight roof over sensation and covers it, shingle by overlapping shingle; it envelopes the passion for life with a kind of tragic halo. Camus's entire technique is already there. To make human beings, life, the entire universe bear witness; to raise them to the dignity of the symbol—or rather, to choose a person, a place, an instant that represents one of life's summits; to abandon oneself to their rhythm, their logic; "to live Tipasa," to live Algeria, to live the Strange and reconstitute that exemplary experience without reserve and without provocation.

The lesson of Tipasa[11] is a lesson of love; the same as that provided us by the stultifying sun and by the sea, a fine animal devouring, with "sucking" desire, the farthest rocks "with the sound of a kiss." Scarcely had Camus approached the ruins than he changed from spectator to participant in the great universal love. Vertigo seized the pilgrim: "The absinthes pour out over the whole world a generous alcohol that makes the sky vacillate." It is for man to open himself without reservation to the passion for life and happiness. Passion indeed—and this is a key word for Albert Camus—since that carnal excess, this life-fever that will also animate both the Don Juan and the Conqueror of *Le Mythe de Sisyphe* are only an ardent replay of the "great licentiousness of nature and the sea."

Camus is not the only one to know the lessons of Algeria. He shares that knowledge with an entire people, a young and poor people who have as their entire "treasure only the warmth of the water and the brown bodies of women." A people without horizon, completely given up to the flesh—it, too, terrifyingly endowed for happiness and pleasure. It has often been said, the African has no sense of time, he is without a future, almost without a past. Has he not slowly but surely corroded away the empires built successively upon his soil? He is unaware of that sophisticated frustration of desire in which Gide took such pleasure, and tastes

[11] A small town west of Algiers, noted for its Roman ruins [trans. note].

only of an insolent and naive satiety like that of the Greeks.[12] Young men racing on the beaches of the Mediterranean are in touch with "the magnificent gestures of the athletes of Delos." Like the noontime sun, like nature at Tipasa, the Algerian does not "construct" his life; he "burns" it. Here, everything is munificence and carnal profusion.

An almost animal innocence: "I believe that virtue is a word without meaning in all Algeria." Neither moral code nor calculation of any kind. Nature has erased the polish of civilizations and "the ruins have turned back into stones." That pure spontaneity, that absence of constraints and rules that the Genevan Rousseau demanded of the forest of Montmorency or the lake of Bienne, Camus, free from all Calvinist reminiscence, expected from Mediterranean exuberance. However, the unimpeded freedom of Tipasa is not man's freedom, the murderous Nietzschean hubris of a Caligula. The kinship between human flesh and the world for a brief time delivered us from our humanity—but that deliverance takes the form of release subject forever to the natural order of the world, in harmony with its breathing and its sighs. At Tipasa, one escapes from oneself only to become whole and fulfilled in the glorious burst of a spring day.

Frustration of the senses, then, has its limits; and that natural licentiousness, its own morality. "The sun, this sea, my heart leaping with youth, my body with its salty taste and the immense setting in which tenderness and glory meet in the yellow and the blue; to capturing this, I must apply all my strength and all my resources. Everything here leaves me intact, I abandon nothing of myself, I don no mask whatsoever; for me it is enough to learn patiently the difficult knowledge of living which is worth more than all their worldly know-how." The conquest of the sensual world is man's first task, not his only one. For this, two virtues are necessary, patience and honesty: the latter frees us from conventions, lies, and false modesty; the former provokes the blossoming of the senses and transforms the vocation for happiness into a veritable revelation: "At Tipasa, I see is equivalent to I believe." A simple faith, but far from commonplace in its deep-seated paganism; unshakable faith in the resources of this world and in the power of the senses; a proud faith also, and full of a secret scorn for those who do not acknowledge "the duty to

----

[12] During this period (1937), Camus thought of writing an "Apology for Satiety."

be happy" and do not think of "having any better account of their lives than to slip through it and escape from it, than to pass by and avoid it."[13]

However, that joy, that ardor for life never ceases to be alien, as if everyone in that burning land were playing a role, as if it were not a question of an effort which, having carried us to the limits of solar communion, would be bound to leave us with the sense of our own insufficiency. At moments, men have the sensation "of having entered into a destiny created in advance, to which they have suddenly brought life and breath with their own hearts." But this destiny is not entirely theirs; they cannot model themselves upon it indefinitely. Joy recedes, as in the eventide of ecstasy, and solitude reappears. At Tipasa, the ruins hide in vain beneath the heliotrope; they remain no less ruins. "Even here I know that I shall never come closely enough into contact with the world."

After the day comes the night. The sun and the caressing sea will slip into the shadows and the gods of darkness will come forth: "and for all their being more somber, their ravaged faces were nonetheless born in the heart of the earth." For hatred, like sorrow and death, is human; as strange as happiness and the joy of living, but no more so.

This is the lesson of the so quickly fleeting Algiers twilight; the lesson of its exalted lives, burnt out at the age of twenty or thirty, then quietly sapped away by horror and boredom. It also is the lesson of Djemila.[14] Djemila, the Roman city, the dead city, the absurd city: "it is not a city where one stops and from which one goes on beyond; it leads nowhere and opens upon no countryside." It is the image itself of death with its ancient columns graven by the wind, gnawed through to the heart of the stone: "Like the pebble smoothed by the tides, I was polished, worn through to the soul . . . Soon, scattered to the four corners of the world, forgetful, forgotten by myself, I am this wind." Wind of strangeness, which detaches man from himself, fiber by fiber, and draws him into the implacable whirlwind of the world.

What Tipasa is to life, Djemila is to death. Yet, this is the same sunlight, these too are Roman ruins. But there they are conjured away, annexed by nature; here, they are stripped and naked. There, the sun

---

[13] Montaigne, *Essais.*

[14] A city in Algeria, east of Algiers, between Constantine and Sétif; also the site of Roman ruins [trans. note].

fecundates and sets ablaze;[15] here it desiccates and nothing escapes its pitiless clarity. The flowers will not grow again, the ruins can do nothing against the wind; each day, each hour here, will be just like all the others.

It would seem that at this point we might be on the traditional paths to meditation upon ruins; paths beaten by the Du Bellays, the Diderots, and the Chateaubriands. But humanist pride, patrician melancholy, the noble elevations of the self-pitying soul are out of place here. In the desert of stones, Camus, ill from tuberculosis, finds himself near to that "heavy, seamless sky" which, for him, respresented a destiny. The immobility of the ruins invited him to silence; the muted colors of the mountains, the desiccating funnel created by the wind, the barren beds of the ravines, impressed upon him a veritable presence of nothingness, in which he soon participated with all his force of indifference. Therefore, the words strike harshly against one another with the same clash as that of the sun and the stones—in order to evoke that "arid splendor."

Everything at Tipasa invited us to join in the pagan communion, and one could summon up Eleusis and the rites of Demeter. Everything at Djemila tastes of ashes and forces us to fall back upon contemplation. Here we are surrounded by an aureole of cold lucidity like Lazarus by a funereal halo. We are in the world, and yet we are not of the world—neither vegetable nor animal, but man—conscious of being mortal; separated from the world by the desiccating light of the mind and capable of approaching it only if we assume fully this glorious flaw.

But how to assume it when everything in us—precisely all that Tipasa exalted—rebels against the evidence! When, with Chénier's young captive,[16] the flesh rebels, and he who knows he is doomed repeats tirelessly: "I do not want to die yet!" Must we elude that fear, divert it into some myth? Camus rejected such a temptation with all his might. The pride born of his illness was too great for him not to accept destiny's challenge with a sort of painful rigidity. Face to face with death —and however much the flesh may rebel—he intended to avoid every

---

[15] "Too much exposure to sunlight," Camus wrote in an attempt to explain his illness. Like *La mort heureuse, L'Étranger* emphasizes this ambiguous quality of the sun, by turns beneficent and murderous.

[16] A reference to the subject of André Chénier's (1762–1794) poem, *La Jeune Captive,* a young woman sentenced to die on the guillotine during the Reign of Terror [trans. note].

illusion and, in order to accomplish this, to kill hope. With all his power of logic, he wanted to see in this nothing but a game, a diversion, worse, a form of dishonesty. He took, as his own, stoicism's bitter and haughty protest against evil.[17] Now, at the end of this confrontation with Djemila, he had only to recover the innocence which shone in the eyes of the ancients confronted by their destiny. "One day, calm will once more settle over this living heart: there is all my insight."

There is nothing then that does not encounter its limits. "There is no love that is not painful."[18] Tipasa, however, in imposing upon us a duty to live dangerously at the limits of desire, reiterated this for us. Pain and suffering also find their limits in acceptance of fatality and in the fascination of nothingness. In the movement that carried a now keen sensibility from vehement revolt to a sort of voluntary numbness, Camus frenetically exhausted his reserves of hope. "All my idols have feet of clay." There is something bitterly triumphant in the irrevocable condemnation of every absolute. Burning his vessels in order to attain the most complete destitution, Camus rediscovered, then, the lessons of poverty.

A shimmering modesty would thus be the Algerian land's ultimate teaching, if there did not remain a word for us to say about the soul. Camus discovered it at the intersection of the desire to live and the fear of death, at that precise point where deep insight detaches us from the one as from the other. This soul has nothing to do with consciousness of a sin, a conception toward which Camus appeared to be absolutely refractory— rather, he indicted it—no more than it has to do with the imprint of the creator on the creature. The soul is that flaw in the process of universal becoming, that bitter kinship between man and the world, that impossible desire to remake a homeland for oneself: "For those who are too tormented by their own being, the homeland is the one that denies them."

The negation of man is, in fact, what this implacable and indifferent sun is. Still more, negation is the torment of living that abides in man and lifts him to happiness—but a fragile, doomed happiness. "In the Algerian summer, I learn that one single thing is more tragic than suffering, and that is the life of a happy man." Hector's tender farewells to Andromache

[17] "Read Epictetus in the hospital. He helped me to hold on."
[18] Louis Aragon.

in the presence of the child Astyanax's laughter, the naive joy of Euryalus of the gleaming helmet:[19] without these manifestations of beauty, love, and risk, "it would be easy to live"[20] and to die.

The mind is nothing other than this consciousness of the tragedy of happiness, of its necessity and its impossibility all bound together. "The grandeur of man is great because he knows that he is miserable," Pascal said; and he added immediately: "All those miseries prove his grandeur." (Camus would have said, "splendor.") Thus Camus made an effort to keep alive his human suffering for the same reason he kept alive his sense of revolt; he meant to maintain a perpetual tension between the forces of life and the forces of death, as he did between "moderation" and "transcendance." The mind, then, is that little flame of life, totally aware of its fragility and which, however, does not resign itself—that fermentation that makes the present burst into bloom like the bud aspiring to become the ephemeral flower—and proclaims at the same time the profound originality of "perishable and generous" human love.

But Algeria speaks to us of the mind only by way of antithesis and implication. It is in Italy that we must seek out its history. To be sure, Italy contentedly arrays itself with a sensual and easy grace, that "of the pink laurels and blue evenings of the Ligurian coast." A lighthearted music which should introduce us to a singing deeper within us. And one of the first lessons we learn here is that much patience is necessary in order to accede to "higher illuminations," to that "living love" which Camus was henceforth to make his nourishment.

The mystical nature of this feverish vocabulary cannot deceive us. The only mysticism here is carnal; but in Italy, man more than nature is the grand master of life—and in the very first instance, it is the painter who is. The North Africans, all with their identical destinies—and to whom Camus felt he was a brother—contented themselves with passionately burning up their bodies. The painter eternalizes the body; he seizes in passing the most fugitive of living matter: a gesture, a movement, a smile. He restores it by the superposition of two inert materials, canvas

[19] Euryalus is one of Aeneas's companions; he and his comrade, Nisus, are killed by the Rutulians when Nisus attempts to rescue Euryalus who has been captured because he was weighted down by booty taken from warriors he had slain (*Aeneid*, Book IX) [trans. note].

[20] From a 1938 review of Sartre's *La Nausée;* reprinted in *Essais*, pp. 1417–19.

and color. Yet, from that silence more eloquent than any number of voices, rises "the black flame which, from Cimabue to Francesca, the Italian painters have raised up amid the Tuscan landscapes, like the lucid protest of man hurled upon an earth whose splendor and light speak to him, without ceasing, of a God who does not exist."

There, Camus found the moving reflection of his own preoccupations. Attentive to nothing but the life of the perishable body, painting is a school of gratuitousness. It neither prophesies nor offers from within it any reason to hope. Like the very life that it seeks to save from the body's debacle, it is an unjustifiable passion. Its purity is all the greater for the certainty of its failure. "I do not see what uselessness takes away from my revolt, but I see clearly what it adds to it." Painting, like revolt, flies to the aid of lost causes.

To paint is further to unite asceticism to enjoyment of pleasure. Must one not, in order to paint, contemplate objects and the world, impregnate oneself with them, and, in a certain manner, "enjoy them twice . . . for in our pleasures," as Montaigne liked to say, "moderation depends on the greater or lesser application we give to them."[21] Such application does not function, however, without method or mastery. And the art of painting evokes an art of living, with its rules, its constraints, and its joys.

This reflection on painting in which Camus is engaged is no more than an indirect reflection upon himself. In face of the certainty of death and its immediate threat, he hastily threw up barricades. The mad munificence of Tipasa is now behind him. There remain prudence, planning, and choice—so many words borrowed from the bourgeois economy that his rebellious youth could not accept. In order that it might not be said that his vehemence was forever dead, Camus systematized his planning, rendered prudence impassioned and, making of vice a virtue, in Nietzsche's fashion chose asceticism out of love of pleasure.

This is the same wager that he saw in the life of the monks of Fiesole. The perfumed and flowered courtyards responded to the austerity of the cells as the senses respond to the mind; and the death's head placed on each table finds its justification in the little watering can abandoned in a corner: "An extreme point of poverty always touches upon the luxury

[21] *Essais.*

and richness of the world." The austere world of the Fiesole monks
suggests a virtuous application less than a profound passion for life, that
of a Saint Augustine, of a Father de Foucauld,[22] to mention only two
examples. From these Christians of Africa and Italy, Camus borrowed
self-discipline and method. He consented to channeling whatever life
forces remained to him in order to increase their intensity; his prodigality
was from now on concentrated in order "to assure a greater life and not
another life."

Thus, love and revolt are reconciled. People often speak of a world
in proportion to man. On the shores of the Mediterranean there are, in
reality, men in proportion to the world and to their condition; men
capable of living in harmony "with the hymn of the entire earth" and of
accepting their limits "in the double awareness of their desire to endure
and their destiny of death." In face of the universe that denies them, they
draw out of that very negation a full "flowering of consent," the consent
of love, the consent of happiness, the consent of beauty. But these springs
can gush forth only for those who know never to be unfaithful to their
thirst.

I have dwelt so long on this little book the better to show that, at its
completion, the dawn of a certain wisdom was already rising for Camus
—that Greek wisdom on which *L'Homme révolté* closes. Happiness is at
the end of revolt and wealth at the very heart of avid lucidity.

With *L'Envers et l'endroit,* Camus had come to full awareness of his
solitude and the bonds that moored him fast to poverty. Still left were the
flowers, the sea, the sunlight, all the luxuriance of the Mediterranean. He
discovered its splendor at the same time as its fragility. The painless
malady that gnawed at him heightened carnal passion as the scope of the
sensible universe shrank. There was a new equilibrium to be conquered at
the heart of passion, through which he could compensate "the readiness
to flee with the readiness to seize."[23]

With *Noces,* a very young man tells us the story of a very old

---

[22] Father Charles Eugène de Foucauld (1858–1916), a French explorer,
became a missionary to the Sahara tribes, the Touaregs and the Hoggars, and was
assassinated by them [trans. note].

[23] Montaigne, *Essais.*

couple, the ceaselessly imperfect and ever renewed love story of man and nature. Nature marked by man where the flowers, the ruins, the monastic cloisters intermingle and harmonize; nature made for man, even in the desert of Djemila, for his amusement, his reveries, his fervor. The hillsides have lines that are reassuring; the sea's madness is spent in embraces. The sun alone strikes straight down. Dead cities, beaches, Florence, all these are so many monasteries cramped and shut in "between flowers and columns" (*CN, I,* p. 75), enclosed spaces where one collects oneself for new departures.

Strange ascesis in which paganism imparts religious accents to meditation! Without doubt, the tone has something ritualistic and ceremonial in its protestation, which evokes the grandiloquence of a Chateaubriand. But is not that equilibrium between "the evidence and lyricism" in which the sentence strains to hit its mark, the expression of a thought bound entirely by the limits of this earth—"no salvation outside the world"—and which attempts to contain within it, despite everything, two contradictory forces: the fervent desire to live and lucidity?

The Nazi concentration camps overflowed with victims, Czechoslovakia dismembered, war was approaching. Camus knew all that. But the world was beautiful! What appetite to live among ruins and secular masterpieces. *Noces* exalts the perishable goods of this world: "sea, sunlight, and women in the light," in face of the doctrinaire abstraction that tears the world apart. A certain entirely natural barbarism counters the calculated violence of the powerful, a spontaneous vehemence opposes cold oppression. Camus suspected that this barbarism might be "excessive in its lyricism,"[24] that it sometimes lacked that irony that bathed *L'Envers et l'endroit.* From the hillsides of San Miniato, casting a last look upon the city of the Medici, "where men nevertheless die," Camus could at least proclaim man's strangeness and kinship to the world, his wealth and his misery. "Florence! one of the only places in Europe where I have understood that at the heart of my revolt a consent lay sleeping" (*N,* p. 88).

[24] "Presentation," *Rivages* (December, 1938); reprinted in *Essais,* pp. 1329–31.

3

The Fall of an Angel

> "If you loved life, you would
> see unleashed that monster
> or that angel you carry
> within yourself."—*Carnets*

Caligula[1] follows upon *Noces* as the intellect follows upon the flesh and the will for power upon enjoyment of pleasure. For conquest of the body comes first, and after it that of the mind.

Already in *L'Envers et l'endroit,* however, old men in the night and youths in the sunlight figured as so many tragic personae. Later the instinctive protest of *Noces* initiated, amid ruins, the insurrection against Destiny. Let the artist draw a black circle around the banality of things; let him concentrate in a few pure countenances everyday life's scattered meaninglessness; let him involve them, finally, loaded with an explosive passion for living, in a sustained and succinct adventure, and as naturally as night follows day, we open the door upon tragedy.

"I still have to answer you concerning the theatre," Albert Camus wrote to an Italian correspondent. "I know that this portion of my activity is considered minor and regrettable. This is not my opinion. I express myself there as much as anywhere else. But perhaps I am not a good judge of myself . . ."

[1] It was essential to treat *Caligula* before *L'Étranger* and *La Mort heureuse.* All these works—including *Noces*—were elaborated at the same period. To be sure, the first notes concerning *La Mort heureuse* are anterior to those that foreshadow *Caligula* (January 1937), but the manuscript of *Caligula* itself predates that of *L'Étranger,* as is indicated by the Madison manuscript in the possession of Christiane Galindo.

Critics may well regret that the Algerian review *Rivages* was unable to devote a special number to the theatre in 1940 as planned and that an essay on tragedy, conceived as early as 1941, never went beyond the initial stage. At least, we have at our disposal today a lecture on the future of tragedy and an "outline" for a television presentation in which Camus explained his preferences at length.

It is incontestable that the stage was for him a place of predilection. "Why do I work in the theatre? Well, I have often wondered . . . quite simply because a stage is one of the places in the world where I am happy." Loyalty? Excitement? The theatre was the monastery at whose portals external agitation died. Camus could give free reign to the instinct for acting that he celebrates in *La Mort heureuse* and *Le Mythe de Sisyphe,* and that he actually incarnates in Caligula and in Jan of *Le Malentendu.* He was an actor in daily life; his associates on the editorial board at Gallimard report that there was scarcely a meeting in which he did not enliven the group with a comical routine. His friends know how much he loved to act out a scene, read aloud a text, in short, to act. There was no platform on which he was not at ease.[2] He gladly replaced an ailing performer at a moment's notice. He expressed his fascination with actors in *Le Mythe de Sisyphe* equally as well as in a series of short articles devoted to the theatrical figures Madeleine Renaud, Copeau, Béatrix Dussane, Hébertot, Marcel Herrand, Marcel Marceau, Guy Saurès and Claude Santelli. "It seems to me that I could have been an actor and have supported myself in that profession."

In the theatre he rediscovered " 'the community' . . . the concrete responsibilities and the limitations every man and every spirit needs." It was this very feeling that had led him in 1936, as a substitute for the soccer team he had had to abandon, to found the Théâtre du Travail within the framework of his other collective activities. The name is a program in itself; it was a matter of founding a popular, revolutionary theatre: "To take cognizance of the artistic value inherent in all mass literature and demonstrate that art can come down from its ivory tower, the sense of beauty being inseparable from a certain sense of humanity" (*PL, I,* p. 1688). The theatre began by playing—out of anti-Nazi senti-

[2] "I used to think," Jean Grenier writes, "that with his gifts, he had been called to play a great political role."

ment—Malraux's *Le Temps du Mépris;* then came Gorky's *The Lower Depths,* Ben Jonson's *The Silent Woman,* Aeschylus' *Prometheus Bound,* and finally Pushkin's *Don Juan.*

Along with political-thesis plays, he staged works from the eternal theatre: Prometheus and Don Juan—as Caligula would later on—played out their lives, rejected commonplace morality and the supernatural, and invested themselves with a provocative solitude at the core of a regal and threatened freedom.

Then came the break with the Communist Party. The Théâtre du Travail became, symbolically, the Théâtre de l'Équipe. The actors were the same as before, all "buddies" in one way or another. "One had to be," said one of them, Blanche Balain, "a little crazy, crazy about the theatre, about beauty, and madly unselfish . . . I was struck certain evenings by a purity of intellectual and moral atmosphere which itself came from a certain passion and a certain firmness that filled the best among us . . . The center of it all was that tall young man, tireless although he was ill . . . from that moment on, Albert Camus was the man to bet on." Fernando de Rojas' *La Celestina,* Vildrac's *Le Paquebot Tenacity,* Copeau's adaptation of *The Brothers Karamazov,* and Synge's *The Playboy of the Western World* were placed on the program for 1938 and 1939. In this bouquet of plays that he adapted or staged can be found the great themes dear to Camus: the Absurd in Pushkin and *The Brothers Karamazov;* the happy couple in love in *La Celestina* and *Le Paquebot Tenacity;* solidarity and revolt in *Le Temps du Mépris, The Playboy of the Western World,* Gide's *Le Retour de l'Enfant Prodigue* and *Prometheus;* justice and poverty in *The Lower Depths.*

In the meantime, Camus had the opportunity to travel all over Algeria with the Radio-Algiers troupe. They needed a young lead; they hired him. He played a great many roles from the French Classical repertory, including Molière, whom he venerated. There, he learned from an old actor, Max Hilaire—who was well named—"how to breathe and to plant oneself on stage." From these early beginnings a photograph of Alec Barthus' troop has survived, made one evening when Banville's *Gringoire* was on the bill, and in which Camus played the role of Olivier le Daim.

He never abandoned the theatre: he either wrote original plays for it (from 1938 to 1949), adapted other authors' works (from 1936 to

1939, then from 1953 to 1959) or he acted (he even dreamed of doing a film), or, finally, he directed productions.[3] In 1952 he applied for the directorship of the experimental Théâtre Récamier. In 1959, André Malraux, named Cultural Minister by de Gaulle, offered him the direction of the *Comédie Française.* However, he preferred a more modest house and one more given to innovation.

The attention that he gave to the stage corresponds to his vision of the world: the universe is only a theatre (he loved amphitheatre sites, a forum backed up against a hillside), life a tragedy or a comedy in the broadest sense of the word, and man a "character in search of an author."

One must recall that for him, the symbol, like tragedy, was only a way of projecting his nostalgia and his anguish in concrete terms and giving them universal value. Before our eyes, a countenance, a gesture reconstructs a yearning for eternity; a landscape, the emptiness of existence under the fullness of the sky. With tragedy, we merely take another step further along the path of art. Characters borrowed from history or legend and living for us their ultimate moments take upon themselves the author's temptation (the absolute, violence, the dream of "the abode," justice, or peace of soul) and amplify them.

Tragedy also returns to its Greek sources. The theatre of Aeschylus and, to a lesser degree, that of Sophocles offers us not so much characters as metaphysical passions. The myth of Prometheus celebrates the creative will of men and their rebellion against the gods, even though they must be paid for by eternal torment. Sophocles' *Oedipus Rex,* if one is to believe Nietzsche, teaches us that "even he who resolves the enigma of nature—that hybrid sphinx—must also, as murderer of his father and husband to his mother, overturn the most sacred laws of nature."[4]

Tragedy, according to Camus, answers the exceptional needs of a civilization in a state of rupture, still prey to obscure forces, submitted to the ascendancy of the sacred and imminently threatened by individual

[3] In 1939, he was to have given Vitrac's *Le Coup de Trafalgar* (November 3), Malraux's *La Condition humaine* (December 29), and Goldoni's *La Locondiera*; in March, 1940, Jacques Copeau's adaptation of *Hamlet* and in May a play of Aristophanes. The war interrupted all these projects. In 1944, he almost staged Sartre's *Huis Clos.*

[4] *The Birth of Tragedy.*

reason: Aeschylus and Sophocles in Greek antiquity; Shakespeare and the Spanish Golden Age at the dawn of modern times. "The forces that confront one another in tragedy are equally legitimate, equally founded in reason . . . each force is equally good and bad . . . Antigone is right and Creon is not wrong" (*PL, I,* p. 1703).

In a certain way, *Révolte dans les Asturies,* that collective creation inspired by Camus, is in the tragic tradition. The defeat of the insurgents monitored by the radio, the hymns, explosions, discourses and trials, everything seems to fit into the order of things. It is Antigone's defeat in her combat against the powers that be. No one in the play is entirely pure. Nonetheless, the work attempts to be politically committed, revolutionary. By turns, it is akin to the medieval mystery plays (the scene is situated everywhere and nowhere, at Oviedo, at Madrid, in a café, and at the Council of Ministers) and to the experimental techniques of Piscator and Brecht (use of radio newscasts, peoples' choruses); it is an attempt at total theater in which the revolutionary epic invests itself in a tragic design.

Caligula takes as its province this rebellion against an abortive universe. But it introduces ambiguity into it. Camus's Caligula is barbaric but also refined; rebellious but possessed of a Dionysian will to live; impassioned with being, right up to the totalitarian obsession that grips him as soon as he stumbles up against evil. His stare is fixed upon Apollonian respect for moderation and, on top of all this, upon the metaphysical consolation that "snatches [one] momentarily from the grinding wheels of ephemeral migrations." "My freedom is not the good one," Caligula will affirm; however, he was not wrong in his mad intransigence—and Cherea and Scipion are both right.

Caligula was an old acquaintance of Camus. Jean Grenier, in his courses, loved to cite Suetonius' *Twelve Ceasars* "from a romantic and D'Annunzian point of view."[5] He saw in it the nostalgia for the absolute,[6]

[5] Jean Grenier, *Albert Camus.*

[6] M. Gay-Crosier (see *French Review* [May, 1968], pp. 818–830), is correct in seeing some indirect relationship between *Caligula* and the following notes from the *Carnets* of 1936: "Question of will = push absurdity all the way = I am capable of . . . Let us seek the ultimate experience in absurdity." And again: "Annihilation and the taste for death, the true tragic climate and not the nighttime, as in the popular notion."

a certain indifference, "a pantheistic exaltation that made short shrift of ethics." In 1933, in *Les Îles,* Grenier emphasized this trait of the mad Emperor: "one day, he had all the accused, witnesses, and lawyers involved in a trial killed, crying out: 'They are all guilty.' " This word takes on its full meaning if we transpose it to that desperate quest for innocence formulated in both *la Mort heureuse* and *L'Étranger.*

Camus read Suetonius and Seneca closely. He knew of his hero's past generosity spoiled by a delirious will for power; his insomnia, his "moonings," his incestuous love affairs with his sisters, especially Drusilla, his flight, his return in a daze, his sexual caprices, his cruel acts. The legendary and historical Caligula scorned the great, mimicked the gods, held poetry competitions. Even some of his very words are historically authentic: "kill him slowly so that he feels himself dying" . . . "I am still alive."

But Camus gave Caesonia a tenderness and Cherea a courage that history did not accord them. He makes Scipion the charitable "double" of Caligula. As for the mirror, it plays the same revelatory role as Meursault's tin plate. To Caligula, whom he had hoped to portray for the Théâtre de l'Équipe, he attributes his own physical characteristics: "tall and thin, his body slightly bent." In the development from one manuscript to the other, Camus suppressed the delirious eroticism of his character, his brutal and desperate lyricism, moving him somewhat away from his physical horror of death in order to draw him more toward the tragedy of the mind. At the same time, a character, absent at the beginning, carves out for himself an ever more important role: Hélicon, the master-slave of this "Barbaric Nietzsche," cynical and cruel ringmaster, actor and role-player par excellence, accomplice and detached spectator of that crisis of the intellect of which Caligula is at once the denunciator and the prey.

Tragedy, then, protests against a certain theoretical optimism and the many incarnations of humanistic lukewarmness. That is why the tragic hero as conceived by our modern authors from Pirandello to Anouilh suffers destiny less than he provokes it. A Henry IV, a Caligula, an Antigone have this in common, that they exist only to shatter ugliness, stupidity, lies, and convention. They are truly iconoclasts. In differing degrees they appear to us as lunatics, but their madness is composed of sincerity and betrayed purity. Any inclination they have for scandal is none other than a fondness for truth.

There could be a great deal said about the utilization of eccentrics in literature. Etymologically speaking, not only are madmen, from Caligula to Henry IV, eccentrics, but so are the monsters, like Pier Lagerkvist's Dwarf; the intransigents, from Molière's Misanthrope to Anouilh's Antigone; the saints, like Corneille's Polyeucte; the chosen ones from Vigny's Moses to Lazarus and even including Ghelderode's Mlle. Jaïre. Viewed by the wisdom of nations, they have only their strangeness in common. If our modern theater has made them a major product, it is because these characters on the margins of society serve as useful debunkers of mystification. Every form of satire has its screen; the eighteenth century used Persians, Hurons, or giants borrowed from Rabelais. The entire intention was to indict manners and institutions. Anouilh, Pirandello, Camus—and many others—who go at the very roots of the human condition, at the mystery of life, employ more disturbing personages.

The instinctive self-defense and skepticism of the spectator must be dealt with. He is allowed the means of evading a part of his responsibilities in order to better make him take on the other part. There are undoubtedly only two means of attracting attention: strangeness and death. When Caligula cries out painfully, "yes, I wanted the moon!"[7] we dismiss him with a shrug of the shoulders. But he looks at us with his disturbing stare: "the moon!" We shudder; useless to tell ourselves that this is absurd . . . however, if it were true, if this were indeed the only problem, if the Absurd were the truth about the world? "When madmen begin to talk, they wreck everything: Conventions fly into pieces . . . they shake to their very foundations all the things that we have built within ourselves, around us, the logic, the logic of our conventions."[8] It is not that they are illogical. On the contrary, they are following their reasoning to its very conclusion, as Caligula does. While we attempt to halt time by petty artifices, they claim to smash it totally; or on the contrary, they accept inconsistency and instability without reservation and plunge straight into the abyss. "You use all your strength to plant yourself firmly and they let themselves go."

---

[7] For Camus, the moon, starting with *L'Envers et l'endroit,* symbolizes the rebellious rejection of a fleeting existence.

[8] Pirandello, *Henri IV.*

All right, we say, but they are lunatics. Not exactly. All the skill of the tragic author, that of Camus in *Caligula,* consists precisely in disarming us by the mixture of the normal and eccentricity, of cold logic and macabre humor, of mysteriousness and banality. Bad taste? Obliviousness? Sadism? Caligula ceaselessly eludes us. He leaps from brutality to laughter, from cruelty to tenderness. Whom is he deceiving, and when does he deceive us?

Caligula "was a perfect emperor," an adolescent like so many others. As Scipion says: "He said that life was not easy, but that there were religion, art, the love that people bear us."[9] An idealist without excess, up to now he has had his place in the world, the modest place of a well brought up young man, respectful of rules and the established order; he merely existed. Suddenly, the day after his sister's death, he fled. Something within him had brutally collapsed. As the curtain rises, he is awaited with some concern. It is a lunatic who returns, a lunatic who will henceforth tyrannize his coterie, organize the Absurd, have this one and that one killed arbitrarily, until at last he himself succumbs under the blows of those whom he has finally succeeded in rendering rebellious.

Caligula is a sort of male Antigone. He has her bitter lucidity and intransigent purity: "Everything around me is lies, and I, I want to live in the midst of truth." He will cause men to perish because he loves them with an imperious love. He loves their warmth, their heroism. He rejects in them only their calculation and their lukewarmness. He feels a fierce tenderness for them: "Men weep because things are not what they ought to be." But he vomits their resignation in face of the absence of any true life. To this emptiness, he opposes the harsh rigorousness of those who consent to burn up their life out of a yearning for the impossible: "I need the moon or immortality, something that may perhaps be depraved, but which is not of this world."

A tender bitterness floats around his initial revelations, the same that marks Scipion's dreamy countenance. Caligula's soul, still naive and trembling in its nascent monstrousness, is that of a rebellious poet. In his presence we are far removed from the distastefully cunning and dubious adolescent Néron of Racine's *Britannicus*. From Rimbaud, "the blond archangel" of Charleville and his descendants, Caligula has inherited a

[9] In the Madison manuscript, Scipion says: "I learned everything from him, and first of all, to be a *just man.*"

melancholy fervor charged with a secret vehemence. The slightly raucous
and constricted sweetness of his voice betrays a mingling of weariness
and heroic pride, a similar liking for both high summits and bottomless
pits.

The death of her brothers excited in Antigone the thirst for the
absolute. Caligula has stumbled over the body of Drusilla, his sister-lover.
However, with the one as with the other, these were but occasions. "Her
death is nothing, I swear it to you, it is only the sign of a truth that makes
having the moon a necessity for me . . . men die and they are not
happy." Caligula would gladly have remained faithful to the illusions of
his childhood. "How hard it is, how bitter, to become a man." Vain
regrets! One cannot renounce the knowledge of evil. "I have wept," he
might well say, paraphrasing Chateaubriand, "and I have ceased to
believe." The total collapse of tradition's relative values leaves place only
for nothingness or unconditional exaltation of the being.

In these conditions, the only thing that remains for him is to
organize evil, to kill it by the very excess of it, to go all the way to the
end and touch the bottom-most depths. "It is because one never holds out
to the very end that nothing is ever obtained. But maybe it is enough to
remain logical right to the very end." Antigone denounces the Absurd by
her passivity. Caligula denounces it by his unfailing activity. She dies; he
causes others to die before succumbing in his turn, like a just man. She
abandons a world she no longer recognizes for her own. Caligula is a
revolutionary—are not great revolutions metaphysical after a certain
fashion?—who claims to rebuild the world from top to bottom and to
mold it in the image of his desire. He plunges into the current of history
the better to eternalize it: "I shall give to this century the gift of equality.
And when everything shall be leveled, the impossible, earthbound at last,
the moon in my hands, then, at last, men will no longer die and they will
be happy."

To achieve this, men need severe lessons. Therefore, Caligula's
undertaking and his crimes are essentially pedagogical. He claims, in his
way, to be evangelizing a world "deprived of knowledge and which lacks
a professor who knows what he's talking about."[10] This professor of

---

[10] The same pedagogical concern is found in Musset's *Lorenzzacio:* "The
world must have some idea of who I am *and who he is.*" The characters Bindo
and Tebaldeo are the respective counterparts of the Patricians and Scipion in
Camus's play.

thought and life is the emperor himself. Thus paradoxical as it may be—but humanity only progresses thanks to paradox—"there is finally come an emperor who will teach you the meaning of freedom."

An implacable logic[11] and deadly decisive experimentation are the bases of this curious pedagogy: nihilist logic in which the classic demonstration by the Absurd is rigorously triumphant. If men cannot have the moon, then nothing else matters. "Everything is of capital importance, I tell you, the grandeur of Rome and your attacks of arthritis." The world is only chaos. One is tempted to seek out the guilty parties among the gods; but have men not had the generosity to take upon themselves the sins of the world? Would one die if one were not guilty? Caligula's murderous irony denounces this sophism in the famous syllogism: "One dies because one is guilty. One is guilty because one is Caligula's subject. Now everybody is Caligula's subject. Therefore, all the world is guilty. From which it follows that everybody dies. It's just a matter of time and patience."

Here, we pass beyond the stage of simple demonstration. We now stand before the bar. Caligula demonstrates and Caligula indicts. He crushes us under the inhuman weight of divine jurisprudence. He borrows from the gods their arbitrariness and their freedom: "One is always free at someone's expense." The gods are free at men's expense and Caligula at the expense of his people. The logic of the all-powerful: men submit and the gods crush them in order to conform to the decrees of Destiny; if they revolt, as Prometheus did, their revolt is punished; this is the deadly dilemma in which Caligula ensnares Meréa. "No one understands Destiny and that is why I have become Destiny. I have taken on the stupid and incomprehensible face of the gods." Antigone forced the powers of this world and of the other to accomplish their will for death. She overwhelmed them through her martyrdom. Caligula parodies them, takes their place with even more rigorousness than they possess, like a god that men would not have made in their image, a god endowed with a limitless power, even unto denying man and the world.

Caligula's mime is accompanied by a series of ballets in which the emperor reveals his deep-seated liking for disguises and mystification. Caligula is a born actor and a talented stage director. He plays with the naive Scipion, organizes blasphemous or satanic buffooneries—here

---

[11] . . . the absurd effect is connected to an excess of logic" (*MS*, p. 205).

again one thinks of Rimbaud. All of Act IV is filled with these pranks, which are deliberately gross or mocking, like a shadow play.

It is now men's turn to dance. To every lord, every honor; bring on the Patricians. These he makes pirouette until they are literally deflated like a beaten bladder. These capitalists love money; but "if wealth has any importance, then human life has none." And yet they dance! They are attached to their holdings, their honors, their wives. Caligula will force them to betray all to save their lives—a few days of life. This is the famous ballet of fear. "Honesty, respectability, what will you say of them, wisdom of nations, nothing means anything any more." Everything disappears in the face of fear.[12] They turn now to degrade themselves, to crawl. They will intone his litanies; Mucius will deliver up his wife, Lépidus will laugh on the very next day after his son's execution. These debased puppets, without flinching, will bear being called "my pretty." And not a one of them rebels!

The same exact thing, with the poets. They too are going to dance, these mountebanks . . . he teaches them to speak only of what they know, to respect the true meaning of words, to bring their thoughts and their actions into harmony. Caligula tears away all their masks, "he tests hearts, just as death does." He forces everyone to think—"insecurity, there is what makes people think." And here one thinks of that famous text from *La Republique du silence* in which Sartre wrote: "Never were we so free as under the German Occupation.—The often atrocious circumstances of our fight made us truly live, without masks and without veils, that unbearable heart-rending situation called the human condition." Caligula, like the Occupation, like the plague to which it is comparable, like death, obliges each of us to appear in all his truth. Each of Caligula's crimes tirelessly repeats, "all men are mortals." And at each of his blows, one man reveals himself a coward and a cheat, or a pharisee, another as courageous, capable of resistance, rebellion, and love. Cherea is quiet courage; unselfish love is Caesonia; honor and tenderness intertwined is Scipion, that transparent soul "pure in goodness" as Caligula, his spiritual brother, is pure in evil.

This intrusion of the dance and mime—in short, of the theatre on the stage itself profoundly modified the character of tragedy. Ordinarily it

[12] Vehemence and scornful derisions explode with even more brutality in the earlier versions of the play.

assumes that the spectator sympathizes at least partially with the hero, that he suffers or hopes with him. Modern tragedy, because of the intentionally strange characters it holds before us, cannot demand of us this effort at communion. Moreover, the reappearance of the chorus considerably modifies the perspectives. We no longer follow "directly" the phases of the action; they are retransmitted to us, reverberated by the chorus that observes them and comments on them.

But the chorus, if it places a distance between us and the stage, at the same time reintroduces us to it. If tragedy is to be something other than a diversion, if it is to be an edifying spectacle in the sense that one can say that Racine, with *Athalie,* composed an edifying work, how can the spectator be prevented from evading the blows one wishes to lay upon him? Precisely by placing him indirectly on the stage, or, if not him, at least his image. The chorus, in *Antigone* and similar plays, is a delegation of average spectators, invited to observe things from close at hand. This presence of the chorus on stage means that we are much more concerned than we might wish to be. The staging of mystery plays, by the very numbers of its participants, reminded the audience in the same way that the Passion was the affair of them all. In brief, the chorus, by situating us beneath our very own eyes as direct spectators of the tragedy, imposes upon us a kind of double self and invests the theatre right in our own consciousness.

If a great number of modern plays have therefore reintroduced the chorus either openly or in some incipient form, it is not by chance. In any case, it is not enough for the dramatist of the Absurd to force us into a state of detachment or lucidity; he must snatch off our masks as well, force us to distinguish within ourselves the authentic from the impure. An Antigone will denounce hypocrisy only in words—which is perhaps what accentuates the gratuitousness of her gesture. She claims to make Creon think; but she only induces him to remember or at the most to admit openly a conflict of which he has always been aware, that of the scrupulous king torn between his feelings and the necessities involved in the maintenance of order. Creon accepts and assumes this division of loyalties, his character is molded by it, and he cannot be drawn out of it.

Caligula goes further. Here the chorus—we may include in it the Patricians, Cherea, Hélicon and Scipion, who all await the emperor's return in the first three scenes—the chorus that thought it possible to remain uninvolved and watch the drama, like the one in *Antigone,* sees itself dragged into Caligula's murderous round of action. Antigone offers herself up as a spectacle before men; Caligula will offer up men themselves as a spectacle. And we see the cowardly Patrician or the courageous Cherea that we are, buffeted, mocked, stripped bare by Caligula's fixed stare. From the spectators that they were, the members of the chorus have become actors; and not only actors, but the hero's playthings. In Antigone's presence we were like a spectator at a football game who sees himself in the midst of the animated crowd on a television screen. With Caligula we are like that same spectator who, having been hit full in the face by the football, then discovers that he is either cowardly or violent or filled with a self-possession of which he himself did not know he was capable.

Here the technique of the ballet and the mime takes on its full importance. Each character is at once himself and another. Caligula, for example, is both himself—a rebel, and others—the gods that he mimics. The Patricians who believed they were indeed what their name implies, at the end of what one could call in music-hall terminology a strip-tease of the consciousness, wind up by appearing in all their flabby emptiness. Racine—*Esther* and *Athalie* excepted—was theatre in the highest degree: actors incarnating the characters played out the action before us. *Antigone* is theatre in the second degree: the characters play out the action for the chorus, which in turn plays it back to us. With *Caligula,* we reach the third degree: the characters play out the action for one another when they are not playing it out for themselves alone.

This house of mirrors which Pirandello brought to perfection and to the very point where tragedy dissolves in a hallucinatory skepticism, astonishingly enough illustrates Montaigne's celebrated remarks on the "farcelike" character of our condition. The theatre in the theatre is a method of demoralization, or, more exactly, of demystification which permits only one authentic value to subsist: life.

Caligula, in fact, just like Musset's Lorrenzaccio, is an actor only out of excessive seriousness, out of disgust with the frivolous. His laughter is a liberation or an avowal of failure. If he let himself go completely, his style would be that of a visionary: there is something in him of the unrealized prophet. He burns with that cold will for earthly salvation that animated a man like Saint-Just. In order for humanity to progress, he sacrificed himself even to the extent of criminality. He took upon himself the hatred of the world as Prometheus took on that of Zeus. At least Prometheus succeeded in seizing fire from the heavens. Our modern Caligula will die for nothing, or almost nothing. The most noble of exigencies becomes perverted, an angel gives in to the sin, no longer of knowledge, but of pride and of pity, a pity that goes all the way to scorn.[13]

In this sense, tragedy derives from the genre of the mystery play: the final scene alone, because of its emotional impact, permits us to speak of Passion. Caligula knows the total inanity of his enterprise. Does he ever clearly envision a hypothetical success? Each of the blows that he unleashes is like a nail that he sinks into his own heart in order to elevate it to a state of divine indifference. And in those whom he tortures, Caligula crucifies, for the edification of men, the impossible love that he bears them. Ultimately, the entire play is nothing but the history of a "superior suicide."[14]

By introducing scene vi into Act III in 1945, Camus intended to emphasize this point. The old Patrician denounces the conspiracy in vain: Caligula, who is not a dupe, however, refuses to believe him: "No, one does not turn back, and one must go on right up to the consummation."[15]

Thus he will die, without doing anything that might spare him the chalice, he who took himself to be a god and whose rage for freedom had ended in the worst possible crimes. He will die in fear, on a "night heavy as human sorrow."[16] Right to the end, the mirror will stubbornly send back to him the countenance of only a man. Caligula has failed to become a god. But the others have become men, and this compensates that failure. To his assassins, pushed by him to courage and revolt, he has transmitted the flame that consumed him. Therefore, in a final outcry in which pain, defiance, and triumph are mingled, he can affirm: "I am still

---

[13] See Vigny's *Eloa* (version of 1824).

[14] *Théâtre, récits, nouvelles*, p. 1728.

[15] See also Act III, scene vii: "Continue, Cherea, carry the magnificent argument that you set forth for me, all the way. Your emperor awaits his repose." Also Act III, scene iii: "I know in advance what will kill me."

[16] The second manuscript version reads: "Ah, here I am afraid. Oh! if you knew this abjection of the heart, this disgust, and this vile taste that comes when, after having despised others, one feels in one's soul the same cowardice and the same impotence."

alive." By his sacrifice, he assures the everlasting survival of that insane urge for purity, justice, and truth that aligns men against their destiny, which, like the everlastingness of evil and death, alone reveals true human quality.

The pedagogue succeeds, but the revolutionary fails. That failure is another lesson, "a modest ideology . . . that I have the impression of sharing with M. de la Palice and all of humanity."[17] Excess in everything is a failing. An excessive inclination toward morality, an overflowing soul, an excessive fidelity to one's own demands, are so many eloquent betrayals of man. Caligula has indeed bestowed an order, the order of cemeteries. Men cease dancing their ridiculous pantomime before him only to die. He did not really know himself: he did not love the living, but the dead. "When you are all there, you make me feel a measureless emptiness in which I can see myself. I am at ease only among the dead." In the eyes of this inquisitor, these at least are aware of an eternity.

Caligula admits his failure, with the triumphant accent of a knight of the abyss. "I know that nothing lasts! To know that! Only two or three of us have really experienced it, have accomplished this demented happiness." He himself disappears as the plague disappears, without our knowing exactly why, because, no doubt, nothing endures. He only decided upon his own death after having acquired the conviction that death could not be conquered. And so that it could indeed be said that nothing any longer has any meaning, he drags Caesonia there with him, in the hope of killing "the only pure feeling" that life may have given him. Should she resist, Caligula could deny love. But she abandons herself to his mortal embrace, "her hands held out a little in front of her," in the ultimate offering.

Caesonia by her death bears witness to love. But here faithfulness to Caligula was too great to compensate the hatred and "offset the hostility of the world." Scipion, who loves life[18] and the present with all his body as Caligula despises them with all his dissatisfied soul, can compensate, however. Their truths are the same. But the pride of the one knew no

---

[17] Commentary on *Caligula* written for its Swiss performance.
[18] This no doubt is why Camus, in a change from the first manuscript version, decided finally to spare him from taking part in the assassination.

limits and the other, by contrast, cultivated Hellenic moderation. Caligula wanted the moon. Scipion consents to poverty. Like the humanist Cherea who "wants to live and be happy," he knows that happy equilibrium of the soul and the body which alone deserves the name of sanity. This is why deliverance will come from them alone. Upon the ruins of conventional morality, they proclaim the generosity of a happiness that "does not live off destruction."

If one is willing to accept that *La Révolte dans les Asturies,* a collective effort, cannot be counted among Camus's own theatrical works, *Caligula,* for being a first attempt, was the work of a master.

A metaphysical play in the ancient manner, *Caligula,* for all that, is not a thesis play.[19] Is one necessarily philosophizing on the stage in giving life to a passion for the impossible, which, all things considered, is equal in worth to many others? *Caligula* in reality takes its place among a number of modern tragedies, Christian or not, which treat of the mystery of man and his relationships with the absolute. In this sense, *Caligula* is akin to the religious theatre, I mean to say to a theatre which recognizes the human ambition for eternity. Without Sartre's *Les Mouches,* Anouilh's *Antigone,* and *Caligula,* the flowering of religious plays that marked the postwar period would probably not have found a public.

In this perspective, which includes *Don Juan* as well as *Polyeucte,* there is no dénouement that does not constitute, whether one likes it or not, the taking of a metaphysical position. But Camus took care to cover up his tracks, and people have often been fooled. They have spoken of a "manual for those in despair."[20] To speak thus was to misunderstand Camus. For, finally, what is the play's last line? Is it the provocative "I am still alive"? Or is it rather that bitter but pregnant observation: "My freedom is not the good one"? Or still yet, is it that sort of metaphysical consolation similar to Oedipus': "fear does not endure either. I am going

---

[19] The proof of it is that when Henri Troyat, in response to a letter from Camus, attempted to demonstrate the relationship between *Caligula* and Sartrean thought, he borrowed all his citations . . . from *Le Mythe de Sisyphe.* See *La Nef* (January, 1946).

[20] Robert Kemp, *"Caligula* d'Albert Camus," *Le Monde,* XII, No. 487 (Feb. 13–19, 1958), 5.

to rediscover that great emptiness in which the heart finds peace." Perhaps we must cease considering our modern tragedies from a different point of view than the one in which we think of ancient or French classical tragedies. There is no tragedy that is not catastrophic. But always in one way or another "the wife of the Pharaoh who commits suicide speaks to me of hope, the marshal who commits treason speaks to me of faith, the duke who commits murder speaks to me of tenderness."[21]

Moreover, Camus took care not to encumber his characters with his sympathy or his antipathy. Caligula's teaching is not Camus's teaching—if indeed one can extract any at all. He did breathe into his hero his own temptation toward the absolute, his "taste for the difficult and the fatalistic."[22]

Had not Camus in 1938 been attracted concurrently by Communism and Augustinian Christianity? But he endowed Scipion with his sense of moderation, and Cherea with his yearning for happiness. Caligula bespeaks the intellect in delirium, Caesonia the flesh in all its fullness; Caligula represents logic put into action, and Scipion represents art which contests it. Caligula is the incarnation of sickness, Cherea that of health.

And finally, the play resumes the great Greek tradition of historical settings. All of European pride—the same that will be scourged in *L'Homme révolté*—finds its tortured countenance in Caligula, this hero worthy of our century. He frequently attains heights of political prophecy. In the play, Nazism is transfigured into all that it could possess simultaneously of the grandiose, the heroic, and the sadistic. And Caesonia's death is not the only evocation of the face of a woman, victim of her fidelity to the tyrant. How many times, finally, have we not had reason to ask ourselves if Hitler's war has really ended, and if his spirit does not triumph in us? In conjoining contemporaneity and legend, a great work gives proof of its necessity.

"Into history, Caligula, into history."[23]

[21] Jean Giraudoux, *Electre.*
[22] *Carnets.*
[23] Restaged several times, *Caligula* has undergone the influence of current events. It seems evident, for example, that the development in the passage in Act II, scene ii from "the family totters, respect is gone, Rome in all its entirety is given over to blasphemy," to its final formulation, "the *family* totters, respect for *work* is lost, the *nation* in its entirety is given over to blasphemy," evokes the famous slogan, "Work, Family, Nation," dear to Vichy.

4

The Birth of Man

The poetic essay, the theatre, and the novel are varied forms suitable to the expression of one particular message and the representation of one particular world. Poetry gathered the joy of living out of the hollow of fugitive sensation; tragedy launched the savage cry of human revolt against Destiny; the novel, which has the advantage of time, recounts for us in detail the eruption of the consciousness of evil within a banal existence.

From one genre to another, there is then, for Camus as for Vigny, who also played on three keyboards, only a difference in scope: the novel's ambitions are less limited, more Faustian. Its demands are satisfied neither by a flowering of images nor by a character caught in a paroxysm of passion; it reproduces a universe in its complexity and its duration. If it is true that a secret complicity binds the modern concept of the tragic to logic as well as to the quotidian,[1] the novel is, paradoxically, better suited than the theatre to express this relationship and to portray day-to-day life, the ordinary behavior of humanity and the traditional social mechanisms. The hero of tragedy lacks familiarity; the novel alone is capable of making of a mediocre white-collar worker a tragic character in the modern world's dimensions.

Therefore, the novel, according to Camus, develops on two planes: the descriptive plane in which behavior is studied in detail in the so-called "realistic" manner of Steinbeck[2] or Caldwell: the author approaches his

[1] See "L'Espoir et l'Absurde" (*MS*), where this idea is developed at length. Camus also devoted to the novel, which fascinated him, a whole chapter of *Le Mythe de Sisyphe:* "Philosophie et Roman," a chapter of *L'Homme révolté,* an article, "L'Intelligence et l'échafaud," in *Confluences* (July–August 1943), a preface to Chamfort's *Maximes et anecdotes,* not to mention the book reviews written for *Alger-Républicain,* the preface to Louis Guilloux's *La Maison du peuple,* and a study on Roger Martin du Gard.

[2] "The American novelistic technique seems to me to come finally to an impasse. I used it in *L'Étranger,* it is true. But that was because it suited my

character from the outside and plants him in his everyday milieu; the moralist does not intervene except in the background; the particular then is joined to the universal and each man carries within him "the image of the human condition."[3]

The more banal reality was, the more significant it revealed itself to be. To that end it was only needed for logic to be injected into the everyday setting and disrupt it. Ever since Bergson, we have been aware of what laughter owes to that form of the Absurd which he called a "mechanism superimposed on the real."[4] Let the mechanism kill, and laughter turns into malaise. In *L'Étranger,* a victim of the mechanism's workings, a man who has up to now lead a disoriented existence, finds his point of convergence in this privileged torture chamber. A second reading, as necessary for *L'Étranger* as for Kafka's *The Trial,* rewards us with the discovery, in detail, of the unity of a life that had seemed to drift.

Thus, freedom and fatality are reconciled: "The end that transforms everything is already there," Sartre had already said in *La Nausée,* "for us the person telling the story is already the hero of the adventure . . . instants have ceased to pile up merrily one upon the other: they are appropriated by the end of the story, which attracts them toward itself, and each of them in its turn attracts toward itself the instant that precedes it." By its very movement, the novel is made in the image of our existence in which the final words are revealed to us only at death. "The novel manufactures readymade destiny" (*HR,* p. 668).

Taking into account Camus's multiple vocations, shall we make of *L'Étranger* the final panel of a Dyonisian tryptich which would include *Noces* and *Caligula?* Or, on the contrary, are we going to place it with *Le Mythe de Sisyphe* and *Le Malentendu* in an absurd trilogy? If we choose according to appearances and Camus's own views, the second proposition ought to carry the day.[5]

In fact, there is nothing more arbitrary than this kind of classifica-

---

purpose which was to describe a man without any apparent consciousness. In generalizing this procedure, one arrives at a universe of automata and instincts. This would be a considerable impoverishment" (*Nouvelles littéraires* [November 15, 1945]).

[3] Montaigne: *Essais.*

[4] Bergson, *Le Rire.*

[5] "I treated the theme that interested me before the war in three different forms: the essay with *Le Mythe de Sisyphe,* the novel with *L'Étranger,* the theatre with *Le Malentendu* and *Caligula*" (from a manuscript notation).

tion. It supposes an absolute conformity between order of conception and order of publication and implies that the work expresses the author's state of mind in some direct way. Now, Camus's books owe very little to "bursts of inspiration,[6] and are the fruit of slow maturation and "daily faithfulness."

The whole matter of composition, then, is only a question of exploration and of determining the proper mixture of various elements. Thus it was with *L'Étranger*. But before *L'Étranger*, Camus had already tried his hand at a novel (*La Mort heureuse*), a work which long remained unpublished, to which the foregoing remarks apply as well.

Publication of this text makes it possible today to deal with it directly. Let us summarize the plot: Mersault murders Zagreus in order to steal his money. Afterwards, in a flashback we discover what Mersault's life had been up until the day of the murder: an existence gnawed by the lack of time and money, by the jealousy that Marthe and her lovers inspire in him, the reflection of which he finds in the character of Cardona, a cooper.

Having become rich, Mersault travels in Central Europe as far as Prague, regains Algiers by way of Genoa, lives in a communal arrangement with three women students, moves with Lucienne, his wife, to the edge of Tipasa and dies from an attack of pleurisy.

It is easy to discover what this story owes to Camus's biography, from Chapter II on: office life and bills of lading, Céleste's café,[7] his Uncle Acault's butcher-shop, the apartment in Belcourt, in short all the author's personal museum. In addition, we can add Cardona, who bears the name of Camus's grandmother, and who lives the life of a poor cooper, as did another of Camus's uncles.

Then there is Prague, visited in 1936, there is the fear, described at length in "La Mort dans l'âme": "the power of anguish . . . evil spell of Prague nights" in which strangeness and human solitude burst forth. And there is the body lying stretched out on the sidewalk (and no longer in Zagreus' room) and the revolt in face of death.[8]

---

[6] See "L'Intelligence et l'échafaud."

[7] Max-Pol Fouchet, in "Un jour, je m'en souviens . . . ," recalls a bistro in the quarter near the City Hall, called *Les Bas-Fonds* [The Lower Depths], that Camus liked to frequent (p. 23).

[8] See Max-Pol Fouchet, "Un jour je m'en souviens. . . ." (p. 21). There he recalls the incident of a boy struck down by a bus. He and Camus had happened upon the accident while returning from La Bouzaréa. "A few meters

Next came the descent toward the sunlight and life in the communal residence, *La Maison devant le monde,* with the cats Cali and Gula, with Catherine, Rose, and Claire, who resemble more or less the three students, Jeanne Sicard, Christiane Davila, and Marguerite Dobrenn.[9] There is Tipasa also, which Camus had frequented not long before with Simone Hié, Tipasa and its absinthes, Tipasa where, the hotel-keeper was fond of saying, "one could die without even getting himself talked about.[10] Names we recognize surge up, which confirms Camus's lack of inventiveness: Bernard, the doctor; Pérez, the old one-armed fisherman. And when Mersault succumbs to sunstroke, at the end of a walk on Mount Chenoua, when he has his first fainting spell, the days and the months file by: the almond trees of January, the apple trees of March, and the great summer wind that dries out the land. Toward noon, after a last look upon the sea, after having breathed in the aroma of absinthe, rosemary, and warm stone, Mersault is able to die.

La Mort heureuse appears at first, in its disjointedness, like the author's imaginative museum with its familiar names, its landscapes, the different milieux that he frequented (the office, the *Maison devant le monde,* the village of Tipasa, its local life, its pretentious colonials). But all his obsessions are also assembled here: ever-present and ubiquitous death, in the first as well as the last chapter, in Prague itself, the death at which Zagreus looks directly, "without turning away his eyes"—it is the murderer who closes them—the death that Mersault listens to rising within himself, with an interior smile that answers the "earth's smile . . . And stone among the stones, he turns back, in the joy of his heart, to the truth of motionless worlds."

Whoever is familiar with the *Carnets, La Peste,* or the voices of *Le Quartier Pauvre* recognizes the obsession of the tuberculosis victim, balancing between passion for life, the taste for happiness, and a kind of indifference. The book's title, on this point, enlightens us against the background of death: it is a question of a slow conquest of happiness,

---

from there, Camus stopped. He turned toward the sea and the sky which were extraordinarily blue. He pointed out the sky with his hand, the passive sky and said to me: "You see, he remains silent."

[9] I cite their names without attempting to establish any direct correspondence between the fictional characters and the real persons.

[10] Letter to Max-Pol Fouchet (1934).

which cannot be obtained without asceticism and detachment. "It seems," we are told at the beginning, "that the only task men have, may be to live and to be happy." Mersault pursues this quest for happiness throughout his conversations with Zagreus: "And you, Mersault," the invalid tells him, "with your body, your only duty is to live and to be happy."

Zagreus thus opens up for him the relationship of time to money and of money to happiness. "I am certain that one cannot be happy without money. That's all there is to it." Zagreus, through his own cynicism, the cynicism of a pure heart, in a way provokes Mersault to murder. Here again, one could speak of a superior suicide. Mersault will make for Zagreus the move that he himself, touching his forehead against the revolver, licking the barrel of the weapon, and gurgling "with an impossible happiness," had never dared make.

All around Mersault, everything seems to support Zagreus' words: a folkloric Céleste, with his door in the form of a slate; René, the tuberculosis victim with his bright-eyed stare; the fellow-workers from the office; Cardona, deaf, half-dumb, alone in his sordid room with his old dog. It is after having found Cardona in his distress that Mersault killed Zagreus. "In face of misfortune and loneliness, his heart today was saying no—and in the midst of the great distress that filled him, Mersault felt indeed that his revolt was the only true thing within him, and that the rest was misery and complacency."

Prague, then, represents a stage in the march toward happiness, the very depths of solitude and strangeness. There, in a faraway country, "time took on its most extreme extension." Like Jan in *Le Malentendu,* "Mersault sought the word, the sentence that would formulate his heart's hope, where his anxiety would be captured. In the state of weakness in which he was, he had need of formulas." At the height of dereliction and abandon, then, Mersault rediscovers "his ties" and affirms "his solidarity with the world in its most repugnant form." Breslau and then Vienna evoke for him, by contrast, Southern lands and his Algerian girl friends.

The slow reascent toward happiness begins. Liberated from monetary preoccupations, finally disposing freely of his time, Mersault is going to learn to live and to die. The liberation from time becomes a near synonym for authenticity. Until now, Mersault has acted out "a degrading comedy." Had he even been jealous of Marthe, with that sexual jealousy which *La Chute* deals with later? He had played at wanting to be happy. Never had he wanted to be so "with a conscious and deliberate will." With Marthe, he yields to vanity, abandons himself to the role-playing that is an evasion of living. Henceforth, he will live in lucidity, condemned to lucidity by that voluntary act, "by that calculated gesture" which had eliminated Zagreus. That long detour by way of Prague and Central Europe, that shock of anguish, will have been necessary in order finally for Mersault to find self-realization. It is a "new being who disembarks at Algiers," shorn of his illusions about love, devoted to the innocent and terrible love of the black god that he henceforth served.

Through a paradox, which recalls in passing the first Christians with whom Camus dealt in his thesis, "what was best in his life had crystallized around what was worst in it." The descent into hell which the murder constitutes and the voyage that prolongs it, open the doors of happiness and of rediscovered time." "Innocent, overwhelmed by joy, he understood finally that he was made for happiness . . . It was with time that he had to bring his being into accord."

Catherine and her friends give an example of that accord with time and the world. Amiability, humor, absence of prejudice, each has her innocence and her own "bag of tricks." "On good days," says Rose, "confide in life, that forces it to respond in kind." But this kind of happiness lacks a tragic background. Mersault "abandons" the *Maison devant le monde* out of a desire for detachment. To Catherine, who questions him about the reasons for his departure, he replies: "There, I would risk being loved, my dear Catherine, and that would keep me from being happy." And he adds: "Do not even expect life from a man. That is how so many women deceive themselves. But expect it from yourself."

Here several of Mersault's traits reappear in concentrated form: that life which "sways every day in the odors of cafés and tar, *detached* from him and from his interests, alien to his heart and to his truth." There is also his taste for silence: "he has something in his guts. But he shuts it up in him. That way, then, one is deceived." But Mersault soon makes a virtue of this natural detachment, in imitation of Zagreus, who used to say to him: "Already then, all that was strange to me. The cultivation of impersonality, that is what occupied me." In a sense, after the invalid's death, Mersault's life becomes oriented toward "the imitation" of Zagreus.

Like him, he is haunted by loneliness and seeks a retreat for himself.[11] He finds it on the train from Breslau where he "passed in review his distraught conscience and his will for happiness which, in those days was, for him, in Europe, like one *of those cells* in which man learns to know man by way of that which transcends him." The *Maison devant le monde* represents a sort of Abbey of Théléme, but Mersault needed an ascesis. He finds it in that house in Tipasa where, at last, after have taken shelter in friendship, confidence, and a seeming security, he will be able "to begin his game."

His is a lucid game which sets aside all lyricism. Between him and Lucienne, there is no love; nothing more than a physical presence. "If you insist on it, I can promise to marry you. But that does not seem to me to be of any use." "You don't love me?" "But, I never told you that I did, my dear." "That's true, and that's why." This liaison does not prevent solitude; on the contrary, it makes solitude all the more conscious: "face-to-face with himself, and for a long time, until the consummation." Thus, when he meets her again for the final walk along the Chenoua, he will be able to say to Catherine: "What alone counts, you see, is the will for happiness, a kind of enormous, ever-present awareness . . . I cannot taste happiness except in the tenacious and violent confrontation that it maintains with its opposite; . . . I needed to leave and find that solitude in which I have been able to confront in myself what was to be confronted, what was sunlight and what was tears."

In the end, Mersault attains a kind of peace composed of detachment. He approaches death with a completely tragic serenity: "At that hour in which his life appeared to him so distant, alone, indifferent to everything, and to himself, it seemed to Mersault that he had finally found what he was looking for, and that the peace which filled him had been born of the patient abandonment of himself which he had pursued and attained with the aid of this warm world that denied him without anger." Happiness near to tears, in which hope and despair are mingled, in which the attraction of death (when one is swimming, for example)

---

[11] Camus often liked to make retreats. Max-Pol Fouchet notes that, agnostic that he was, he was to go several times to the Trappist monastery of La Médéa as well as to the monastery of Saint-Maximin in 1943. That fondness for monasteries, for the solitude that they provide, and the asceticism they impose, is reflected in the evocation of the monastery at Fiesole in *Noces*.

counterbalances the instinctive repulsion that it inspires. "Therein was all his happiness in living and in dying. He understood that to be afraid of this death, which he had looked upon with the wild fear of a beast, meant being afraid of life."

On the whole, Mersault in his disbelief succeeds in what the Christian succeeds at through faith: joy in spite of death and in death itself. He arrives at this through a sort of Nietzschean asceticism, which, from the depths of anxiety, leads him to serenity by way of the slow conquest of a spontaneous indifference. He arrives at it through the consciousness of himself, which, as in *L'Étranger,* is born of death given and death received. Patrice Mersault and Meursault do not know themselves until the day they have killed, and see themselves condemned in their turn. The shock of death is revealing, purifying for one as for the other. As for the death received, is it not also a source of solace? The community, the fraternity of the dead, here takes on the character of a near mystical exchange, but with an entirely human mysticism, of which *Les Justes* will furnish us a new example. "He who had inflicted death was going to die."

At this point *La Mort heureuse* appears as a sort of thematic catch-all: happiness, innocence, lucidity, sexual jealousy, one life for another, harmony with nature, coupling of earth and sun, confrontation of mortal man and the eternal universe, instructional value of travel, natural or acquired indifference. In it are found the dominant themes from *L'Envers et l'endroit, Noces, Les Justes, La Chute,* and of course *L'Étranger.* It is in this sense that I was once able to write that *La Mort heureuse* had come forth to the profit of all Camus's works.

But Jean Sarocchi rightly insists on a more profound kinship between *L'Étranger* and *La Mort heureuse.*[12] It is not so much because Camus had envisaged, among other titles for *L'Étranger, Un Homme heureux.* But rather because the curve of action is approximately the same in both. In both cases, a man who dragged out his life in a sort of grey-toned unconsciousness, kills. With the shots he fires, a universe collapses. Then begins the discovery of life as, all the while, death approaches. The hero grows in that solitude he imposes on himself or which is imposed upon him, grows to the point where he dominates his anguish and attains tranquility.

[12] *Camus* (Paris, 1968).

La Mort heureuse retraces a sort of spiritual itinerary that Camus might have followed in order to surmount his own vicissitudes, if he had not also been the sportsman, the actor, and the journalist that we know. Mersault conquers a sort of individual salvation by way of cynicism, pushing to the extreme the logic of his solitude and transcending the naive and sensual "game" he played before the murder by the lucid "game" of his final moments: "Nothing, no love nor any décor, but an infinite desert of solitude and happiness in which Mersault played his last cards." One thinks of Milosz's Don Juan,[13] whom Camus evoked in *Le Mythe de Sisyphe,* withdrawn into a monastery in the expectation of death. At the extreme limit, the game and authenticity come together in "the abandonment of compromises and the truth of nature" (*CN, I*).

The reconquest of self through financial independence; the reconquest of time,[14] influenced perhaps by a reading of Proust, who, both Jean Grenier and Max-Pol Fouchet tell us, made a deep impression on Camus; the reconquest of that peace of soul which was to remain Camus's obsession, *La Mort heureuse* takes on the character of a progression: the will to succeed and profound indifference to success, fondness for women and the dream of chaste friendship, love of play-acting and obsession with truth, so many contradictions that cause the book to progress toward that final death through which it returns to its beginnings. From Zagreus to Mersault, the circle is closed.

This book, poorly put together, insufficiently rid of its autobiographical preoccupations, laden with literary associations (the assassination in *La Condition humaine,* for example), has not yet found either its form or its style. Several notes indicate Camus's intention of incorporating an alternation of tenses that was not maintained, but from which is derived that systematic exploitation of temporal values which gives *L'Étranger* its mystery. However, if it is true that "the meaning of the book [*L'Étranger*] lies in the parallelism of its two parts," how can we not take note of the fact, along with Sarocchi, that *La Mort heureuse* was reduced from three parts to two, each one ending logically with a death, if one remembers that Chapter I of *La Mort heureuse* is only a chronological anticipation in the form of a flashback. The structure of *La Mort heureuse*

[13] Oscar-Vencelas de Lubicz-Milosz, *Miguel Mañara* (Grasset, 1912).
[14] See particularly the leisurely passage of the seasons in the final chapter.

prefigures that of *L'Étranger,* but its original one-third, two-thirds arrangement lacks the later novel's balance.

Camus, who had decided to write a work elaborated in 1936, could
nor have been aware of these imbalances or of the dispersion of the
themes. He was, while refining them, to reuse certain settings, certain
characters, certain subject matter from *La Mort heureuse.* He was to give
to the character of Meursault an inchoate coherence. He was to go so far
as to borrow the famous Algiers street scene.[15] But he was to suppress all
lyricism except that dealing with the senses; he eliminates all meditation,
deliberately playing the card of impersonality and detachment. From
L'Envers et l'endroit as well as from *Noces,* he retains only muted echoes,
a realism expunged of its refracted poetic outbursts.

Perhaps Camus had in mind *L'Étranger,* the first of Baudelaire's
prose poems:

"Whom do you love best, man of mystery, tell me, your father, your
mother, your sister, your brother?"

"I have neither father nor mother nor sister nor brother."

"Your friends?"

"There you are using a word whose meaning until this day has been
unknown to me."

"Your homeland?"

"I know not in what latitude it may be found."

"Beauty?"

"I would gladly love it if it were a goddess and immortal."

"Gold?"

"I hate it as you hate God."

"And what do you love then, strange alien?"

"I love the clouds—the clouds that are passing over yonder, the marvel-
ous clouds."

If Meursault loved something, it was rather the sun. An Algiers
white-collar worker, he buries his mother; the next day, while swimming
in the harbor, he meets a typist he had formerly known, Marie Cardona,

[15] In the typescript it is set off by three asterisks and brackets (See
L'Étranger, pp. 1143–44: Raymond's account of his street fight [trans. note]).

and takes her for his mistress. He finds himself a "pal," Raymond Sintès, rumored to be a pimp, and does him a few small favors: a letter he writes for him, an appearance as a witness in his behalf. One Sunday, Marie, Sintès, Meursault, and another couple of their acquaintance, depart for an uneventful picnic on an outlying beach. Some Arabs, who have an account to settle with Sintès, watch them from a distance: a scrap, injuries, general retreat—Meursault, who longs to find a cool spot, returns to the beach toward a spring in the rocks. One of the Arabs is napping there: mutual fear, brilliant sunlight, weariness; a knife flashes, Meursault fires one short, then four more.

All these events follow one another by chance, lived by Meursault in all their contingency and neutrality. They illustrate what Sartre wrote about life in *La Nausée:* "When one lives, nothing happens, the settings change, people enter and leave, that's all. There are never any beginnings. The days are added to the days, without rhyme or reason: it is an interminable and monotonous addition."

What we are given in the first part of the novel is pure existence recorded by the hero in a sort of journal. However, in a journal, one focuses, one defines oneself, morally if not physically. Meursault does none of this. We are left ignorant of either his demeanor or his face. Precisely, Meursault is faceless. No interior life bestows unity upon the character. He seems to know only two tenses: the imperfect for description and the compound past, the tense of discontinuity, of completed action. He uses neither coordinates nor connectives.[16] "I had trouble getting up . . . While I was shaving, I asked myself what I was going to do and I decided to go swimming. I took the streetcar to go to the swimming concession in the harbor. There I dived into the channel—I found Marie Cardona in the water." The details accumulate, without the slightest relief, the least nuance of anteriority or of posteriority which might betray the consciousness of duration; from one to the other they form a kind of colorless and odorless current that carries along all his gestures which are, at one and the same time, identically dull and bizarre. The dialogues are skillfully broken up, emptied of that power of commu-

---

[16] See Sartre's excellent study, *L'Explication de L'Étranger* (*Situations III*). (A translation of *L'Explication* appears in *Camus: A Collection of Critical Essays,* ed. Germaine Brée [Englewood Cliffs, N. J.: Prentice-Hall, 1962] pp. 108–21 [trans. note].)

nication that defines them by the insertion of identifying phrases such as "I said, he spoke, he added." The contact is never direct.

With the gunshot, we are plunged into the middle of an adventure. Meursault is arrested and condemned to death. The first four chapters of the novel's second part are no longer made up of day-to-day notations; they constitute an account dominated by the death sentence. The passage from the compound past to the imperfect, the descriptive or anecdotal tense, exactly translates this reversal. Doubtless the book's movement remains slow—but with a calculated slowness, with that skillful slowness that leads tragedies to their dénouement. The reader himself quickens his pace, as though drawn to the end of the story. At the foot of the scaffold, which already looms, all monotony has disappeared. Our hero and we know from now on where we are going: the judge, the lawyer, the prosecutor, all of whom are possessed of a sense of rhetoric and logic to spare, have made us aware of it.

The sun would also have warned us, had we bothered to seek its counsel. The sun marks the rhythm of the work. The sun was high in the sky, bearing down like a man's destiny, the day Meursault buried his mother. It is the same sun that presides at the murder, the same searing rays striking the forehead, the same dullness of the senses. It will reappear, implacable, more suffocating than ever, the day of the sentencing. And who knows . . . ! That searing light in which the entire book is bathed silhouettes each of Meursault's moves in vivid contrasts: the world in which he evolves could easily appear to us as wasted and abstract. However, the tamarinds, the rock-irises, and the sea, now immobile and now heaving "with all the stifled respiration of its small waves," are the same as those to which *Noces* introduced us. We rediscover "the country-side . . . gorged with sunlight," the unbearable brilliance of the sky, and the melancholy gentleness of the Algerian nights.

Is Meursault himself so different from those young Algerians glimpsed for a moment in "L'Été à Alger" (*N,* pp. 67–78)? Like them, he exists entirely in the present. "I was always concerned with what was going to happen, with today or tomorrow." The only thing that counts, quite naturally, is immediate sensation and the satisfaction of desire. "My comrade, Vincent, who is a cooper and the junior breast-stroke champion, has a still clearer view of things: he drinks when he is thirsty; if he wants a woman, he tries to sleep with one and would marry her if he loved her (that hasn't happened yet). Afterwards, he always says, 'That's better' " (*N*, p. 69n).

Meursault resembles Vincent like a brother. When he is sleepy, he sleeps, whether his mother has just died or not. His affair with Marie has an animal-like simplicity. He sees no reason whatever to marry her; he doesn't see any more reason not to marry her. The affair's having begun the day after his mother's death is pure chance. If Marie had not quit her job at the office where Meursault works, it would have happened a long time ago. Marie herself is scarcely more complicated. Doubtless Meursault's black necktie gives her momentary pause—but without further consequence. Their little private games, which they play together in the water and on the beach, are marked by the same healthiness and naive disregard for decency that we saw in their Algiers brethren.

Meursault shares even silence and boredom with Algiers; the silences at his mother's wake, Marie's silences and those of Sintès ("I don't like to talk just to be talking"), the spectators' silences in the courtroom, and those of the condemned man's final night. We are familiar with these silences. Already, in Belcourt, the mother was similarly silent. And the same Sunday boredom: "I thought that it was Sunday and that bothered me; I don't like Sundays . . . after lunch I was bored a little, and I wandered around in the apartment." Sunday, circumscribed and artificial, a bourgeois day.[17]

The soul's day, too—and Meursault knows nothing of the soul nor of morality. "There is nothing here for him who wishes to learn to improve himself or to become a better person" (*N*, p. 67). People, things, do or do not please him, and that's that. Books, religion have no place in his existence. Be it numbness or detachment, Meursault is without spiritual or material ambition: his boss offers him the supervision of a business office in Paris for which he demonstrates no enthusiasm whatever. His ethics are summed up in an elementary code: refuse nothing when one has no "reason" to do so. Meursault responds to whoever speaks to him, renders service to whoever asks it of him. As for himself, he asks no one for anything;[18] initiative eludes him. He is "a pal," "a good guy,"

---

[17] See another description of a Sunday in Sartre's *La Nausée*.

[18] "The book's principal character never takes the initiative. You did not notice that he restricts himself always to *answering questions,* those posed by life or by men" (*CN, II,* pp. 32–33).

say his friends, and Sintès, the pimp, who knows whereof he speaks, states quite simply that he is a man. But the prosecutor, impermeable to that innocence, will not leave off excoriating him: "He said that in truth I had no soul, and that nothing human nor any one of the moral principles that guide the hearts of men were accessible to me."

Meursault is a kind of natural man, unpolished and primitive. Not the good savage, the imaginary peasant that Rousseau willed us, but the man of the people—of Belcourt and elsewhere. He has his simplicity and frugality: "I no longer live in any room except this one, among the slightly sagging straw-bottomed chairs, the wardrobe whose glass is yellowed, the washstand and the brass bed." Wine and *boudin* make up an acceptable meal. He has the diversions permitted by his "forty hours"[19] and his social condition. His passions, too, are proportionate to his poverty and his leisure time. His habits and behavior and his language manifest an absolute scorn for form. The constant use of semi-indirect discourse (I said, he replied) are accountable to the author's well-thought-out art and to the total indifference to art of the character who is a practitioner of the popular form of narration.

Besides Marie and Sintès, he frequents only simple people: old Salamano who, at the death of his wife, "had felt very much alone. So, he had asked for a dog from a comrade at the plant." And when the dog disappears, Salamano weeps quietly. There is also Céleste, the bistro-keeper and his regular customers. At the death of Meursault's mother, "they all felt a great deal of sorrow," and Céleste said: "one has only one mother."[20] This banal remark and the few steps these friends take in silence alongside Meursault, said a great deal more than a lot of ritual expressions of condolence.

Intelligent, but not in any sense intellectual, Meursault is a rudimentary being, a raw consciousness, free of every hierarchy of values. Camus's choice is significant. While Sartre discovers existence through Roquentin, a cultivated, cosmopolitan character, formed by a long period of introspection, Camus gives it expression by way of an unadorned and semiproletarian condition. "I never love this country more than in the midst of its

[19] In 1938, Camus thought for a while of writing an essay surrounding the forty-hour work-week syndrome.

[20] From *La Mort heureuse* to *L'Étranger,* Céleste develops; he becomes more perspicacious and more laconic.

poorest men" (*N,* p. 68). They are without artifice, without masks, close to matter, but in no way its slaves, and capable of baring themselves completely. Down to earth as it may be, their manner of being is not any the less pure for it."

These humble people, easy prey for the social mechanism, are instinctively defiant of its representatives. "I have always seen the faces around me become compassionate upon the passage of a man in the grip of a policeman." In face of the gigantic social apparatus whose functioning they barely understand, they find themselves awkward. Those functionalized personages—I mean to say prisoners of their functions and their social dignity—whom they meet never cease to disturb them. They sniff constraint and mechanization all around them. "I recieved a telegram from the asylum—'Mother deceased—burial tomorrow—most respectfully yours.' That doesn't mean anything." The formalism of the telegram surprises Meursault in the same way as the mechanical process of the burial: "Everything went very fast." The funeral director arranged everyone in his place and the procession, with its four people, began to move. The steady acceleration of the hearse, the stifling heat, relieved the ceremony of all human significance—the nursing home director retains his dignity nonetheless—but old Pérez, the only one for whom the dead woman unquestionably had any meaning, flounders like a puppet on a string, cutting cross-country to catch up with the procession, losing it again, and so on until finally he faints. The funeral mechanism pitilessly ridicules this final, pathetic homage.[21]

The trial even more rigorously denounces society's artifices. When Meursault enters into the courtroom, he is startled by the sight of the spectators: not a single known face, and he experiences the bizarre impression "of being superfluous, something of an intruder." Why that crowd? The newspapers had overplayed his case: "The summer is a dead season . . . and there was only your case and that of the parricide that they could make anything of." Meursault discovers uneasily that he is only an object, a sensational topic for indifferent and bantering newsmen, a head to be severed for the prosecutor (compare Act I of Sartre's *La Tête des autres*), a case-study for the examining magistrate, and a "dirty business" for his court-appointed lawyer. Nothing of himself any longer

[21] See also René Clair's short film in the burlesque and surrealistic mode: *L'Entr'acte.*

remains, nothing of Meursault, the Algiers white-collar worker with his crude love affairs, his boredom. Like Voltaire's Huron (in *L'Ingénu*) or Montesquieu's Persians, he sees enter, not without some curiosity, "a tall thin man dressed in red, three judges, two in black, the third in red." Without grasping very well its importance, he watches the drawing of lots, the calling of the witnesses, and, once again, the interrogation in order to establish his identity. From this point on, and despite the fact that his head alone is at stake, everything takes place over and above him. His lawyer deprives him of all initiative, going so far as to speak, using the first person, in his name. The witnesses in no way distort the truth; yet he, Meursault, cannot recognize himself in the interpretive depositions which the prosecutor will use to manufacture for him a logical existence, a coherent personality entirely consecrated to crime. In that murder which Meursault had lived as pure chance, the prosecutor sees a culmination, a revelation. Little by little, by way of a kind of objective and generalized responsibility, dear to all witch-hunters, Meursault sees himself judged less for his criminal act than for his monstrous indifference "to the most essential rules" of society. For the prosecutor, Meursault's act informs his entire past attitude; and the cigarette smoked in innocence before his mother's coffin, the tears he did not shed, the few instants of sleepiness to which he succumbed, are so many unpardonable crimes. Meursault was a criminal all along; the gunshot merely revealed a deep-seated vocation. And the blade to which he is destined will descend in all its mechanical perfection not on a murderer but on an asocial creature, a primitive being whose greatest sin is precisely not believing in sin.

The prosecutor, for his purposes, uses the terrorist logic of which Caligula had made himself the impassioned herald. At this level, *L'Étranger* can very well appear as a kind of Voltairian *conte philosophique,* denouncing the arbitrariness of the judicial mechanism—or one of the first examples of those literary and cinematographic works, so numerous today, that raise questions about the excessive place the sacrificial rite of the trial has assumed in our universe. In fact, it takes to task the presumptuousness of passing judgment at all, and in this joins Pirandello. Opposite the old people in the nursing home, lined up in a semicircle during the wake, Meursault already felt like an accused—accused of what, he had no idea. "Anyway, we are always a little bit at fault." He knows only that he is being judged; that his boss, the concierge, the nursing-home director, are judging him; that the travelers in the bus are intently watching his foolish gestures.

"The most repugnant form of materialism is not the one of which one ordinarily thinks, but the one that would have dead ideas pass for living realities" (N, p. 82). All Meursault's adversaries are bent on avoiding life. His boss waits until the day after the funeral to find a word of sympathy. "For the moment, it is a little as if mamma had not died. After the burial, on the contrary, it will be a closed case and everything will take on a more official aspect." For him, as for the others, sorrow begins with the black necktie, tears, and all that one ordinarily expects of the orphaned child. Marie herself would like to see their liaison conse-crated by some word—"she asked me if I loved her; I replied that that didn't mean anything, but that it seemed to me that I didn't"—by some official and visible bond—"she asked me if I wanted to marry her—I said it was all the same to me . . ." But Marie is a simple person and her affection undergoes no change because of this. The examining magistrate, who is more complicated, is not satisfied with finding out that Meursault loved his mother "like everybody else." This "Patrician" in a red robe had expected lyricism, great protestations of filial love; he runs head on into an elliptical spirit. He expected remorse, he encounters only a vague regret, a feeling of "chagrin." Clutching a crucifix, he launched into a pompous tirade on the necessity of repentance, to obtain an avowal of which he plays out an emotional comedy. If Meursault is not moved, a whole world will collapse. " 'Do you want my life to have no meaning?' In my opinion, that did not concern me and I told him so." The universe of the judge, the prosecutor, and even the priest—who, however, is so profoundly moved in other respects—rests on a network of words, con-ventions, prefabricated attitudes, and clichés that assures them a material, intellectual, and moral comfort. Not to conform to them is to betray—the lawyer, who pleads momentary insanity for Meursault, is well aware of this, and the society, which kills in self-defense, is even more aware.

We should not think, however, that all this is merely a matter of a Publican being delivered up to a few Pharisees. There are many degrees of pharisaism—but in the final analysis, no one escapes it altogether. We all need myths; the virtuous agitation of the examining magistrate is only a refined form of conformity and escapism. By his very passivity, Meur-

sault appears an iconoclast, a kill-joy. To the mania for judging, which
betrays fear and the need for self-justification, he implicity opposes the
evangelical "Thou shalt not judge," for, as Meursault's lawyer points out,
in this case "everything is true and nothing is true." To verbal artifices, to
ready-made phrases, Meursault replies with silence and an absolute sincerity,[22] whose pedagogical effectiveness is easily equal to Caligula's
flights of fury.

His purity totally escapes the traditional categories of morality—
Meursault is a man of glass. His consciousness records facts objectively,
like a blank paper; it reconstructs them unchanged, without having in
any way adorned them. At one moment the "I" and the "me" are
radically cut off from one another, and the "I" states in an impersonal
manner what the "me" has lived; at another moment they are one and
the same, and every intimate reaction is automatically reproduced for
external use. More than lucid, Meursault shows himself to be translucid.
For him, men seem to dance without his having ever heard their music
and without its ever being possible for him to join in the dance. He is no
more able to join in it than Jaïre's daughter, returned again to life, could
pass for a living person (in Ghelderode's *Mademoiselle Jaïre*), no more
than Dostoevski's Idiot, often recalled in connection with Meursault,
could pass for normal, or Baudelaire for a serious bourgeois. This is precisely the tragedy of *L'Étranger;* doing his utmost to escape the frozen
empire of words and clichés, Meursault winds up being crudely labeled
"monster" or, as the judge says, "Anti-Christ."

For Meursault infinitely transcends the role of innocent victim that
sums up the personality of a Johann Moritz[23] and so many other "symbols
of this exasperating world in which unhappy automata live the most
mechanistic of experiences" (*HR*, p. 669). He is, in the full sense of the
word, the innocent. Meursault adheres completely to the universe in
which he breathes. Different from the madman or the visionary, he
provokes no scandal and never makes a spectacle of himself. The ultimate
in his perfidy—or in his innocence—is his having lived up to now without
anyone's having suspected anything. The gunshot alone opened peoples'
eyes.

[22] "One will however have a more exact idea of the author's intentions if
one asks oneself in what way Meursault does not play the game. The answer is
simple; he refuses to lie" (*Théâtre, récits, nouvelles*, p. 1920).
[23] Gheorghiu, *The Twenty-fifth Hour*.

Meursault, thanks to his imprisonment, made for himself an exemplary destiny of that equivocal innocence. At the moment the verdict was read, the spectators realized this. They evince a sudden consideration for him. He had again become someone, "what is most human in a courtroom";[24] even more, he has become a symbol. This very ordinary Algerian, poor among the poor, has come, in spite of himself, to reveal to us our suffering while taking cognizance of his own. His mediocre life reminds us, "miserable earthworms," that we know only how to crawl. Loneliness is our lot and we are cut off from one another by the double barricade of our habits and our language, like Marie and Meursault by the grills of the prison visiting room. Each of us remains a stranger to himself, surprised by his own voice, powerless before his own image: "I smiled and it [my reflection] kept the same expression."

Imprisoned, condemned to asceticism and bare necessities, Meursault, like Oscar Wilde in Reading Gaol, escapes from his own individuality. His condemned man's journal is basically no more than the illustration of Pascal's remarks on the man in prison—the journal of all the condemned men that we all are. The entire second part of the book has a double meaning: rebelling against the machinery of capital punishment and the pitiless precision of the scaffold, which constitutes his personal and immediate destiny, he takes to task, in a definite way, suffering humanity's very destiny.

The prison experience upsets Meursault's notions. The discontinuity of moments begins to blur. The days flow into one another. Memory erupts into a consciousness up to now devoted only to the present: "I wound up no longer being bored at all, from the moment I learned to remember." His indifference takes on quite another meaning. Meursault is going to die and nothing that is used to justify frantic human activity has henceforth any value in his eyes. He looks upon the world of men with the detachment of a La Bruyère watching cats playing at war;[25] of a Pascal "considering the diverse agitations of men and the pains to which they expose themselves," of the monks of Fiesole looking down upon Florence.

One single thing eludes his indifference: death. "How had I not seen that nothing is more important than a capital execution and that, in one

---

[24] Roger Grenier: *L'Accusé.*
[25] Jean de la Bruyère, *Les Caractères,* Book XII, no. 119 (edition of 1696).

sense, it was even the only truly interesting thing for a human being." He concentrates his attention, formerly so willingly dispersed, on this unique object, this impasse. At his mother's burial, the nurse had said to him: "If you go slowly you risk getting sunstroke. But if you go fast, you are all in a sweat, and in the church you get chills and fever." This was already a crude image of existence. Charybdis and Scylla: hot or cold, hot and cold. In any case, one never escapes from it, one is never again wholly oneself —there is no way out.

If only one could hope in a miracle. If "chance and luck had only once changed something! Only once!" Meursault comes smack up against this mathematical "insolent certainty,"—and discovers the Absurd. At the same stroke he discovers joy: "That terrible bound that I felt within me at the thought of twenty years of life yet to come." Twenty years of life on this earth . . . what indeed does another life matter: at the utmost, he could spend his time there remembering this one.

Moreover, wishing for another life "had no more importance than wanting to be rich, to swim very fast or to have a better-shaped mouth." His life threatened, fleeing in all directions, the sky and the earth alone retain his attention. He cherishes them with anguish, as a mother would her condemned child; he wants to lose no part of them. All consolation is empty of meaning for him. His attitude betrays resentment, rancor. Against whom? against this condition of penal servitude in which we must pay without understanding why.

Fear, pathetic protest, resignation and, finally, melancholy acceptance: doubtless it has not been sufficiently noticed how the last chapter reproduced, just as the last scene of Caligula did, the emotions of Christ on the Mount of Olives. Certainly, the sense of revolt is vehement; it bursts forth upon the chaplain like a storm; it rains down in imprecations that mark the limits of despair. But their sincerity is such that they draw tears from the powerless and overwhelmed chaplain—the same tears that Father Paneloux will shed over the body of the dead child in his arms. Then comes peace—not divine peace—but the world's peace, tender in its indifference and fraternal in its everlastingness. A certain continuity of despair engendered a happiness known by Oedipus: "I felt that I had been happy and that I was still." On the threshold of execution, a final thought brings him back to his mother whom he had been accused of not loving—and to men, among whom he hopes to die, standing forth like

Caligula for their edification: "the only Christ we deserved," Camus was to say many lears later.[26]

There is nothing more incontestable than the fact that Meursault, in certain of his aspects, embodies that temptation toward an active nihilism and impersonality which constitutes, among others, one of the permanent characteristics of Camus's work. However, in this case, impersonality is a conquest. The bareness of the style alone is the effect of an artistic effort. Since *L'Envers et l'endroit,* with its poverty of spontaneous language, we have become acquainted with *Noces* and its passionate luxuriance. Camus's style has been stripped bare in the full sense of the word. And the nothingness that surrounds Meursault proceeds not from a kind of abandon, as a certain moralistic brand of criticism would have it, but from a choice.

Meursault is a poor man—and that would suffice to throw pure intellectuals off the track—but a poor man mutilated by prejudices; a protoplasm of a poor man, a negative factor. He takes up as his own the itinerary from innocence to consciousness, of Valéry's *La jeune Parque;*[27] but in contact with the indecent nakedness of this "transparent" being, an uneasiness overtakes the reader and awakens in him whatever pride in being alive slumbers within him. "M. Sartre," Camus wrote in an analysis of *Le Mur,* "converts one to a view of nothingness, *but also* to lucidity."[28] *L'Étranger* converts us to a view of nothingness in order better to attain lucidity, if not an actual truth.[29]

Just as he had drawn out of Djemila's aridity the highest lessons of clear insight, Camus has made Meursault's dreary and sterile existence bear witness in the trial—taken from Romantic tradition—which he

---

[26] In the preface (1955) to the American textbook edition of *L'Étranger,* eds. Germaine Brée and Carlos Lynes (Appleton-Century-Crofts); reprinted in *Théâtre récits, nouvelles,* pp. 1920–28 [trans. note].

[27] *La Jeune Parque* (1917), by Paul Valéry (1871–1945), is a poem in which the author set out to express "the change of a consciousness in the duration of one night," during which the youngest of the Fates awakens to knowledge of her own complex being [trans. note].

[28] *Essais,* pp. 1419–22.

[29] "It is a question of a still negative truth, the truth of being and of feeling, but without which no conquest over ourselves and the world will ever be possible" (*Théâtre, récits, nouvelles,* p. 1920).

brings against Destiny. A polyvalent and ambiguous testimony in which the victim's silences are so many accusations, in which humiliation touches upon grandeur, in which the strangeness of the hero, in the final analysis, touches our own humanity in order to assume it completely in revolt and in consent. Even before the appearance of *Le Mythe de Sisyphe,* laconically, without raising his voice, Camus had already answered his own question: It is possible to live without appeal; all that is needed is a little love and a lot of insight.

If one will recall, *L'Étranger* is approximately contemporary with *Noces* and *Caligula.* It takes the torch from the just barely aborted *La Mort heureuse.* Camus was not unaware of how much literary vehemence there was in *Noces* and *Caligula.* But solitude, an exalted moment, now appeared to him to be as little literary as possible. As once before in *L'Envers et l'endroit,* the tragic is very well reconciled to a total absence of despair, if not of sadness. The "phony war" could only confirm that impression. The accent then is displaced from the Dionysian to the Absurd.

Meursault, anodine and insignificant, is like Caligula was before Drusilla's death. But he is also Caligula's victim and his pupil, not one of those puppets, worshippers of the golden calf, who dishonored the title of senator, not even a poet or a man of letters, but a simple man that a logic born of blood and steel reveals to himself. Caligula illustrated the perversion of the desire for eternity: with him an angel falls. With Meursault, a man is born to life through the discovery of death.

L'Étranger is, then, a pivotal work. The intimate or external circumstances (the solitude associated with camaraderie, the respite of his illness, the hours spent with the newspaper, the war) seem to have provoked a setting aside of love and happiness to the benefit of strangeness. The ardor to live and desire remain keen, but latent. They hardly appear any longer except in the background or in rare outbursts. The lyricism of *Noces* gives way to a deliberate, spare, almost ascetic style. The hurtling pace of Caligula, its spasmodic or whirling rhythms are effaced by the continuous monotony of a current of insignificance.

Does this mean that *L'Étranger* is, for all that, an autobiographical work? Or even the history of a soul? Surely not: "Our true moralists have looked at the world and they have seen themselves." The internal experience and external contacts reinforce one another. With personal memories are mixed fleeting faces, words caught on the wing and situations from life. *L'Étranger* took form by means of a steady accumulation of details and the successive interweaving of its various layers; after which, it was necessary, taking into account the demands of form, stylization, and meaning, to choose deliberately from among the funds of experience. Far from seeking in *L'Étranger,* then, the mark of a frustrated individualism —which many facts deny—I would rather see in it a blueprint of the bitter and scandalous contact of an existence that discovers its own contingency with a society that takes the form of Destiny, necessary and logical even up to the inclusion of murder. If *L'Étranger* proceeds from an experience, it reflects a consciously mutilated experience, stripped right down to the rock-bottom of indifference.

For a long time, analyses of the book, following Sartre's lead, dwelt upon the satire of justice and social mechanisms. It is true that very early, in reaction against the social constraints, conventions, and the prejudices that pierced his impatient youth, Camus thought of creating a character in a novel who, a prisoner of public opinion, refused to justify himself before it. Developed in that single direction by a journalist accustomed to courtroom proceedings, the initial theme could very well indeed have ended up being a Voltairian *conte.* At the utmost, it would have been a repetition, in a new form, of Pirandello's critique of public opinion.

But, between this conception and the writing of *L'Étranger,* psychology came back into its own. Behind "the *homo absurdus,* living lifelessly in a century whose prophet is Kafka," there reappears "a resolute and haughty choice, a desperate denial, and perhaps a lesson," says Nathalie Sarraute.[30] This makes too much of a certain little sentence—added later, moreover—in which Camus, in an exceptional case, evokes Meursault's student past (*ET,* p. 1154).

Camus himself replied to this comment in 1954, in an unpublished note: "*L'Étranger* is neither reality nor fantasy, I would rather see in it a

---

[30] *L'Ère du soupçon.* I would much prefer Robert Champigny's interpretation in a very solid book with the significant title, *Sur un héros païen* (Gallimard, 1959).

myth incarnate in the flesh of the day's warmth. Many have wanted to see in it a new type of immoralist. That is entirely false . . . Meursault is not on the side of his judges, of social laws, of conformist sentiments. He exists, like a stone, or the wind, or the sea under the sun: none of them ever lies." It is not so simple, however. The gunshots shattered this mineral or vegetal simplicity. Meursault is born to duplicity in the course of the trial. His expression may remain innocent like that of Voltaire's Huron. But, between the smile that he tries to express and the grimace that his tin plate flashes back to him, there is a kind of rift; already, a fall from innocence.

Let us go still further: were the gunshots aimed at the Arab or at Meursault himself? Was he not obscurely tired of the very unconsciousness in which he was exhausting his life? In his innocence, was he not calling down a misfortune that would overwhelm him and lead him to his final convergence? The chrysalis breaks its cocoon; the surfeited young obstinately seek the suffering that awakens them.

Moreover, when is Meursault the stranger? When he coincides with the natural world and remains indifferent to society? Or when he is separated from the world and discovers that he is both exceptional and exemplary? Meursault seems ceaselessly to elude us.

J. C. Pariente rightly notes: "Completely detached from himself, he would not have kept a journal. All the same, if nothing means anything to him, he should not write this book."[31] This man who has no certainty, who lives in indifference, is yet anxious to have us share his experience of indifference and his certainty that the truth lies in indifference.

After having rejected the novels fabricated by others (the examining magistrate, the prosecutor, the lawyer), with the book's last chapter, he writes his own novel. But he does not impose it. And we are free to conclude that the prosecutor understood nothing but that Meursault, despite his sincerity, has not said everything.

"A novel of indifference [which] shows itself indifferent to being a novel," an ambiguous novel par excellence, *L'Étranger* illustrates finally the impossibility of being sincere. It intends to deny literature by the very use of literary artifices. It finds simplicity in a stylistic procedure, impossibility in the irony of its comments. It is a recording eye that sees and sees

---

[31] *L'Étranger et son double.*

itself seeing, which never lies, but selects or eludes, until the day when the blank stare becomes accusing before fading away in a tragic smile.

There is no definitive stranger, but a being who at one moment adheres to the world with all his spontaneity, who at another clings to his own life with all his revolt, until the hour of tranquil acceptance. He is a distorting mirror held up to us so that, in these shadow plays against a background of consciousness, we finally see ourselves, doubly betrayed but fascinated.

5

Sisyphus and the Myth of Salvation

It was doubtless not by chance that *L'Étranger* preceded *Le Mythe de Sisyphe* by more than a year. The essay follows the novel as commentary follows immediate perception by the consciousness. It develops, and reduces to their essence, the hero's integral and bewilderingly living discoveries. This anteriority of the literary work over the essay bears witness to the primacy of the image and the word over the idea.

Camus himself was capable of making a mistake in this respect: "a novel," he wrote in 1938, "is never anything more than a philosophy put into images."[1] He was not long in returning to a more exact conception of his art. He wanted to be a novelist rather than a philosopher insofar as the novel, "faithful to the particular," and wedded to life in its "very unfolding," rejected abstractions and rational arguments in order to devote itself to the representation of the world and to derive all its vibrancy from the continual friction between thought and objects in the world. Was he not "convinced of the uselessness of all principles of explication and . . . of the pedagogical message of tangible appearances" (*MS*, p. 178)? If philosophy there is, it is unexpressed, pantomimed for want of being sublimated.

Under these conditions, what purpose then does *Le Mythe de Sisyphe* serve? It has a double objective: to take stock and to shatter a state of solitude. In general, the work of art calls forth admiration rather than dialogue and exchange of confidences. It imposes on the reader all its esthetic prestige, but it does not necessarily engage his adherence to a common view of things. The essay, by contrast, solicits agreement or, barring that, an exchange of views. In this spirit, Camus always abstained from defending his literary works but very willingly carried on open polemical exchanges on the subject of his essays.

---

[1] *Essais*, pp. 1417–19.

Furthermore, if the work of art liberates the artist from some of his obsessions, it brings no satisfaction at all to the need, so keen in Camus, for coherence and unity. How, in fact, do we reconcile those diverse manifestations represented by *Caligula, L'Étranger,* the report on the Kabylian famine,[2] and the preface to *Rivages,* which exalts "sea, sunlight, and women in the light"? How can we bring into accord that aura of nothingness that Meursault expels and Camus's rejection of nihilism which surfaced at the very moment when war was vitiating all hopes? How finally can we come to a full understanding of that discrepancy between thought and actions which troubled a sense of honesty sensitive to all forms of bad faith?

Le Mythe de Sisyphe, then, represents an effort of organization and definition rendered necessary by the inevitable dispersion of all literary or human activities which, themselves, magnify strength, love, and death, and establish, here and there, forward points whose effects are sometimes contradictory; the effort to organize and define occupies the terrain, clears it by logic, and fortifies it in preparation for new departures. In practice, Camus first takes a position and justifies himself afterwards.

Camus's thought very early developed under the double aegis of Hellenic moderation and Christian zeal. From his acquaintance with Epicurus and Lucretius, Marcus Aurelius, and Epictetus, Camus retained the image of a world without redemption or sin, in which pride in life was allied to a spirit of comprehension. Born "under a happy sky, in the midst of a nature with which one feels a sense of harmony, not of hostility," he had quite naturally "the heart of a Greek."

However, Epicurians and Stoics were in no way unaware of death and suffering, which they tried to subjugate through cunning or force. And the Greece of shadows, of Heraclitus or Empedocles, conferred an unfathomable depth upon the mysteries of knowledge and life. Camus analyzed this Greek serenity and torment in the introduction to his thesis, *La Métaphysique chrétienne et néoplatonisme.*[3] But with the reading of Job, Ecclesiastes, Saint Augustine, anxiety grew, and the foundations of existence were attacked at the root. The desire for eternity gnaws at men's

[2] *Essais,* pp. 902–38; this series of articles originally appeared in *Alger-République* between June 5 and June 15, 1939.

[3] His thesis for the *Diplôme d'Études Supérieures,* directed by Professor Poirier; reprinted in *Essais,* pp. 1224–1313.

hearts and the wounded flesh shudders. Christianity exacerbates our pride
in living in order better to humiliate it in this world: it bestows the keys
to the city both upon the irrational and upon scandal, and opens the abyss
that separates the infinitude of our desires from the relativity of the here
and now. In brief, it gives to being and objects the "tragic and necessary
quality lacking in certain workings of the Greek spirit."

In the first chapter of the thesis, "Le Christianisme évangélique,"
Camus discovered, by way of the Gospels, the existence of physical fear in
face of lonely death, the scandalous incarnation, and the hope of redemption and salvation. He affirms with melancholy: "One has to be Greek in
order to understand that wisdom is learned." The entire thesis is, from
this point on, devoted to the study of various attempts at Greco-Christian
collaboration. One senses in it a certain irritation in face of "the arbitrariness inherent in every doctrine of salvation." However, Saint Augustine
fascinated him. He imagined him torn between sensuality, fondness for
the rational, and the desire for faith that is born of the discovery of
evil—"Greek in his coherence, Christian in the anxieties of his sensibility," Plotinus sharpened Camus's thirst for knowledge; Saint Augustine
humiliated the reason, unfit for full comprehension of objects and beings.

This undertaking, in which the author's personality pierces through
the apparatus of erudition, comes to an end on a note of divided feelings:
on the one hand, there is a sympathy for Christianity, considered as a
rejection of dormant courage and Socratic serenity, and for a sort of
heroism and permanent exaltation in the act of commitment. But there is
also mistrust of Christian prophesying which Camus sees as feeding into a
philosophy of history. The exclusive domination of innocence and Greek
clarity comes to an end; we enter into the world of sin and generalized
guilt. If he had had to choose, perhaps Camus might have felt himself
close to Marcion, the Gnostic who rejected the Old Testament and part of
the New, and who drew a moral lesson from scorn for the law, a man
who was religious without a sense of mystery and who was an ascetic out
of pride. "In that pessimistic view of the world and that proud refusal to
accept, resounds the echo of a wholly modern sensitivity. Moreover, it
originates in the problem of evil."

For himself, Camus vainly attempted to reconcile his fondness for
equilibrium and happiness on the one hand, and the temptation toward
the absolute and the chivalrous on the other. "God is dead," but He has
left an indelible imprint in unconscious hearts. Deprived of His divine

ascendance, Christ becomes for Camus what He was for Vigny, the highest incarnation of solitude and human grandeur in the desert of the heavens.

Next comes the tragic reign of man in history. During this time, humanism degenerates into an illusory and easy optimism, the democratic spirit rots beneath the Pharisean formalism of dominical discourses and science succumbs to fetishism, fostered concurrently by both the naive and the technocrats. In his contacts with Spengler, Sorel, and Malraux, Camus fortified his conviction that our epoch is only at the dawn of its vicissitudes.

On the day after the French capitulation in 1940, the highest civil and religious authorities initiated a critique of the times: France had loved life too much. If Camus had had a reproach to make to France, it would have been that she had loved it too softly, in too bourgeois a manner, an attitude to which *Caligula* bears witness and in which human-istic optimism is rudely shaken. But Christian eschatology having gone astray into questions of "moral order" exasperated him even more. *Le Mythe de Sisyphe* is a challenge flung at the exploiters of the nation's misery. In opposition to so many false ascetics, in the midst of so many ruins, he gave voice to the desperate appeal of a happiness whose throat was being cut. He asked reasons for living of the earth alone. Europe was dying, not so much for having loved life too much, but for having loved it badly. In opposition to the spokesmen of appeasement, *Le Mythe de Sisyphe* claims the right to vehemence, in opposition to the nostalgic the right to solidarity, in opposition to the prudish the right to cynicism, and, finally, in opposition to the totalitarians the right to indifference or simply to modesty. For all those who deny the Absurd, who soften it, or who adorn it are without argument its best providers.

For years running, its manifestations had succeeded in appearing sporadic or partial. They took the form of Belcourt's limited horizons, the mute weariness of the workers, the wall of poverty, the bereavements— all that which did not provide an answer or which no longer provided one. The war was to break off the last dialogues, and Camus's recurring illness was to shut off the last exits. In any case, from sensual experience to clear-sighted consciousness, the Absurd changes character; from an open wound in our flank, from a subjective element of our existence, it expands into an objective relationship of man to his own life or to the world that surrounds him. The Pascalian man was at once an object of

the world which he understood physically and a subject of the world
which he was alone in conceiving intellectually. Man, according to
Camus, experiences the Absurd at the same time that he notes its existence and combats it.

That is why the first lines of *Le Mythe de Sisyphe* set forth its
ambition and its limits: "There is something of the provisional in my
commentary . . . The Absurd is here considered as a point of departure."[4]
A modest attitude whose exact significance the author would better seize
on the threshold of writing *L'Homme révolté.* The earlier work, which
combines painful passion, cold analysis, and the spirit of struggle, represents a sort of critique of existence which it rids of a certain number of
myths that encumber and falsify it.

For the time being, what mattered was the "description, in its pure
state, of a sickness of the spirit." More prudent than Chateaubriand, who
was constrained to condemn in retrospect René's morose delectations,
Camus makes clear that his description is to some extent clinical and that
it presupposes the will to be cured. A precision that is all the more
necessary since the first observations seem to confirm the ultimate and, to
sum it up, the incurable character of evil. But we must understand: if one
cannot cure oneself of being man, if evidence of the Absurd is incontestable, at least we must rid ourselves of the multiple temptations of fear and
despair.

All of this accounts for both the book's richness and its difficulty. It
is tempting to discover in it some confidential revelation, and, in one
sense, nothing is more true. Camus describes the evil of the Absurd so
well only because he had profoundly experienced it. Perhaps at the time,
as would be natural, he even attached an importance to certain states of
his thought that he would have contested at a later time. His attempt
remains nonetheless an effort to detach himself from this evil, to turn
upon it and borrow from it a style of life and of writing.

"The last pages of a book are already present in the first ones" (*MS,*
p. 106). The exposition of motifs in what follows those first pages does

[4] In *Alger-Républicain* of March 12, 1939, Camus had already written: "to
take note of the absurdity of life cannot be an end but only a beginning" (*Essais,*
p. 1419).

not reveal a certainty conquered by dint of reason, but "the feeling that all true knowledge is impossible." Thus, in an initial intuitive experience, there is less an affirmation of a certain historical relativity of thought than of the mind's basic inability to know. But once the limits of knowledge are established, reflection develops, under the valid pretext of description, in an exercise of purification and deliverance. To what extent are the author and his book not transformed by each other, as happened with Montaigne, since in any case the observation of evil is a means of partially delivering oneself from it without, however, the bond that unites man to his rock ever having been definitively broken?

Camus has nothing to demonstrate. In this rigorous and seemingly detached book with its philosophical tone, he undertakes a critique of philosophy in the name of existence.[5] He proceeds from an intuition, an elementary reaction expressed in the most simple and colloquial form: the nausea of the traveler lost in a totally strange city, fatigue, disgust with existence as they are felt by the housewife weary from polishing the same household objects day after day, the worker worn out from repeating indefinitely the same gesture in front of the same workbench, the mother powerless to save her child. "What do we do in this world?" Not what are we, in essence, or whence do we come; not a problem of destiny or of reality, but of existence and of meaning: "at the bottom of it all, we wonder why we live," that is to say, why do we not commit suicide in spite of everything or because of everything? "There is but one serious problem: suicide."[6]

Camus refused to pose purely metaphysical questions. First of all, because he thought them insoluble, because they belong to the realm of play-acting, at least in so far as they do not threaten existence. Thus, his scorn for certain philosophers or poets, the singers of suicide and murder, who are too refined to take part in the acts themselves.[7] What use to treat of Destiny if our existence is not modified by it: faith, yes, but not without works (and this is addressed to so many of the completely

---

[5] See *Carnets, I* (p. 89): "To have or not to have value. Create or not create. In the first case, everything is justified. Everything, without exception. In the second case, complete Absurdity. There remains to choose the most esthetic form of suicide: marriage plus forty hours or a revolver."

[6] See *L'Homme révolté* as well (p. 500ff.) on surrealism and suicide.

[7] See preceding note.

obedient faithful). Men are judged by their acts, because acts alone are known with certainty; what do we know of intentions? The Stranger, his being split between his acts and the intentions others impute to him, learns this at his expense. It is not that he was badly judged, but simply that he was judged. All true knowledge, then, of man as well as of the universe, is impossible.

If Camus avoids exclusively metaphysical problems himself, he takes no greater interest in those others have posed and supposedly resolved. Sartre reproached him for having only a secondhand knowledge of the works he used and of not understanding them in depth. It is true that his knowledge of German existentialism (Husserl, Jaspers, Heidegger) came by way of Profesor Poirier's philosophy course and Gurvitch's works on the subject.[8] Camus pretended to be neither commentator nor exegete. On occasion he even made very free use of texts, as in the case of that "all is well" attributed ten times to Oedipus and which we seek in vain in Sophocles. But what of it! He borrowed ideas or citations less than he did attitudes signifying a mode of being. He held valid little that was beyond the lived experience (physical, moral, or spiritual) and not bookish experience: "the soft lines of these hills and the hand of night on this troubled heart teach me far more." His book falls open at Djemila and Florence more than at Husserl or Scheler. He meant to have no other master than nature, certain of drawing unadulterated lessons from her. Above all, it was the cry of the flesh and the senses he listened to, always renewed and each time unique.

One lives a long time without hearing this cry, because of a kind of fast pace of living which we acquire: "We assume the habit of living before having acquired that of thinking." Thus Meursault lived before hurtling against the bars of the prison; thus Marie lived with all her bronzed body. Sleepwalkers, deep in that sleep so necessary to life, which blurs the worst suffering, secretes impossible hopes, and lulls the pangs of our omissions and our denials.

One day the searing light of consciousness erupts: "To begin to think is to begin to be consumed." From such a painful birth Valéry drew some of *La Jeune Parque*'s unforgettable lines. Thought divides, destroys;

---

[8] On the other hand, he knew Chestov, Nietzsche, and Kafka—as well as Kierkegaard—remarkably well.

or rather, to think is to become sensitive to the contradictory forces of the universe of which we are a part—and for that there is no need whatsoever for books.

In this sense, *Noces* marked the farewell to the "sleep necessary to life," the passage from the life of the body to that of the mind, from the vegetable to the human. The body, upon discovering death, lost "its lead." The mind, which, as we knew already, is a quite different thing from the rational intellect, is born of that encounter. Death is the inevitable product of that ferment, and medieval Christianity had understood it well. From that discovery on, each of us carries within him his lost paradise, the paradise of innocence and childhood loves which the collective imagination embodies in Adam and Eve before the fall, in Rousseau's natural man, and perhaps also in the Greek so dear to the humanists. But once the mind is awakened—that mind which, to be exact, is less a mechanism than a grain of sand slipped into the mechanism of the instinct—the manifestations of the Absurd multiply and "passion" is born.

First of all, it is the fundamental discovery of time. "Tomorrow, he longed for tomorrow, when his whole being ought to have rejected it. That revolt of the flesh is the Absurd." The same urge that makes us desire new harvests and new sunlit days carries us to our death, and our yearnings bear in them their own poison. No one has better evoked that progress toward ardent and agonized torture than the seventeenth-century bishop and orator, Bossuet. But "let us take care not to toss poetry into so repugnant a business . . . to understand that a dead human being is fit to be thrown on the garbage heap, to persuade ourselves that memories make no difference, these mark true spiritual progress."[9]

Does man at least respond to man, to that desire for solidarity that haunts him? Not to any greater extent, or rather, quite poorly. Upon slavery follows serfdom and upon serfdom the proletariat. And other forms of servitude, whose strange births are recounted in *L'Homme révolté,* are substituted for the proletariat or coexist with it. Having parted from a desire for liberty and unity, that one should finally come logically to slave-labor camps and periodic purges is only yet another evidence of the Absurd or, if you prefer, the Plague.

Communion with the world? It is henceforth impossible. Even in

[9] From a variant in the manuscript of *Le Mythe de Sisyphe.*

the almost mystical exaltation of Tipasa a weakness subsists. One can never fully coincide with a world that is opaque and primitive in its hostility. One peels an onion in vain, its core is never reached: one skin after the other is stripped away and things retain their mystery. "If one had to write the only significant history of human thought, it would have to be that of its successive repentances and failures."

To be sure, man has tamed nature; ore torn from the soil becomes metal, then machine. But what image of man does the machine reflect? Which one serves the other? Simone Weil, a metallurgist, did not share the technician's optimism on this point. In his desire to possess things, man, as Rousseau feared, enslaved himself to that fetish, money. And even if he no longer had to serve the machine he would still have to tremble in fear of its capabilities. Science has its limits beyond which man himself finds his own existence in question.

Thus, from point to point, from conquest to defeat, we hurtle up against the Absurd, even in that rational intellect of which we are so proud: "What is absurd is the confrontation of that irrationality and this desperate desire for clarity whose call resounds in the deepest part of man." Pascal, confronted by the star-filled heavens, already examined the two infinites of "a measureless universe" off which a "blind reason" rebounded wildly; he assigned to the latter "its own order in which it is effective; [it is] precisely the order of human experience," whether it be scientific or everyday and practical. Whoever wishes to go further, steps into the grand play of vicious circles and false problems, or, through feats of acrobatics, attains the summits of excess like Hegel, for example, and his totalitarian offspring. In the process, one stifles a breath of life that one pretended to amplify and purify.

Up to this point, nothing new has been added. There is nothing that has not been said already from Epicurus to Montaigne and from Pascal to Vigny. The Absurd is the proof for man that he is part of the world but at the same time not all of it; it is the intuition of his changeability with all the potential for hate and love it contains, or, more exactly, the hatred born of unrequited love. Thus Caligula out of excessive love turns to scorn, madness, and murder; thus too, according to Sartre, the members of the proletariat, pushed into the margins of a society that uses them and rejects them at the same time, detest those who importune them. The Absurd is born, then, of the desire to find a meaning in the world and give it form. At the extreme, it resides in the absolute form of an exigency wrecked upon the chaotic reality of the universe. The solution, in this case, could consist in not loving too much in order not to hate too much.

From this comes man's tragic situation—in other words one with no real issue—in the world, torn as he is between a lucidity that confronts him with unacceptable realities and the undefined nature of his desires (lucidity is, all things considered, only the other side of this unsatisfied desire), "between his yearning for unity and the clear vision that he can have walls that close in upon him." At this point, man's essence is the passion, the cross, or, more exactly, the rock to which Prometheus clings, the tree of temptations to which Tantalus succumbed and that indefatigable couple, Sisyphus and his rock. Interminable passion in which anger corresponds to resignation and denial to consent.

For the victim does not suffer without struggling. He protests, shouts his innocence. Already desire is charged with revolt. Revolt holds high that demand for unity, that thirst for the absolute that creates researchers, artists, conquerors, and the dissatisfied (and who isn't at some time or another?). But how can he forget that silence in which this outcry dies? Revolt protests, rises up, but without hope. Prometheus, who condemns Jupiter, knows he is weak and subject to the god's whim. And the same urge that causes us to lay claim to unity forces us in advance to renounce any hope of complete success.

The living man is only a paradox and it is because of this paradox that Camus holds to man's lived experience. Pascal proceeded from the undemonstrable and secret character of the divinity to the truth of His existence, from the Absurd to Truth. Camus infers the necessity of living from the insupportable character of existence. Despite appearances ("if I judge that a thing is true, I must preserve it"), there is no rational argument in this. What evidence is there of it? Even supposing that human nature might be "truly" so torn apart, why would one have to preserve it, not in spite of, but because of its being torn apart? Rather, I see in this a sort of youthful defiance, a fondness for risk, another way of laying claim to the impossible and of proclaiming one's revolt, one's desire to live in spite of everything—as is confirmed by this definition of truth: "I call truth all that which continues" (*N,* p. 79)—in spite of the insecurity, the suffering, the inevitable failures, or rather because of all that, out of fidelity to his childhood and to his mother. Doubtless, this daring is allied to a sort of unconscious Mediterranean faith in the order of the world, to the acute sense of man's necessity in the world, and, in sum, of his primacy, contested though it might be. Montaigne deemed that life without death would not be life. Camus, likewise, implicitly supposes that the Absurd perfects existence: "it will be so much better lived for not having any meaning."

If the Absurd is little else than a negative relationship (as that of the two lovers who reject each other) between human exigency and the reality of things, it comes to mind that this relationship can be easily modified by the transformation of one of the terms. Remove man through suicide and the Absurd disappears—at least as far as the suicide victim is concerned. Such a solution, as we have seen, would profoundly misconstrue the tragic nature of humanity. Let one destroy human exigency, set it adrift, or dominate it, and you have Montaigne's humanistic renunciation as well as religious submission:[10] the one calms life's sharp appetite or seeks to extend it in depth as it diminishes in duration, the other bridles it or channels it toward spiritual ends. Again, playing on the other term of the relationship, one can destroy the universe (*L'Homme révolté* was to treat of this nihilism), declare it rational like certain Hegelian-oriented existentialists, or finally, one can transform it along Marxist avenues, another object of meditation for *L'Homme révolté*.

Through some curious aberration, no one perceived for a long time that Camus's attitude was radically anti-existentialist. Despite his reiterated denials,[11] people refused to see that *"Le Mythe de Sisyphe* was directed against the philosophers called existentialists," whom he reproached precisely for ultimately arriving either "at divinity by way of the critique of reason," or at "a divinization, which is simply the deification of history," with which *L'Homme révolté* was to claim to deal definitively.

Once again, Camus's effort is less a matter of establishing a com-

[10] "I except the hypothesis of acceptance. It is a mockery" (from a typed manuscript).

[11] See the interviews in *Nouvelles littéraires* (November 15, 1945), and in *Servir* (December 20, 1945); also the letter to M. le Directeur de *La Nef* (January, 1946); the two interviews are reprinted in *Essais*, pp. 1424–29; the letter to *La Nef* in *Théâtre, récits, nouvelles*, pp. 1743–44.

mentary than of drawing from various texts something that resembles an exemplary attitude toward life. "What interests me is knowing how one should conduct oneself." Whatever profound esteem Camus might have had for Saint Augustine or Pascal, the existential leap that they inaugurated seemed to him a juggling act: "The Absurd become God."

Faith is henceforth the most deeply moving form of escapism. The incomprehensible provides access to a higher comprehension; the greater the scandal, the more radical the antinomy, the more exasperating the paradox, in short, the more total the Absurd and the nearer salvation. The blackest night foreshadows the most radiant of days. This game of "losers-take-all," with the "sacrifice of the intellect" that it carries with it, is contestable. The great misfortune is, in fact, that the irrational is not total nor the Absurd absolute. If this were not so, what link between man and the world would subsist. The residue of this world's experiences does not perforce constitute the key to the next one. Basically—and it is here that strict adherence to texts loses its importance—Pascal, like Chestov, Kierkegaard or Jaspers, sought to be cured of this metaphysical illness. Camus too wants to be cured, but the others postulate a sure cure in order to better escape the illness:[12] a procedure with a real but relative effectiveness. The will to live does not hinder us indefinitely from dying; in any case, nothing of the kind is revealed to us. All the rest is literature or "frustrated lyricism."

We can attempt another reduction, for which Husserl furnishes the model: the universe reduced to eternal reason. Phenomenology keeps company part of the way with the exponents of the Absurd. It describes the world without explaining it and proclaims the equality of all experience. Then, through one of those acrobatic exercises, the secret of which belongs to philosophers, modesty becomes assurance, and essences, camouflaged behind tangible appearances, are unveiled in all their majesty. The universe, of which we perceive only the surface, finds a third dimension. Under the coarse design of human reason, the filigree of divine reason takes form and the Absurd vanishes. "One no longer believes in God, but one believes in history" (*PL, II,* p. 1427).

The longing for totality triumphs, then, over the perceptible evi-

---

[12] "I refuse especially to believe that in the metaphysical order the need for a principle necessitates the existence of that principle" (letter to Pierre Bonnel [March 18, 1943]; reprinted in *Essais,* pp. 1422–24).

dence and creates the illusion: the desire to reconcile all contradictions raises many difficulties which will reappear in the long run. This is why nothing is more tragic than the happiness of the completely convinced, gorged as they are on the irrational. In any case, the true characteristics of human reason are isolated and revealed by counterproof. In its first stage, reason is ambitious and a motivating force: it wants to understand, understand everything, and is drunk with logic. Contact with the irrational, death, and evil force it into a withdrawal and a bitter reservedness. Nor for long, however; scarcely has it taken cognizance of its weaknesses than it sets loose the cry of revolt and repeats it tirelessly in order to be able better to measure it afterwards through awareness of its limits. In this back and forth movement the reason is both motor and brake: "the Absurd is lucid reason that discovers its limits." The phrase is worthy of Montaigne, as is this one: "I can understand only in human terms." The surreal universe or the supernatural world, then, were to have only a psychological or poetic value for Camus.

Similarly, the present alone is an object of experience: the future eludes human capabilities and at a stroke every predication, religious or political, is impossible. To the "hell of others" that obsesses Sartre, "the hell of the present" replies. In short, in the period during which the reason tirelessly demands that the world have a meaning, it challenges everything that adorns itself—improperly from its point of view—with a suprahuman significance. It chooses the present over the future, the certitudes of the earth and the flesh over the elusive and hypothetical soul, human tenderness over impenetrable divine love. Over abstractions and metaphysics it chooses poetry, that most sensual of human expressions—at least, that poetry which limits itself to the "lyricism of forms and colors." Rather than contemplation it prefers creation, which, rejecting the world's obscurity, reinvents the world in its own mode, but without illusions; rather than saintliness, it prefers nobility of heart and mind, a still imprecise form of revolt of which Meursault in death and Rieux in life provide us with the surest examples; and finally, to sin it opposes a freedom composed of innocence, ignorance, and openness to life, illustrated once more by Meursault at the foot of the scaffold, free at least from hope and remorse as Epicurus was from fear.

It is at this point that Sisyphus sees values reborn out of a world deprived of meaning and to which he stubbornly refuses to impart a meaning. Where indifference and fatalism seemed to have reigned, gran-

deur arises: the grandeur of the role to be played in the infinite multipli-
cation of experiences (thus it is that the actor should be one of the priests
of the Absurd, for he multiplies himself by assuming different masks),
experiences of compassion and hatred, of action, of movement and creation, like the bee gathering honey from flower to flower or Don Juan
from woman to woman chasing after the satisfaction of his inextinguish-
able desire. *Nihil humanum a me alienum puto* ("I think nothing human
to be foreign to me"), the rallying cry of eternal humanism which Camus
rejuvenates by inviting us "to choose the form of life that brings us the
utmost of human substance."

Hungry for the absolute, the "absurd" man finally turns to humanity
to fulfill this appetite. Once it is admitted that profundity is barely a
human dimension, he engages resolutely in a policy of quantity and
surface experiences. This is doubtless an explanation of why the book
may appear lucid and luminous but not to have any of those lightning
flashes that for sudden moments rend our intellectual universe. In return,
as deliberately superficial as they may be, these experiences demand a
concern for continuity, an obstinacy, and to sum it up, a pride that gives
the book its loftiness and its dignity.

A pride, in fact, that justifies "the unbearable wager" of the Absurd.
The eternal, for those who seek it, is their comfort, their final refuge.
Happily for them, at the very moment they think they grasp it from here
in this world, the earth disappears from beneath their feet—and discomfort remains the lot of Pascal, Saint Augustine, and the mystics, just as it
is the lot of Sisyphus; but with him it is conscious and claimed as a right.

One senses all that is aristocratic in this attitude (as with the
stoicism of the slave Epictetus, who had earlier "helped [Camus] to hold
on," in the hospital[13]), yet it is derived from reflections common to all of
us. If there is any equality in the world, the lucid consciousness grants it
to the "conqueror" just as it does to the post office employee. But at the
same time, they will both have the same scorn for the utilitarian or, more
exactly, the same indifference toward productiveness, the same absence of
remorse, an introverted form of hope, and the same sense of responsibility
that compels *Les Justes* to pay for their deeds as men of responsibility and
not as men of guilt.

Such is Don Juan, prey to the instinct of the flesh, thirsting for

[13] From Viggiani's notes.

happiness, delivered from regret, without morality but not without honor. He knows that a specific instant of love will never come again—"love what one will never see a second time"—that his pleasures are without tomorrows, fleeting and unique. That bitter knowledge transforms his sensual pleasure into asceticism. The most frivolous of existences ends in the most tragic of contemplations. Camus never stopped pursuing the dream of bringing to the stage the legend of Don Juan—that of Vencelas de Milosz—betrayed by his body and ever afterward "kneeling in the void."

The same fondness for the perishable, the same illusionless determination to make their mark in the sand, comprise the lesson we learn from both the conqueror and the actor as well. The conqueror becomes a part of the present and of history, and he discovers the true value of human life even on the humiliated or mocking countenances of his adversaries. The fearless, reproachless combatant, too, ends by seeking his victory in the defense of "lost causes." In the conqueror there is something of the black knight of medieval legends.

Revolt, which Don Juan must proffer in the form of blasphemy, and which enlivens the actor's parody (Bossuet saw this clearly), the conqueror carries as his standard. Don Juan insinuates himself into the flesh of the "other" of a thousand faces; the actor into his soul; the conqueror strives to make contact with "others," or rather with their heads, he rises up against Destiny, proclaims that human grandeur lies in its fleshly frailty, and rediscovers in suffering and fear the way to pity and solidarity. He knows that he will not remake men; but at least he must "make as if." The modern conqueror is a kind of revolutionary anarchist for which Lawrence of Arabia and Malraux might at one time have furnished examples.[14] From the desert of the Absurd where only indifference and cynicism seemed to flourish, a promise rises in all naturalness: "There is one single luxury . . . and it is that of human relations . . . upheld faces, threatened brotherhood, friendship so strong and so modest, these are the true riches since they are perishable." Resolutely turning his back on the eternal, facing history rushing down upon him like Sisyphus' rock, the

---

[14] "Nothing of the conqueror endures, not even his doctrine." And from the manuscript: "The end of the conqueror is betrayal. Fear nothing. Like everything in this world, treason itself is transfigured in my somewhat proud heart. There are betrayals that liberate and magnificent traitors in history. There are honorable treasons."

absurd man discovers that the instant of life that still flutters is alone precious and, beneath the blow of a common threat, leans for strength upon his companions in misery and in glory.

More than honor and solidarity, artistic creation bears witness for man. To create is less to become the equal of God than to "re-do" his work. For is existence anything else but "an exaggerated mime beneath the mask of the eternal"? Everything in this world is a role, as Pirandello would have it, and it is not without reason that actors are thought "to create" new roles. "To create is to live twice," and to live in the fundamental fiction of the universe in which man sees himself condemned endlessly to build on sand, to undertake without any certainty, in short, to make "as if" he were eternal. By no means can creation constitute an escape from the Absurd. When a jazz blues song reveals the existence of art to Roquentin, the hero of Sartre's *La Nausée,* he is not any the less freed from his nausea, but a joy, an "absurd joy," rises up out of his disgust, born of art's inner necessity in an obscure and contingent world. "If the world were clear, art would not exist." In the hands of man the Absurd sometimes blooms forth in beauty and the artichoke becomes an acanthus.[15]

It is self-evident that if creation is not an escape from the Absurd, it derives relatively from the same indifference as the remainder of human activities. "The absurd creator does not put great stock in his work—he could give it up." At least, he ought to be able to, as did Rimbaud and as did Roquentin, who frees himself painlessly from the historical work he had begun. But like everything that is absurd, creation is ambiguous. It too is acceptance and refusal, moderation and excess, Romantic fervor and Classical discipline. And one thinks of this statement of Vigny in this connection: "The work of art is a piece chiseled out of experience, a facet of a diamond in which the internal brilliance is contained without being limited."[16] Creation rises from the individual to the general, from sensibility to lucid consciousness. It clings obstinately to the life that it re-initiates in order to perfect it. But it takes care never to forget that life cannot truly be made over, that all this is only a game, a grandiose illusion. And, in order not to be caught in the trap of hope, it "says less," finally moving in

[15] "Every artichoke bears within it an acanthus leaf, and the acanthus is what man would have made of the artichoke if God had asked for his advice" (André Malraux, *La Psychologie de l'art*).

[16] See *La Maison du berger,* ɪɪ. 199–205.

accord with our longing or rather constraining that longing within the limits of lucidity. Thus, a new classicism is defined in which order responds to passion and in which the wild outcry is submitted to a rhythmic cadence; a school of patience and clairvoyance, whose father could be Baudelaire, covering over the mute drama of an absurd existence with strange sensual images.

This classicism is a teacher of life: "In it one learns to give form to one's conduct" (*PL, I,* p. 1892). Morality, "that great torment of men" (*PL, II,* p. 1108), haunts minds avid for coherence. Gide's immoralist deceived himself as to his own aims: haltingly, he sought a style of life beyond conformism. True moral values scorn moral codes. For pleasure, exactly like art, conquest, or acting, is not without its own demands. "That which bars the high road gives rise to the footpath," Marcus Aurelius said. Camus retained scarcely anything else from Stoicism. For years, his life was resumed in a simultaneous combat against death and against himself: to concentrate his strength, free himself from the weight of vanity and the desire for wealth, to pass finally from indifference to detachment. Without the Absurd there is absolutely no need for ethical values. The Christian freely imagines that were it not for the commandments, morality would be finished and done with. The "everything is permitted" of Ivan Karamazov is the cry of an emancipated Christian. The absurd man states more modestly that nothing is forbidden. The Absurd, in fact, suffices for him. God's silence is the most impassable of barriers. If it is true nothing is forbidden, there are so few things that are possible, or that are possible, at least, without force of will and effort. Now, from his past participation in sports, Camus retained a fondness for disinterested struggles, for honor: "What I am finally most sure of about morality and men's obligations, I owe to sports."[17] The game, once begun, is played right to the end. The rules are good for what they are, but they are the rules. The essential is that the melancholy smile of the glorious defeated blooms again on Sisyphus' exhausted countenance.

Le Mythe de Sisyphe thus offers us the décor[18] of a world emptied of the divinity, of eternity, and of the hope they engender. Within it, a

---

[17] *Racing Universitaire d'Alger* (April 15, 1953).

[18] "What seems to me to be a 'given,' in fact, is not values, nor even being; it is the world, the framework, the décor, if you will" (letter to Pierre Bonnel).

personality evolves, a stranger to himself, to his fellow men, to the universe and, at the same time, quite close to them, if only through his longing. A character who senses that he was made for happiness, eternity, and dialogue, and who by the feebleness of his intellect, his physical and moral strength, is condemned to anguish, frailty, and uncertainty. Bound to the living world by intertwining desire and disgust, he has to admit that contradiction is his true nature and that no dialectic whatever can free him from it. From the intuition of the Absurd, we have come now to the tangible evidence of the Absurd: all true knowledge is impossible.

At the extreme, Camus admitted, "perfect absurdity would be silence. And why not?"—a statement he was later to repeat to his friend, the poet Francis Ponge. But is not to live, to speak and to judge? "The Absurd apparently impels us to live without value judgments and to live is always, in a more or less elementary fashion, to judge."[19] Meursault learns this at his expense. Backed up against those contradictions that are the warp and woof of our existence, it remains for man to live in spite of everything, to re-initiate ceaselessly the impossible dialogue, even if it entails merely hearing the echo of his own voice, to answer for his own acts since nothing else answers for them, to give himself a style of life in which refusal is balanced against acquiescence and heroism is fused with clear-sighted simplicity. In short, without questioning in any way the value of human life—which is to say its frailty—it is a matter of no longer fearing evil and of suffering less from its effects. The world does not always have meaning, but little by little it becomes once again liveable; and the love man bears the earth, without being a justification, becomes at least his reward.

To be at home within these walls without falling into new illusions, to transpose the struggle against evil into modest combats against accessible, particular evils; thus appears the absurd man's policy in outline: "those political attitudes alone are acceptable which are concerned with the event, with the housekeeping of the city, without demanding submission to any code of ethics or any metaphysics."[20] This manuscript statement is elaborated in a brighter tone one year later, in a letter to Pierre Bonnel: "I believe it perfectly possible to link an absurd philosophy with a political one concerned with human perfection and which places its

---

[19] Letter to Pierre Bonnel. In the same spirit he wrote to Jean Grenier that "there is no absurd thought," since every thought brings judgment with it.

[20] From the manuscript of *Le Mythe de Sisyphe.*

optimism in the realm of the relative." For the time being, Camus forbade himself to speak out on "what one can do" within the framework of the Absurd, to come back to it later with his study of revolt. At what price can men establish among themselves the dialogue that Heaven denies us?

"Relative optimism." The expression may seem strange with respect to *Le Mythe de Sisyphe*. The book has deceived more than one reader. People have not always distinguished, behind the apparent logic of the text, the lived experience that flashes here and there, despite the author, in bursts of rebellious lyricism. *Le Mythe de Sisyphe* is a personal adventure shared in by a whole youthful generation, the confidential statement of a young man, hungry for life, plunged into sickness and war, who strove to rediscover a balance midway between a hope that did not touch him and a despair that he rejected. Should one be surprised to learn that the study on Kafka, written in 1938, and completed for insertion in the chapter "La Création absurde," originally bore the title "Kafka, romancier de l'espoir"? Doubtless, Camus was here again concerned with freeing himself from the temptations of hope by means of a dearly conquered indifference. But the very fact that the author had to make so many efforts and that unendingly, a relatively optimistic vocabulary wells up beneath his pen, is evidence enough that "metaphysical pessimism in no way means that we must despair of man."[21] If *Le Mythe* is, as Camus was to repeat in his letter to Bonnel, "the description of ground zero," it was because he intended to improve his odds in the great game of existence.

In all, *Le Mythe de Sisyphe* is no more a philosophical work than *L'Étranger* is a true novel. It is neither chronologically nor in fact the intellectual skeleton of *L'Étranger*. The novel (*récit*) spends much more time on the pre-absurd man, the difficulties of human expression, the social comedy of which the essay speaks not at all. *L'Étranger* describes the everyday world, the discovery of consciousness by way of the experi-

[21] Letter to Pierre Bonnel.

ence of evil. *Le Mythe de Sisyphe* establishes a logical diagnosis and an individually tailored prescription.

"Why am I an artist and not a philosopher? It is because I think according to words and not according to ideas" (*CN*). This is why in the essay itself, he had to have recourse to the Apollonian myth that enlightens, delimits, and sometimes desiccates. Therefore, we should not be astonished if the clinical character of the work and the will for recovery that it implies have sometimes, with the critics as well as with the author, favored abstraction. "The three Absurds are finished. Beginnings of freedom," he cried on February 21, 1941 (*CN, I,* p. 224). What an illusion! There he stands, "absurd as before."[22]

[22] See "L'Enigme" in *L'Été.*

6

The Return of the Prodigal

The first step in an analysis of *Le Malentendu* must begin with *L'Étranger*. This detail alone emphasizes the limits of Camus's imagination as it does his spirit of continuity. Meursault, in prison, discovers between his mattress and his cot a shred of old newspaper, "yellowed and transparent" like a Greek myth. In it is related a brief news item: the murder, by his mother and his sister, of a man who, returning to the family-run inn after a long absence, had decided to register there incognito. From one point of view the story "was unlikely. From another it was quite natural. In any case, I found that the traveler had a little deserved what happened and that one should never play games" (*ET*, p. 1180).

It was in the heart of the winter of 1942–43 that *Le Malentendu* was written. Privations, recurrences of his illness, living in exile in Europe reawakened in Camus "an old anguish there in the hollow of my heart, like a bad wound that every movement irritates." He was alone in Le Panelier amid the immense and somber backdrop of the Mezenc mountains, far from the sea and sunlight. He remembered Prague and the nausea he had felt there. Hemmed in on all sides by hostile countries, delivered up to Nazi rapacity by the cowardice of Munich, Bohemia, cold and shoreless, represented in his memory the epitome of the alien land.[1]

At that period the logic of the concentration camps, prophesied by Caligula, touched us less directly than the banality of our days of national shame. Denied by their brethren, crushed by the rage to live of some and the weary resignation of others, men by the thousands were dying in the midst of the general apathy. Horror daily became more natural. From this

---

[1] The theme of the play dates from at least April, 1941. At that time, Camus was still in Oran. That is to say that his actual exile in Europe was not at the origin of the play's conception; but, as is often the case, life lends concrete support to the initial idea.

state of affairs, doubtless, arose the idea of recreating on the stage an atmosphere of emptiness, impotence and fatalism which, however, would be rent by a breath of love.

It was a gamble, and Camus always held for *Le Malentendu* that tenderness that one holds for great undertakings that miss their mark. He had the troubled feeling that *Caligula* was not an authentic tragedy: Caligula seeks death in a superior form of suicide, he does not submit to it as though to an absurd destiny. He mingles in his acts too much pedagogical ambition, and even when the game did not live up to his expectation, he remained from start to finish the leader of the game.

Camus wanted a modern and more pure tragedy in which the tragic appeared in all its nakedness. This explains the completely classic bareness of the theme. After an opening scene full of expectation and mystery, everything focuses on the simple question: will Jan leave the inn alive or not? *Le Malentendu* is the play of missed opportunities. The mother hesitates to kill, out of weariness. Maria, the foreign wife, multiplies her efforts to dissuade Jan from a course of action that she senses is fraught with danger. If the old man should discover Jan and Maria together, if Martha should check Jan's passport very closely, the situation would be saved. It would take little more for Martha, annoyed by Jan's lack of discretion, to refuse him hospitality and death. During all of scene vi, imminent recognition hangs in the air; a word seems enough to bring it about, but another word postpones it. When Martha, under the pretext of bringing him towels and water, comes to see her brother, she hesitates once again. But the evocation of the sea in the sunlight and of Mediterranean splendors will reawaken in her the taste for blood. The words that ought to have brought the brother and sister together separate them for once and for all. When the mother finally intervenes and when Jan decides to flee, it is too late, there is no turning back.

The subject lent itself to melodrama (as in the film, *L'Auberge rouge*),[2] to spectacular repercussions. Camus reduced it to "nothing." The action ultimately is entirely internal: nascent scruples, hesitant pity, anxiety. Each step forward by one of the characters produces an involuntary retreat by another, as with two like magnets that repel one another, and the very reasons that ought to set everything to rights merely worsen

[2] The film is situated in the region of the Mezenc mountains about forty kilometers from Le Panelier.

the situation. Jan's fate and that of his murderers is played out in nuances. Everything is only a question of instants, words, and elementary gestures, all summed up in the anodyne cup of tea. The tragedy lies less in the almost absent or muted passions than in their blind interplay. A ray of sunlight is all it will take for Martha and her mother to become the barely willing murderers of the prodigal son.

In *Le Malentendu,* Camus avoided ancient history as a source, but not the realm of legend. In France and abroad the songs and stories that recount similar "incidents"[3] are numerous. *Le Malentendu* is related to the story of Oedipus: a natural course of events leads the least likely of men to murder and incest; all it took was for the goad of curiosity to compel him to answer the Sphinx. Jan assumes Oedipus' curiosity, pride, and fondness for complications. Martha and her mother in this case play the role of the unwitting murderers. All three are prisoners of a destiny that is imposed by the most natural of circumstances. In Caligula's madness there was a provocation of Destiny, a heroic defiance. The ways that lead our three characters to their death are without apparent grandeur. They all go to their end like beasts to slaughter, for want of a word's being uttered.

Caligula is the center of everything, whereas Jan has scarcely confirmed his decision to spend the night at the family inn than the future eludes the protagonists. In any case their happiness is compromised. Jan would never have been able to forget the glacial atmosphere in which his mother and his sister breathed. Martha could never console herself for her lost chance, and her conqueror's spirit would not have been satisfied with a happiness lavished upon her. Not one word is spoken that does not, unbeknown to all of them, widen the abyss that separates them. Finally,

---

[3] I had pointed out that Zacharias Werner, a protégé of Goethe, had composed a romantic drama, *The Twenty-fourth of February,* based on the same basic theme. In a letter to Richard Thiberger, Camus explained that he had not read this play but had encountered the anecdote in a newspaper. Now, Professor David G. Speer has discovered in the French press of 1935 a dispatch, dated January 5, that reported an exactly analogous story, except that it was not situated in Czechoslovakia. It can be conjectured that the Algiers press picked up the dispatch, that Camus read it and that, deliberately or unconsciously, he transferred it to Czechoslovakia after his personal visit in 1936. True or not, the story nonetheless takes on a legendary atmosphere (For Speer's article see "Meursault's Newsclipping," *Modern Fiction Studies,* XIV (1968), pp. 225–29 [trans. note]).

Le Malentendu, more than any other tragedy is a work of disillusionment: Jan's good will butts up against the wall of Martha's reserve, the tiny light of decency that had begun to flower in the Mother's heart is stillborn, and Martha dies unfulfilled.

Camus wanted to make of *Le Malentendu* a desert where alone would flower "the blue of sand thistles." Therefore he purposely adopted a style of indifference. Poetry crops up only in very rare moments. The passport scene very precisely sets the tone. Its sentences are short, uttered sometimes as though by chance. The dialogue is as disconnected as Meursault's monologue. It seems as though contact is impossible to establish: "Do you have any family?" Martha asks. "You could say I used to have. But I left them a long time ago." "No, I mean are you married?" Each one secretly pursues his dream, each behind his own wall of words, playing upon hints and implications: "I am not very poor," Jan says, "and for many reasons, I'm glad of it." Most often passions are suggested and are expressed only by silences. Martha dreams, she "visibly has her mind on other things," and suddenly she stiffens. The sentence stops short, but it has the cutting edge of a guillotine blade. The utterances become rapid, stacatto, aggressive. However the dryness of the tone deadens their effect. Martha's bursts of anger are not the kind to which one abandons oneself, but like those one shuts up within oneself. Martha's speech cuts, erupts in machine-gun bursts, but she scarcely ever becomes openly excited. Whether they pass from the utterance of formalities to accusations, from emotion to weariness, the characters always have in their voices a certain neutral and colorless quality. There hovers in their wake an odor of boredom and loneliness.

Camus strove equally to relieve the murder of its dramatic facility. He emphasizes its banality—great real-life tragedies often carry in them a dash of mediocrity. The murderers' "occupation" and their almost professional application are made strikingly obvious. In one sense, Martha and her mother are presented as some kind of shopkeepers of crime. From this contrast between the technical indifference of the pair's occupations and gestures and the gravity of their consequences, Camus anticipated an effect of cold horror, perceptible from the opening scene.

But can tragedy easily support the double indifference of both action and language? These are essentially novelistic techniques which had contributed in part to *L'Étranger*'s success. Emptiness is not in itself theatrical unless one succeeds in stylizing it. The stage implies a certain communication between the spectator and the characters, and it is a dangerous gamble to show us characters whose passions are repressed and each of whose gestures betrays detachment. Between us and both Martha and Jan, contact is as difficult as between Jan and Martha themselves. Most often, by decree of their creator, each of them fails to give off either heat or light.

Indeed it is not enough for the characters to be murderers or victims in order that the tragic dimension be conferred upon them. Madness created a curiosity about Caligula, which depended upon his ambiguity. Meursault benefits in like manner from what one might call his transparency or his strangeness. The former sacrifices himself even in the midst of his crimes, the other was a victim despite all appearances. Murderers move us only to the extent that the human and the monstrous is allied within them.

Camus somewhat increased his difficulties when he denied his heroes the excuse of blindness or of a passionate outburst. Their murders are premeditated and methodical; they are fully conscious of their aim and the motives for their actions. They put specifically human qualities, lucidity and professional conscientiousness, to the service of inhuman tasks. The tragedy derives solely from an error of the victim's identity. They are given no attenuating circumstances other than the misfortune that preys upon them, and no grandeur other than the cross they themselves have raised for their own torture.

Camus's attempt could sustain itself, then, only by the tragic power of the characters' personalities. But, while the decision to stress an atmosphere of indifference led him to compose with blurred strokes, the decision to give the play symbolic force constrained him to simplicity. Hence there is a certain imprecision in the conception: at one moment the lines are sharp and the character is easily reduced to a formula, at another he is dissimulated behind the coldness of language or seems to dissolve into the general meaninglessness around him. The point of equilibrium is difficult to locate between too much familiarity and a too great dignity of tone.

Thus, Martha could be a disturbing character. This woman of repression, this puritan of crime belongs to the race of Cromwell or the Inquisitors. "No one has kissed my lips, and even you have not seen my body uncovered. Mother, I swear to you, that is going to have to be paid for." In her eyes she has that evil light which is like a reflection of the seas of which she dreams. She is a feminine Caligula who loves life, aspires to happiness and detests faith, the ultimate recourse of the weak: "Oh! I hate this world in which we are reduced to God." The little old woman of *L'Envers et l'endroit* too had been reduced to God; she at least, had lived. "But me, I suffer from injustice; I have not been treated right . . ." Martha is abrupt, rebellious, totally prey to her obsession: the sea, the sunlight, escape from the greyness of the Slavic lands. She is sister to those young Nazis who wanted for their country "a place in the sun." She mistrusts any feeling of pity and avoids it by force of severity and logic. She tends hatred in her heart out of a longing for love. One might say she is an intellectual obsessed by the flesh.

The character of the mother touches us more perhaps. Her weariness, that fondness for religion that comes to her with age, her old woman's scruples, that mixture of tenderness and hardness whenever the prodigal son is evoked, all that reminds us of faces already glimpsed. She kills without knowing exactly why: out of what has long since become habit, almost as a vocation. She has lost the sense of murder as others lose the sense of words. She is a living corpse in whom human feeling flares up for brief moments. She has known suffering and misfortune; her husband is dead, her son has abandoned her. She murders with the same detached sadness that she puts into all her material tasks. But the consciousness of her crime will be brusquely awakened in her by maternal love, and she will rejoin in death the prodigal son of whom she never ceased to dream in silence.

Jan moves us through his naive good will and his awkwardness. He shines with the desire to make happy those he had left behind. But he is afraid of words. This adventurer has the heart of a child. He is devious because the moment of reunion frightens him much more than any of the struggles that gained him his wealth. Once his fortune was made he began to remember, to feel fondness for his past, and he cannot rest until he has found his family home again. But he preferred to return there, if I dare say so, by breaking and entering. For himself alone he wanted it to be by surprise. He meant to assault its solitude, the better to break down his own, the solitude of happiness.

But the most pathetic of all is Maria, the happy wife. She understands nothing, neither Jan's demands nor his anxiety. To lose nights of love when a single word would take care of everything! For this woman of flesh and blood, firmly planted in happiness and health, these are chimeras, a spoiled child's games. We share the sympathy Camus had for her. For him she is the woman in love, a younger and more conjugal Caesonia, a less carnal and more tender Marie Cardona. He projected into her his conception at the time of feminine love, demanding and simple, which blooms forth in various scenes from *L'État de siège* and especially in *Les Justes.* On hearing of Jan's death, her great dark eyes radiate a smile, rejecting the truth with all her confidence. "You're joking, aren't you? Jan told me that, already when you were a little girl, you took pleasure in disconcerting people." She alone is openly moving in the midst of her happiness, first threatened and then destroyed.

All these characters, however, lack roots. Martha is without a past. What is the source of her passion? Childish obsession, the reaction of a single girl getting on in years, capriciousness? No one knows. We perceive Jan obliquely rather than meeting him head on. Why had he run away? What has he retained from his childhood? We never know the circumstances of the mother's first murder. And Maria will turn to God without our having been, up until that moment, in any way aware of her faith. All of them are limited to the present. Meursault appeared strange because of this; they merely seem mutilated, deprived of an essential dimension, time.

Each of them is important as much for what he represents as for what he is. Camus, in portraying Maria, yielded somewhat to a conformist idea of the wife because he meant to oppose her to Jan as happiness and equilibrium are opposed to anxiety. Jan has the urge to know, to understand beings and things from within. He aspires to reconciliation, to the home of the soul: "To live among one's family the rest of one's life . . ." He embodies metaphysical instability, that virile agitation which gives rise to problems and duties and directs us toward moral conduct. In this sense, he is the perfect victim, innocence whose curiosity delivers him up to the executioner. Maria, the passive lover by contrast, suffers and knows only how to weep. She speaks of the suffering flesh, ignorant and crucified humanity. Martha and Mary, the Gospel pair, whom Camus dedicates to the Absurd. Maria loves and contemplates; her idol has feet of clay. Martha has chosen action, dirty hands; she is the kitchen-maid, but rebellious this time, and hospitable in the treacherous fashion of the gods.

Camus felt the need to prolong his final scene in order to have love and revolt confront one another, and in order better to subordinate Maria's suffering to the final exchange with the mute servant. We had already come to understand clearly the author's intentions when, in Act II, scene iii, Jan rang from his room for service. To be sure, this would be an excellent means of justifying the cup of tea, and Jan's action is explained by nervousness and lonely anguish. But the old servant has barely left the room when Jan cries out: "that is not a response." That suffices to transport us brutally into the metaphysical sphere. Was not the play, after all, to have borne the subtitle: "God does not answer"? The servant seems indeed to have no other *raison d'être* than to embody Destiny, which is "mute, blind and deaf to the outcries of living creatures." The symbol, our journalists would say, is "telegraphed."

Le Malentendu, in fact, makes use of the double-meaning technique to the fullest. I do not mean merely the hidden meanings that separate the characters: Racine's Néron and Athalie also make use of threats they alone understand; but with what suppressed hatred they make them, while Martha is without real cruelty. It is rather the metaphysical double meanings that I refer to. A sentence like this one—"it seems to me that we were not so much strangers to one another as all that"—sums up the two techniques. Behind the guest's simple amiability the brother's mental reservations are silhouetted; and all of this overlays the metaphysical pretention to biblical reconciliations or to Greek recognition scenes.

It is important to note that the manuscript provides us only with nameless characters: the Old Man, the Sister, the Mother, the Son, the Wife, thus establishing only symbolic bonds of relationship. For the stranger[4] that Jan, in his success, has become, his return is that of the Prodigal Son. The word *demeure* [abode] comes frequently to his lips, as the privileged locale of reunions, of peace of soul, of unity. The essential matter is to find the suitable "language." And on this theme there are superabundant variations.

Doubtless the principle of the double meaning is defensible, since the Greek theatre as well used it in an almost identical fashion. At least it had the advantage of being able to evoke Destiny and the gods. But we

---

[4] "One cannot always remain a stranger."

moderns who believe more willingly in progress than in Destiny, or who tolerate it only when it is subjugated to the logic of the heart and the unconscious, have lost our footing. The mother has enough substance to symbolize, unknown to Camus perhaps, Ronsard's "stepmother Nature" or the bankruptcy of the maternal instinct. It is too much, on the other hand, to freeze upon the lips of a faceless old man "the eternal silence of the divinity," of which Vigny speaks.

Camus attempted to attain the symbolic level without losing all contact with realism. Psychologically, Caligula's quest for the moon was explainable by his madness, and the passage from the metaphysical to the real was effected through the appearance of an interplay of the normal and the abnormal—Camus's great skill consisting in this instance of never giving us the wherewithal of deciding what the norm is. This mixture, in spite of the skillfully created atmosphere of indifference, could not be achieved in *Le Malentendu.* The rhythm of the play is broken by it, our attention wandering ceaselessly from the characters' personalities to their symbolic meaning, depending upon whether the symbols take root or not.

The language is often the cause for a given scene leaving us with an impression of being tacked on. In the next to last edition of the play, in the presence of Jan—who lies in drugged sleep—the mother meditates on happiness. "Yes, we have much to do, and that is the difference between him and us; he is now relieved of the weight of his own life . . . he no longer carries the cross of that internal life that forbids repose, distraction or weakness. At this moment he no longer makes any demands upon himself, and I, old and weary, I am tempted to believe that this is what happiness is." Spoken by one of the murderers, these words had seemed to me to ring false. Moreover, we did not expect from the mother, an old, simple woman, so ample a metaphysical consciousness and especially not so abstract a language. Would one not have thought that she had abruptly taken the measure, not only of what she was, but also of what she symbolized?

Camus took into account such criticisms, and the work that he never ceased to do on the play tended to lighten it of its overly philosophical burden, to veil the symbolism, and to give more impact to the diction. The televised presentation was infinitely more restrained in this sense. But he could not bring himself to cut deeply into the final scene in which Martha is opposed to Maria, the occasion of a vehement dissertation: "It is difficult to be more clear than I have been . . . If you want to know, there has been a misunderstanding . . . Let us exaggerate nothing, you have lost your husband and I have lost my mother: we are even." Martha reasons, demonstrates, dissects. "I cannot," her sister-in-law replies, "I cannot bear the tone of our language." There is indeed much artificial coldness in this young woman who, at the very threshold of death, hurls at her whom she has no reason whatever to hate: "Before leaving you forever, there is but one thing left for me to do: to deprive you of hope." And we reply along with Maria: "Where do you find the strength to speak coldly of what should send you running into the street and draw from you the cries of a beast?"

The characters in *Le Malentendu,* with the exception of Maria, are afflicted with a dangerous lucidity. It seems that nothing of themselves, or of the intentions with which the author has laden them, can escape them; at least they seem sufficiently persuaded of this to impose upon us a clear view of their roles. They reason with insistent complacency in order better to reveal to us the secrets of a destiny that thereby loses in power and mystery. Superposition of symbolic meaning does not suffice, however, to create ambiguity when the various planes of meaning remain distinct like oil and water. It is curious that Camus, elsewhere so sparing with his words, on this point should not have been the man of understatement and silence. Perhaps he himself, experienced in all forms of introspection and asceticism by long self-familiarity, sometimes overestimated the powers of lucidity?

Le Malentendu remains a relative failure. Technically speaking, it belongs to the experimental theatre and constitutes a daring and interesting attempt to renew tragedy. It would be wrong to describe as powerless a simplicity, a deliberate bareness of plot, reflected also in the setting and mode of expression. It would be unjust to criticize a rejection of psychology which is deliberate and of which other weaknesses, in fact, make us aware. One perceives in the play a nostalgia for lost happiness, an obsession with sterility, silence and solitude, a latent claustrophobia,[5] but these do not grip us like a great misfortune or a nightmare. Kafka

[5] M. Gay-Crosier, *Les envers d'un echec: étude sur Albert Camus* (Minard).

gave his phantoms a body, he renders the Absurd tangible for us. *Le Malentendu* succeeds in this only here and there, more often through its silences than through its exchanges of dialogue. We see opposed the amorous couple and the murderous couple, the executioner and the victim; we see brought into play between the mother and the son the impossible dialogue of repressed tenderness; and finally, love and hatred confront one another in a verbal duel. Doubtless, each executioner is equally a victim and a certain kind of love resides in the heart of the murderers. But this complexity smacks of calculation.

In this play, Camus seems to have paid the price, in artistic terms, for the effort of clarification and coherence that *Le Mythe de Sisyphe* represents. Clinical preoccupations and concern for integrating the war and its problems into the absurd universe led him unconsciously to renounce the spontaneity that qualifies all living complexity.

At least Camus's course of action for the immediate future had become clear.

The time to act had come. The world scene had not changed. At that time, even more than in the preceding years, the anguished appeals of man abandoned on a both familiar and inhuman earth went without reply. But two lessons were extracted from the wartime adventure: a lesson of frankness and of simplicity—of honesty, Rieux would say. Jan complicated everything. Nemesis struck him down for his childish demands. Maria notes with good reason: "When one loves, one does not dream of anything." The second lesson is precisely that we should respond to insoluble metaphysical problems only with love for humanity. The mother dreamed as well. She woke up just in time to discover that "in a world in which everything can be denied, there are undeniable forces, and that on this earth where nothing is assured, we have our certainties . . . the love of a mother for her son is now my certainty."

Jan's return is also equally significant. He possessed wealth and happiness, all of which he compromises out of loyalty to those half-dead souls, his mother and his sister. He leaves the sunlight for the cold, tears himself from Maria's arms and walks toward his family, his heart laden with promises. He goes forward, fragile and naked in the heart of the cold winter, and he succumbs from lack of simplicity.

The time is not distant when *Les Lettres à un ami allemand* will appear. Camus too had his certitudes; there is no wilderness without boundaries. Abandoning the drunken and perverse Dionysus, of whom Martha is the last incarnation, he will henceforth draw his strength from Socrates. No, *Le Malentendu* is not "the manual of those without hope," but rather the tragedy of a happiness lost through excessive ambition— and the triumph of relativity.

7

The Pen and the Sword

The forlorn quality of *Le Malentendu* indirectly poses the problem of action within the course of history. To hear certain Christian or Communist critics speak,[1] the negation and absurdity that is presupposed by the thought of Malraux, Sartre, or Camus could logically only end in despair. Parting from the death of God, the argument is pushed to the very end, to the point where everything appears to be a matter of indifference, where every value definitively collapses, giving free reign to both hedonism and conquest. There is nothing left but to permit oneself everything or to permit everything, which comes down finally to the same thing.

"But," Camus wrote to his imaginary former German friend, "you lightly accept despair, and I have never consented to it." Never, or at least never with any continuity, never in the depths of his being. Similarity of language cannot deceive us. "In truth, I who believed I thought like you, saw scarcely any argument to oppose to you, if not a violent fondness for justice which seemed to me as little founded in reason as the most sudden of passions" (*LA*, p. 240). Although it can be justified logically, revolt against nihilism and against the barbarism that follows it owes little to abstract reason. It wells up from a pure passionate impulse.

Cut off from hope in the divine, that entire generation of writers and men found themselves at the same stroke condemned to the earth: "We want to think and live within *our* history" (*A, I*, p. 312). But is wanting it enough to assure success? Sartre does not think so. In the polemical exchange between him and Camus in *Les Temps modernes* in 1952, it appeared to him as though Camus's entry into the Resistance Movement was only the fruit of a conversion to sacrifice rather than to history, an accident rather than an act of fidelity. Camus, in Sartre's view, suffered

---

[1] Georges Adam in *Les Lettres françaises,* and Georges Raboud in *L'Aube* (1945); see also *Actuelles, I,* p. 311ff.

from a nostalgia for the eternal, and the invincible force of his natural inclination carried him outside the margin of history. Basically, in spite of this nostalgia, Camus was an intellectual whom a movement of pity, paralleled by a need for coherence, had snatched from the green paradise of childish loves; in the midst of the difficulties and harsh demands of political action, anxiety soon seized him: he had no peace until he had regained the feathered nest of his bourgeois virtues.

This view makes very light, however, of an entire childhood that was not always untouched by envy. Because Belcourt was near to Tipasa and the beaches of Algiers it was not any the less Belcourt, and the distance between the Camus family apartment and the well-to-do dwelling of the neighborhood doctor was more than the width of a street. Doubtless, Camus's fidelity to the world of misery derives more from memory than from common action—and that is the price paid for success. But where did one get the idea that the working-class world was the mirror image of its revolutionary elite and that it was one with history? The fishing party, the Sunday football match, and the random walks in the sunshine are so many prosaic Tipasas. The working-class world certainly exists within history, but it can get along without it, and more than one proletarian has his own personal world. Only an active minority makes of political action "man's whole concern." Here again Camus appears to us as an average Frenchman endowed only with an exceptional sense of exigency, as he himself said.

The fact that he came to literature by way of a novel set in poverty, or that his first theatrical work should have paid vehement homage to the dead strikers of Oviedo in a text in which the class struggle erupts with virulence, could be only a literary accident or the result of a crisis of political puberty. However, among the writers who have counted during the past fifty years, Camus is one of the rare ones—along with Aragon or Eluard—to have played an active role for several years in a political party, and more precisely, the Communist Party. Out of a sense of solidarity with the people of "mutes" of whom his mother and his uncle reminded him, out of revolt against the inequality of position and civil status that distinguished Europeans and native populations in Algeria, out of a taste for action, Camus had joined the Party in 1934. Jean Grenier had urged him to do so, dreaming of a political role for him in a disciplined movement which was badly lacking in members. He joined upon his return from a visit to the Balearic Isles. He meant by doing so to avoid "pseudo-idealism" and "readymade optimisms."[2] But how many misunderstandings there were in that commitment! He sought in it "an ascesis" preparatory "to more spiritual activities." He hoped to see the doctrine evolve. How could one be a Communist in 1934, when one spoke of a "false rationalism tied to the illusion of progress," when one worried over the "struggle of the classes and [a] historical materialism interpreted in the sense of a finality whose end would be the happiness and the triumph of the working class alone"? On the whole, Camus adhered less to Communism, from which his sense of the tragic and his mistrust of reason separated him, than he joined the Communists as one returns to the sources of one's childhood and one's sensibility. "I have such a strong desire to see diminished the sum total of misfortune and bitterness that poison men."

Being practical, he concerned himself with developing the propaganda effort among the Moslems. He opened a cultural center, formed the *Théâtre du Travail.* Did he clash, as he himself believed, with the Party over the effects on the Party's colonial policy of the Franco-Soviet Pact of 1934, or because of the conflicts of influence which, in 1937, opposed Messali Hadj's *Étoile Nord-Africaine,* a Moslem nationalist political grouping, to the Communist Party? The two explanations add up to the same effect. Still, it is undoubtedly the transformation of the *Théâtre du Travail* into the *Théâtre de l'Équipe* which fixes the actual moment of the break. In any case, Camus was never orthodox. His aim to found a Mediterranean collectivism, different from Russian collectivism, his persistent reticence with regard to the word "progress,"[3] made of him a heretic that a schism could not fail to carry off. No doubt Gide's *Retour de l'U.R.S.S.* and Jean Grenier's essay on "L'Esprit d'Orthodoxie" contributed in their time to that awakening.

Yet, Camus did not turn away from politics. *Alger–Républicain,* an Algiers left-leaning daily, which Pascal Pia invited him to join, was to furnish him with the opportunity for renewed combat. He protested against France's policy of non-intervention in Spain, against Daladier's

---

[2] Letter to Jean Grenier, published by the latter.

[3] See *La Culture indigène, la nouvelle culture méditerranéenne* (*Essais,* pp. 1321–27): "I have spoken of a new civilization and not of a case of progress within civilization. It would be too dangerous to fiddle with that maleficent toy that is called Progress."

executive orders of 1938, against the Algiers municipal government's abuses of power. With passion, he wrote the accounts of three trials in which the colonialist mentality revealed itself in all its hideousness: those of Michel Hodent, an agricultural agent falsely accused of misappropriating grain entrusted to him for storage, of Sheik el Okbi, and of the arsonists of Auribeau. In the first case, an agricultural agent, a warehouseman, and six Arab workers were the victims of an effort at illegal grain manipulation; in the case of the Sheik, we have a nationalist who is accused of murder by proxy; at Auribeau, a group of migrant farm workers were handed over to the courts on the false charge of willful arson. "Injustice, Monsieur le Gouverneur, brooks no delays. It cries out from the instant that it appears. As for those who have once heard it, they can never forget it, and they themselves, who were not involved, feel themselves henceforth responsible."

He devoted a series of articles to the question of poverty in which paternalism and charity were rejected for their lack of effectiveness, and in which racism is pitilessly denounced. Camus, superficially impregnated with the elementary principles of Marxist analysis, dwells at length on economic problems: unemployment, standards of living. And defending four leaders of the *Parti Populaire Algérien,* a nationalist organization, he cried: "The only way to abolish Algerian nationalism is to do away with the injustice that gave birth to it."

But the approach of World War II, for a time, removed these problems from the area of immediate concern. Camus devoted a series of articles to chronicling the origins of the war, in which the Treaty of Versailles is severely criticized. He picked up reports from British radio. He launched a guerrilla war with the censorship officials in which his weapons were blank spaces, the conditional (the French tense of probability), humor, and, indeed, refusal to obey regulations. In the end, the publication of the newspaper was suspended and, for lack of work,[4] Camus had to go to Metropolitan France.[5]

At the end of that two-fold experience, both as a militant and as a

[4] *Alger–Républicain* was born on October 4, 1938. It disappeared on October 28, 1939. *Soir–Républicain* was launched, in anticipation of *Alger–Républicain*'s demise, on September 15, 1939. Its publication was suspended on January 10, 1940 by military order.

[5] He was to have gone to work in Algiers for a printing firm but the *Gouvernement Général* of Algeria threatened to cancel all its orders to the firm if Camus were hired.

journalist, we can better assess what his position was: a determination to take part first of all, a position of solidarity confirmed by his attempt to enlist in the army. What! here is a pacifist, little inclined toward the use of arms, rejected by the army for reasons of health, who tries nonetheless to join up with the combat units! Not at all. He simply refused to be a suspect, halfway citizen. How could he pursue a normal existence when so many men of the people, hardly any more bellicose than he himself, were living day after day amid the fear and boredom of the most bizarre of all wars? Camus rejected comfort and solitude.

We find the same attitude when the witch-hunts against the Communists began. He did not hide the fact that "Stalinism did not seem to him the ideal policy to be sought after." But anti-Sovietism worried him; he wanted to keep his head. He accepted the need for censorship applied to military information, but refused any limitation on the free expression of opinions. He consented to combat once it became inevitable, but he insisted that "the means of concluding a durable peace" be envisioned: "Obstinacy in acts of justice can only be conquered by obstinacy in acts of justice." Long hostile toward Hitlerism,[6] he sought the explanation for the phenomenon "in the despair of an entire people."

Undoubtedly there was some naiveté, some quixotism in this attitude that sought, in the midst of crisis, "to grant all that is just, while rejecting all that is unjust"; there is in it, too, an ignorance of the terrible concatenations of history. But one can discern in all this a man who is far from all forms of fanaticism, rigorous, concerned with truth to the point of intransigence, incapable of hatred, and full of a tireless good will.

A pacifist then, was Camus to drift into indifference? The invasion took him by surprise while he was working as a layout man for *Paris–Soir,* a job he had found through his friend Pascal Pia. He went south to Clermont-Ferrand; then to Lyons, where he married for the second time, attended by Pia and four typographers. *Paris–Soir* "collaborated" from the beginning and scuttled its Lyons edition. Camus returned to Algiers. Upon leaving Lyons, he said to an editorial room comrade, "I am

---

[6] As early as 1934, he participated in the anti-fascist Amsterdam–Pleyel movement with Max-Pol Fouchet, who represented the young socialists.

counting on you in Paris the day of the liberation."[7] On January 25, 1941, he wrote an article with the meaningful title, "In Order to Prepare the Fruit,"[8] which is an appeal for moral resistance in face of the spirit of resignation. Three months later, in an article with veiled meaning, he protested against the sense of collective responsibility that the Pétain regime was developing in the French public.[9] In it, he seems to be seeking an active reconciliation between the absurd philosophy that he was analyzing at the same time in *Le Mythe de Sisyphe*,[10] and a will to resist, to which Emmanuel Roblès has borne witness.

He then taught in a secondary school in Oran founded by the Jewish community and to which flocked the Jewish children fleeing from the anti-Semitic laws of Vichy. Quite logically, he was led to create with several friends[11] an underground railway for threatened Jews or liberals. But his health remained unsteady. In August he left to take a rest in the mountains of the Haute-Loire. His wife returned to Algeria alone in September. He was to continue his stay for two more months. The Allied landing in North Africa was to dictate his permanent installation in France.

Living at Le Panelier, near Cambon-sur-Lignon, in the middle of the dark woods, in a both grandiose and cold setting, he led a hard-working and solitary existence.[12] But his trips to nearby St.-Etienne[13] permitted him to push on as far as Lyons, where he met Pascal Pia and René Leynaud, another journalist. It was they who introduced him into the Resistance movement. In the same way, he met Francis Ponge, a Communist *résistant* at the time; Michel Pontremoli, an Ecole Polytechnique graduate, who was to fall under German bullets; Father Leopold Bruckberger, the future chaplain of the Resistance. From that time on, he devoted himself to gathering information and, soon after, to clandestine journalism.

It was in the autumn of 1943 that his activities were to become more definite. Under the pseudonyms of Beauchard or Albert Mathé, he

---

[7] See *À Albert Camus, ses amis du Livre* (Paris, 1962).

[8] "Pour préparer le fruit." This article which first appeared in *La Tunisie française,* was later reprinted in *L'Été* under the title "Les Amandiers."

[9] "Comme un feu d'étoupes" (May 24, 1941); *Essais,* pp. 1465–66.

[10] Completed on February 21, 1941.

[11] According to Emmanuel Roblès and Henri Poncet.

[12] He began work on *La Peste* and finished *Le Malentendu*.

[13] Where he underwent pneumothorax insufflations.

participated in the bi-monthly edition of the clandestine news sheet, *Combat*. After Pascal Pia's departure, he became its director and he had to recruit contributors (in 1944, he joined with Mascolo and Sartre), in order to continue the work of a team which included Georges Altschuler, Marcel Gimont, Albert Ollivier, Jacqueline Bernard, and Pierre Seize.[14] Jacqueline Bernard, who played the role of editorial secretary before being deported, was able to say of Camus that he had "played a determining role at a moment when each encounter and each initiative brought with it grave risks."[15]

People have wondered sometimes why Camus's *Carnets* said nothing of his resistance activities. A supremely innocent question! It was not the usual thing—on the contrary it might have been dangerous—for a clandestine operative to record his various states of mind and his movements. Why his silence in this respect after the Liberation?[16] The simple answer is modesty, when so many comrades died carrying out the same tasks, and a certain chagrin at having survived, as though one had not done enough: "in a revolutionary period, it is the best who die." Still again, following being awarded the Resistance medal: "I did not ask for it and I do not wear it. What I did is a small thing and they did not give it to friends who were killed at my side." (Letter to M. Louis Germain.)

The disappointments of the days following the Liberation, the bitter feeling that the Great Day was only a beginning, sufficed moreover to justify his silence. The Resistance was the moment of great truths, the shining hour that one cannot recall without betraying it, and which leaves those who lived it with that taste of solitude and emptiness which haunts Corneille's young Horace on the very evening of his triumph.

At least, it is an established fact that action was soon to offset the bitterness of exile. The preciseness of the aims pursued and the quasi-ascetic rigor of life in the Resistance embodied a principle of satisfaction

[14] Most of these are newsmen who wrote for post-liberation *Combat* and other Parisian newspapers [trans. note].

[15] "I came to know him in that little bistro in the rue de Lille where, from before the liberation and a long time after, those who had not capitulated met" (Jacques Piette, a companion of the liberation period).

[16] He was, however, to evoke the Resistance in a Preface to *Combat Silencieux* by André Salvet, in the introduction to the *Poésies Posthumes* of René Leynaud, in *Silences de Paris,* and in the Preface to *Écrivains de la Résistance française* by Konrad Bieber, all of which are reprinted in *Essais*, pp. 1470–91.

which, without depriving the Absurd of its reality, verified, however, the preface to *Le Mythe de Sisyphe:* "that means that the Absurd is really without logic. This is why it cannot be lived" (*CN, II*). Arid as Djemila, blind as the knife which obsesses Meursault, the war, by contrast, gives rise to values from out of a world that had seemed deprived of meaning. Not of course that one henceforth knew the whole truth; but at least one knew what was a lie. Doubtless nothing precise was known concerning the nature and the reality of the mind; but about murder, its opposite, one soon had learned everything. Good and evil were not going to be opposed to one another like day and night (Camus left this Manichaeism to the Pharisees and fanatics). Between the two of them there would be a simple nuance, one of "those nuances that are as important as man himself" (*LA,* p. 224).

In this spirit, from the moment Paris was liberated, Camus strove to imprint a new style upon the French press, and by way of a hoped for reaction to it, on French political life as well. He retained sad memories of the sordid atmosphere that poisoned the Third Republic.[17] He condemned at the same time conformism, submission to readers' weaknesses, the prostitution of the commercial press, and its anesthetic methods. At a time when one could still hope for a pure and strong, honest and virile regime, Camus perceived the full importance of "information, the key to democracy," of which he wrote in *Combat* on August 31, 1944, and on June 27, 1945. For him, as for Alfred Sauvy, it seems that between the extremes of scandal and purge, "the least painful constraint of all would be the constraint of truth."[18] Objectivity and courage, independence and clarity—such were, in his eyes, the merits of the press, the fourth estate. The problem, however, is still with us.

The first concern of the free press had to be opposition to formalism[19] as well as all vestiges of the totalitarian spirit—incitement to hatred, insults, violence of language—which stifled all possibility of dialogue. The excesses of the post-liberation "purification," the outra-

---

[17] See *Alger–Républicain* "Petit portrait dans le goût du temps" (December 18, 1938), and "Le Dialogue entre un Président du conseil et un employé à 1800 francs par mois" (December 3, 1938); the first of these is reprinted in *Essais,* pp. 1375–76.

[18] Alfred Sauvy, *L'Évolution économique: les faits et les opinions.*

[19] *Combat* (September 8, 1944).

geous sentencing of a journalist, René Gérin,[20] manifestations of latent racism, the persistence in Algeria as in Madagascar of a colonialist state of mind,[21] were so many defeats for mankind. It was necessary by turns to defend this group against that, then that group against this one, in the name of the few elementary truths conquered during the clandestine struggle.

The key problem was that of violence. Against discreet violence (entirely natural, the Pharisees said), against the moral order that covered injustice, Camus took an unequivocal stand: "We are determined . . . to declare that we will eternally prefer disorder to injustice."[22] The Marxist criticism of the capitalist world was perfectly admissible. In the immediate moment, however, it was a question of open repressive violence versus the risks of revolutionary violence. In the Resistance, everything was simple. Others had unleashed the battle; in any case we were launched into it. "It is not incompatible at the same moment," the poet René Char has written, "to re-establish a bond with beauty, to be sick oneself and be struck, to return the blows, and to disappear."[23] Revolutionary violence demands more continuity. One has scarcely committed oneself to it when a logic of murder and fear carries one away. The victims condemn the executioners to always more and more killing, and finally to institutionalizing murder.

Camus knew too well that one cannot completely avoid repressive or revolutionary violence. "In sum, people like me would like a world, not where there would be no more killing (we are not so insane!), but in which murder would not be legal."[24]

Revolutionary justice can only be an exceptional form of justice—an exception, in fact, rather than a form of justice. Fundamentally, without denying that social combat is one of the forms of permanent struggle men engage in, Camus held to the traditional distinctions between military combat and political struggles. The passage from one to the other, in

[20] Gérin, a literary columnist for *L'Œuvre,* was a pacifist; already at the end of 1944, Camus, along with others, had protested against the execution of the novelist, Robert Brasillach, who had been convicted of collaboration with the Nazis.

[21] *Combat* (May 10, 1947).

[22] *Combat* (October 12, 1944).

[23] "Recherche de la base et du sommet," *Empédocle, I.*

[24] "Ni victimes ni bourreaux," *Essais,* p. 334.

the form of historical realism, leads ultimately to the generalization of the state of war. Capitalism has its legal crimes, so forcefully analyzed by Balzac, and there people cut throats quietly in the shadow of cathedrals and strong-boxes. To put an end to all that, was it enough for socialism, which Camus called for with all his strength,[25] simply to have the frankness to kill in broad daylight?

From a practical point of view, all this led him to feel a deep concern, from the moment of the Liberation, for the opposition between the United States and the Soviet Union. "The only urgent problems of our century are those that concern the accord or the hostility between these two powers."[26] The rivalry between the two greatest economic powers on the globe placed France in a position of "dependency."[27] I cannot resist the pleasure of citing here these lines in which the fearful consequences of the realism of our statesmen is denounced by the pen of an "irresponsible intellectual": "In Cold War terms, we would have to subordinate everything in France to the struggle against the Communist Party, which presupposes certain limitations on the idea that, rightly or wrongly, we have of democracy, and bend every effort to the necessity of developing our military power, which will not be done without serious difficulties for our economy. When I say that these difficulties will be borne first of all by the workers of all classes, it is likely that I place myself beyond the limits of likelihood. In foreign affairs, in order to serve as a realist in the Cold War, you will have to pass over certain of your repugnances. If Tsaldaris serves you better against Bolshevism, you will have to close your eyes to executions in Athens, to penal colonies, and to the policy of repression . . . Since Franco has given military assurances to the United States . . . you will have to support him, wish for his prosperity, and, on occasion, shake his hand . . . The partisans of the Cold War are therefore obliged to accept the idea of preventive war or of

[25] "It is quite true that I would no longer have any fondness for living in a world from which what I will call the socialist hope would have disappeared" (letter to R. Quilliot).

[26] *Combat* (May 7, 1947).

[27] In the light of these observations he advocated both the rejection of power blocs and the "construction" of a united Europe. See "L'Embarras du choix" in *Franc-tireur*, October 7, 1948, and more particularly, "Remarques sur la politique internationale," *Renaissances*, No. 10 (May, 1945), pp. 16–20; reprinted in *Essais*, pp. 1583–86 and pp. 1572–76 respectively.

running the risk of hearing men who are more realistic than they, say one day: in not declaring war at once, you are serving Russian imperialism."[28]

The necessity for France to take a mediational role appeared all the more imperious to him in that the discovery of atomic power placed upon the world the burden of a terrible threat. In these circumstances revolutions could not, at least in Europe, but degenerate into ideological wars; that is to say, "we are not free as Frenchmen to be revolutionaries."[29] Problems were henceforth on an international scale and the movement toward emancipation of colonial peoples seemed to him to have to weigh in the international balance as one of the essential phenomena of the decades to come. Internationalism was from that time on the most reasonable utopia. Collectivization had no meaning except on a planetary scale.[30] The germ of the idea of an atomic pool, so dear to President Eisenhower, is already present in "Ni victimes ni bourreaux," that series of articles that will have to be recognized one day as constituting one of the most lucid documents of our epoch.

If one sticks to the facts, then, it seems somewhat risky to deny Camus's constant concern with understanding history in the process of being made and of acting within it. Committed for better or for worse to his times, he did not hesitate to commit himself in words and acts every time it seemed to him necessary. A keen sense of fraternity prevented the artist that he was from consecrating himself uniquely to beauty and compelled him to participate. "There, we watched the night fall. And at that hour when the shadow which descends from the mountains on that splendid land brings ease to the heart of the hardest of men, I knew, however, that there was no peace for those who, from the other side of the valley, gathered together around a cake made of bad barley. I knew also that there would be sweetness in abandoning oneself to that so surprising and so grandiose evening, but that the misery whose fires grew red before us placed as though an interdict on the beauty of the world" (*A, III*, p. 909).

This long citation, taken from the report on the Kabylian famine, written in 1939, would suffice to prove that the artist remained ever

---

[28] "Réponse à l'Incrédule" [François Mauriac], *Combat* (December, 1948); reprinted in *Essais*, pp. 1589–94.

[29] See also "Ni victimes ni bourreaux," *Essais*, pp. 331–52.

[30] "Ni victimes ni bourreaux," *Essais*, p. 338.

present behind the journalist and refused to sacrifice artistic form. Certain people, however, will see in the dignity of this writing only dilletantism and literature. As if sincerity were measured by slovenliness or vehemence! Suffering and beauty resounded simultaneously in Camus. Must one speak of dispute and anguish as these lines might invite us to do: "One with this world in which the flowers and the wind will never be able to pardon the rest" (*CN, II*). If Camus consistently places himself on the side of those who suffer, it is not in spite of, but because of happiness and beauty. "I have chosen justice, on the contrary, in order to remain faithful to the earth" (*LA,* p. 241). The taste for happiness and the struggle against suffering are complementary.

Revolution would have appeared to him then as the best means of serving happiness, if only he had not been convinced that happiness had always and forever to be recreated. From that moment on, he moved away radically from modern revolutionaries out of the conviction that, as miserable as man may be, he always has some little scrap of joy to defend. "There is history, and there is something else, simple happiness, the passion of human beings, natural beauty."[31] A statement based on experience and which explains his deeply *résistant* attitude. He was not enough of a pessimist to contest the existence of all real value in this world of injustice; he was not enough of an optimist to be assured of tomorrows that would sing. One might say that he was ceaselessly on guard against hope and despair, against the eddies of history and against the tranquillity of cloisters. Camus is mistrustful for fear of falling into disequilibrium. He feared nothing so much as that double urge that carried him on the one hand toward commitment and on the other toward withdrawal. In the heart of every proletarian sleeps a gardener; within him the public figure and the man of solitude also coexist. We live in a collectivity, but when it comes to dying, we are alone. In choosing the vocation of writer, Camus doubtless hoped for nothing more than to achieve that impossible reconciliation.

The fact remains that one senses him less moved by the creative possibility of the collectivity than by the forces of disintegration that threatened it. He lacked imagination with regard to the future. Shall I say

[31] "Réponse à E. d'Astier de la Vigerie," *Actuelles, I,* p. 368; see also p. 385: "These men should try to preserve in their personal lives that part of joyousness that does not belong to history."

that his behavior, similar in this to that of Epicurus, reveals a man accustomed to struggling against illness and to giving himself new respites? Had it not been for that experience, he might have advocated during his youth a socialism of strength and *élan vital* in the mode of Spengler. Quite to the contrary he had to define his right to life in the face of obscure forces. This detail undoubtedly explains his hesitation to point a finger at the guilty. He could with some justice have taken the social order to task: all these are very erudite observations. Poor as he might be, the invalid would never lay blame on his poor environment nor even on poverty. A few days earlier, conditions had been the same and he had not been sick. Let us add that his honesty rejected uncertain denunciations. Therefore his criticism remained most often on a general level. In 1939 as well as in 1945, Camus the journalist was inclined to believe in the general good will, except for blaming ignorance: "My personal position, so far as it can be defined, is to consider that men, if they are not innocent, are guilty out of ignorance."[32] The author of *Caligula* willingly conceded to Socrates that "no one is deliberately wicked." He was akin to the lawyer or the witness, but in no way to the prosecutor.

After all, Marxist materialism as Sartre had excellently demonstrated in his "Matérialisme et révolution" should, in all logic, "refrain from passing judgment: a bourgeois is only the product of a rigorous necessity."[33] The Marxist dialectic proceeds at once from this to the bourgeoisie's destruction. Camus would consent to the destruction of the bourgeoisie but not of the bourgeois. Pacifism, nonviolence, will you say? There are enough facts to weaken any such suppositions. But myths die hard. With regard to history Camus is more Corneillian than Marxist. For him the nobility of actions is still the surest guarantee of their effectiveness. It is notable that his entry into the Resistance was at one and the same time perfectly natural and extremely painful. Natural in fact because one cannot fail to be struck by the simplicity, I would almost say the banality of his reasons, which had to do with neither heroism nor sacrifice, much less devotion to some overriding idea. Simply a certain

[32] Interview published by *La Revue du Caire* (1948); reprinted in *Actuelles, I*, pp. 279–383; see also "Ni victimes ni bourreaux": "What strikes me in the midst of polemics, threats, and outbursts of violence is the good will of all men."

[33] *Situations, III*, p. 193.

limit had been passed, a certain manner of being was threatened in which friendship, love, honor itself still retain some meaning in the face of hatred, jealousy and violence. But such evidence in no way diminishes the internal anguish. It has been written of Corneillian heroes that "they are pushed into tragedy in spite of themselves." Like them, a number of resistants were unenthusiastically combative. Their folly lay in "wanting to reconcile everything." But the time came in which the enemy's slap in the face became intolerable: "we have in fact admitted that in certain cases the choice was necessary" (*LA,* p. 235). Psychologically the *Lettres à un ami allemand* are the *stances*[34] of the clandestine combatant.

I need only cite their tone itself as proof. The multiplicity of affirmations ("we know," "we have learned"), the seeking out of percussive phrases, the constant effort at justification ("we had to"), show quite well that, if the determination to win grew ever stronger, all intellectual and moral scruples were not overcome. Like most men, Camus fought without joy if not with bitterness; but also with the implacable lucidity of whoever has something living to defend. In reading these letters, one cannot help but think of the frightening dialogue between Horace and Curiace in Corneille's *Horace,* a Curiace who might have read Vigny's *Servitude et Grandeur militaires.*

Camus's originality lies not at all in the way he thinks, which is the same way as Meursault or Céleste, the Algerian bistro owner, or the majority of Frenchmen as well, but it lies above all in the logic with which, once he had thought like everybody else, he lived in accordance with his thinking. Like the greatest number he had an equal horror of servitude and war, of injustice and blood. In 1945 a controversy over the difficult problem of the "purification" placed him at loggerheads with François Mauriac. In opposition to Mauriac, he sustained for a short time the necessity for a calm but implacable repression.[35] This was his guiding principle. But in face of the excesses into which the trials soon fell, he was seized with disgust; horror of capital executions created in

[34] "Les Stances du *Cid"* in Corneille's play, refers to the lyrical soliloquy of Rodrigue in which he struggles with the dilemma of being forced to follow one of two conflicting lines of action: either he must kill his beloved Chimène's father, thereby avenging his family name and losing Chimène, or risk the dishonor of failing to avenge his father, thereby risking paternal and social censure [trans. note].

[35] *Combat* (January 11, 1945).

him a feeling that approached nausea and trauma. For whatever reason, Camus suspended his activities for *Combat* in order to stay within the limits of his scruples. Finally he returned to his editorial duties only to state his firm resolution not to add in any circumstances by his word or by his acts to the madness for murder to which Europe had abandoned herself (*A, I,* p. 371). Historically speaking, this was a weakness and he knew it: "Artists do not make good political victors for they are incapable of accepting lightly the death of their opponents" (*A, I,* p. 406). What does this mean if not that they have no confidence in history: man has nothing to hope for from a natural evolution, whether it be mechanical as viewed by the Enlightenment or dialectical as seen by the Marxists. Camus rejects the idea of historical finality. The march of time is unpredictable; that is why he gives it the blind face of Destiny. But, some will say, history is no more than the conjunction and cross contacts of the diversity of human currents. We might as well say that the encounter of human wills, passions, and desires on the one hand, and of technology and civilizations on the other, leads to the same indifference. Events remain foreign to us in their causes or in their consequences. In any case, man's essential desires cannot be fully satisfied. "History is only the desperate effort of men to give form to the most clear-sighted of their dreams" (*A, I,* p. 346).

All this leads us to a form of pessimism which is as much relative as active. "I continue to believe that the world has no superior meaning," he wrote in July, 1944. "But I know that something within it has meaning and that is man, because he is the only being to demand that there be one" (*LA,* p. 241). Such a statement would be enough to justify every revolutionary enterprise if it did not at the same time confer upon them a high responsibility. Every economic transformation implies simultaneously a moral preoccupation in the broadest sense of the word, one for which René Char gives us the definition: "To give new value, even arbitrarily, to the prodigy that is human life in its relativity";[36] that is to say to preserve it from destruction and from all demeaning forces, whether it be a matter of sickness, poverty, the dictatorship of money, technology or the machine, and—last but not least—from the will for power. A politics of prophylaxis in profound opposition to the Marxism

[36] "Recherche de la base et du sommet," *Empédocle, I.*

defined by Henri Lefebvre: "Marxism is not interested in the proletariat because it is weak, but because it is a force . . . not because it is rejected by the bourgeoisie into an inhuman world, but because it bears within it the future of man . . . In a word, Marxism sees in the proletariat its future and its potential." Camus, on the other hand, takes his point of departure from the present in its mediocrity and its suffering.[37] He aspires less to the proud blossoming of strength than to a modest equilibrium. Counter to Nietzsche and Hegel, he invokes Socrates by way of a kind of moral opportunism: "It is a question of strategy" (*A, I,* p. 379).

One can see the kind of spirit in which the flirtation between Camus and Christianity was initiated in the days following the Liberation. Let one not be deceived: nothing had changed in the framework of his thought.[38] Like Vigny when he wrote *Daphné,* Camus was preoccupied with bringing together all men of good will on the modest basis of an individualistic form of socialism. He always reproached Christianity for presenting to man only a humiliated image of himself. He fired back at Christians their own indictment of pessimism: "It is not I who invented the human creature's suffering nor the terrible formulas of the divine malediction." He obstinately rejected resignation. The attitude of the high-ranking clergy under the occupation, its distance from the people, the Vatican's discreetness in face of the Nazis' acts of extortion, and the blessing which the Church of Spain generously bestowed upon the Falangist riflemen were objects of his unceasing indignation. From that time, he foresaw the evolution of Georges Bidault's Catholic *Mouvement République Populaire* toward a charitable and resigned conservatism (*A, I,* p. 386). But the time was past in which he had viewed Christianity as merely a source of comfort. René Leynaud and many others had taught him that faith could be only a "tragic hope,"[39] a tireless searching. It seemed to him that a common moral ground could be defined on the basis of respect for life and the individual (*A, I,* p. 375). His vocabulary

[37] Cf. J-P. Sartre, "Le Congrès de Vienne," *Le Monde* (1953): "One may smile at this conviction based on a surge of sensitivity. I do not believe however that our realists of today, even if they be Machiavellians, would be wise to underestimate the emotions."

[38] *Actuelles, I,* p. 372: "I do not share your hope and I continue to struggle against that universe in which children suffer and die."

[39] *Actuelles, I,* pp. 297–98, 326, 371.

(salvation, purity) betrays that attraction. From that time on, he borrowed from Marxism its critique and its demands, from Christianity its love,[40] and from the Absurd, finally, its sense of the earth and of modesty.

Diverse circumstances led him to abandon the honest predication he had taken upon himself. Fatigue, *Combat*'s financial difficulties, and the disintegration of his editorial team played their part. It seems also that Camus may have yielded at first to an inclination toward retreat into silence and art,[41] or, more exactly, to the desire to escape the eddies of current political events in order to withdraw to some distance and in some way purify himself. The publicist's vocation carries harsh demands. One has sometimes to force one's convictions, hide one's doubts and concerns. At the very moment when he was affirming the possibility of reconciling justice and freedom, Camus feared he would soon have to admit his error. Thus imperatives, exhortations (we must, we have to) crop up in each paragraph. This mixture of determined faith and deep uncertainty gives to his thought that stubborn and taut quality in which Sartre sought to see unjustly "a kind of somber self-complacency." "We are not sure that we have always avoided the danger of seeming to believe that we have the privilege of clairvoyance and the superiority of those who are never wrong."[42] Moral predication brings on sclerosis.[43]

Discouragement must also be included among the causes: "Something within us has been destroyed by the spectacle of the years that we have just lived through. And this something is that confidence in man that has always made him believe that one could always draw human reactions from another man by speaking to him the language of humanity" (*A, I*, p. 331). Bloc politics left the journalist no resource but to cry

[40] See Paul Viallamis, "L'Incroyance passionée d'Albert Camus," *Revue des Lettres Modernes* (1968).

[41] He was absorbed by the final rewriting of *La Peste*. The formation of the Gaullist *Rassemblement du Peuple Français* brought about keen disagreements between the "Gaullists" (Pascal Pia, Albert Ollivier, Raymond Aron) and others on *Combat*'s staff. See *Le Choix*, the editorial of April 22, 1947 in *Combat* (*PL, II*, p. 1559–61): "After all, a certain number of Frenchmen think as we do that the national problem is not absolutely equivalent to the de Gaulle–Thorez dilemma and that it is still permissible to maintain a cool head."

[42] "Autocritique," *Combat* (November 22, 1944).

[43] *Actuelles, I*, p. 403: "And our writers know it well, they all wind up by appealing to this miserable and dried up substitute for love that is called morality."

in the wilderness or to keep silent. "For a time, still unknown, history is being created by police powers and powerful financial interests counter to the interests of peoples and the truth of men" (*A, I*, p. 386). Because the course of events eludes governments themselves and obeys the logic of fear, day-to-day politics resembles some vain and gratuitous game.

Camus was clearly aware of the frailty of his position. Already in 1945 he felt himself caught between God and history. All his difficult efforts were directed only at re-establishing an equilibrium between metaphysical revolt and historical revolt, between the acceptance of the human condition and adherence to history. To refuse to make a final choice is to make of oneself "the witness of pure freedom." It would be better, as soon as one feels oneself incapable of sacrificing either human flesh to history or history to the flesh, either justice to freedom or freedom to justice, to rejoin the impotent crowd and live with them their contradictions and their anguish. Except to prepare in silence "the modest reflection which without claiming to solve everything will always be ready at any given moment to fix a meaning upon everyday life" (*A, I*, p. 351).

Camus returned then to a kind of clandestine activity, the simple tasks of resistance and of preservation against all forms of violence from wherever they may come.[44] Like Rousseau gone astray among the *philosophes* of the Enlightenment, he sequestered himself "in deliberately non-current concerns" (*A, I*, p. 320). It is true that it is anachronistic to plead for internationalism at a time when nationalistic outbursts are conquering continents;[45] anachronistic also to speak of peace in a world that resounded with the clicking of weapons, to hold up the atomic threat before peoples tired of trembling in fear and avid for sleep, to make an appeal to modesty when totalitarian states were mutually reinforcing one another. The sad thing is that each of his protests isolated him still more. The anonymous crowd of those who thought as he did most often took refuge in skepticism, indifference, or disgust. Frightened

[44] "Dialogue pour le dialogue," *Défense de l'homme* (July, 1949): "Until there is a new order, unconditional resistance—and against all forms of madness anyone may propose to us."

[45] It is thus that he sustained, in a kind of spirit of provocative quixotism, the "world citizen" Garry Davis, of whom he humorously wrote to Grenier that he had "the style of a skinny Sancho Panza with the mad whims of his master."

peoples look for prophecy not dialogue. Intransigence, the determination to deal only with the dominant problems of the era, separated him from the crowd at the very time when he believed, and rightly so, that the crowd shared a number of his points of view. It is false to claim that Camus withdrew from history: "The world being what it is, we are committed to it, whatever we may say" (*A, I*). He took his place there as a sniper, as a rebel, and as a protester. Being unable yet to act upon history, he contented himself with being a conscience to it. It is false that he devoted himself out of spite to art. He never produced so few literary works as from 1948 to 1954. It is false, finally, to claim that his positions represented no one but himself: his solitude was in direct proportion to the renunciation of all those who thought like him. But it is true that events and men momentarily rendered utopian his refusal to choose between two forms of violence.[46] It is true finally that it made no sense to be right too often, to speak of détente and coexistence before peoples and their leaders had had the time to take full measure of the depth of their madness. History tolerates neither those who lag behind her nor those who are ahead of her.

[46] See *The Artist in the Arena* by Emmett Parker, one of the best studies on Camus's relationship to politics.

8

The Days of Our Death

La Peste is the most massive of Camus's works and probably the one whose completion cost him the most difficulties. Is it a novel? To be sure, in it Camus brings to life for us characters and destinies. We watch Rieux, Tarrou, Rambert, and Paneloux live and suffer. We learn to know little by little their past, their loves, their anxieties; one of them, Grand, a modest civil servant, still grieves over his wife who left him out of disgust with a too cramped style of life; another, Tarrou, has broken with his bourgeois origins in order to seek peace of heart through revolutions and travels; still another, Cottard, is obsessed with fear of the police. In one sense they are indeed individuals and, when we take an interest in them, we feel we can forget our own real lives for their imaginary fate.

However, the work was not classed as a novel by its author; it is labeled a chronicle. The book owes very little to the imagination. Moreover there is not, in a manner of speaking, any plot. On the other hand, Camus accumulated in it concrete details observed day by day. Secondary characters such as the old man who spits on cats or the old Spaniard were sketched from nature. The fabric of events, their logic, are such as they would be in reality.

Nevertheless as early as 1939, date of conception of the work's theme, Camus, under the influence of Melville,[1] deliberately chose the symbol of the plague;[2] the simple statement of the titles of his works reveals that evolution: men (*Caligula, L'Étranger*) are effaced in favor

---

[1] He was to write of *Moby Dick* that it is "one of the most overwhelming myths that has been imagined concerning man's struggle against evil and the irresistible logic which ends by opposing the just man first to the creator and creation, then to his fellow men, and to himself."

[2] See "L'Exhortation aux médecins de la Peste" (*PL, I,* pp. 1959–63), which constituted one of the ironic digressions, in the manner of *Moby Dick*, originally destined to alternate with the narrative.

of a problem (*Le Malentendu*) or a myth (*La Peste*). The myth is to history what the plastic arts are to the human body. He extracts from it the event, circumscribes it, rids it of its dross, imposes upon it a logic and a direction. It is through myth that the novel becomes "that universe in which action finds its form, in which final words are pronounced, beings delivered up to beings, in which all life takes on the shape of a destiny" (*HR*, p. 666). *La Peste* marks the revenge of suffering over triumphant forgetfulness. It brings form and completeness to what we knew as a mournful succession of moments devoid of meaning and, on this level, history becomes an exemplary fate. Like Giraudoux speaking of tragedy, Camus was able to write, "if the novel speaks only of longing, despair, the unattained, it still creates form and salvation" (*HR*, p. 666n).

   Camus chose for the theme of his book the story of a plague epidemic in the city of Oran. The plague offers the double advantage of being the most terrifying of scourges and the least well known today. Its near disappearance and the relative antiquity of its manifestations only add to the mystery that surrounds it: *major e longinquo reverentia.* Language alone sufficed to introduce the element of the miraculous that myth demands. The multiple uses that the vernacular makes of it is evidence enough of its extraordinary resonance. Better still, the plague appeared and disappeared like the devil in Germanic legends. Its epidemic character requires that a state of plague be decreed. Thus Oran cut off from the world takes on an aura of strangeness. Forebodingly distant like Moses or Meursault in his prison, nonetheless it, like them, remains curiously close to us.

   This combination of familiarity and mystery confer on the myth of the plague an ambiguity which gives it its value. Its interpretations are multiple. Camus could very well have recounted for us the history of the occupation and the clandestine struggle in a straight chronicle. He could even, as Steinbeck did in *The Moon Is Down,* have disencumbered the history of its anecdotal aspects and its subjective details. To have done so would have amounted most certainly to limiting the scope of the story: a tale of occupation would have evoked all past and future occupations and that only. Camus had a higher ambition. He felt it necessary to remove the event from the preciseness of people's memories, put it out of reach of the reader's natural egocentrism and in its place give him the spectacle of a city prey to the legendary scourge of humanity: the plague. "It is as reasonable," Daniel Defoe reminds us in the epigraph to *La Peste,* "to represent one kind of imprisonment by another as to represent no matter what object that exists by something that does not exist."

Thus the book in its completely puritanical simplicity presents a triple meaning. In the most literal summary, the city of Oran[3] is caught in the clutches of an epidemic of the plague which appears, develops, reaches its apogee, and disappears. This provides us with a medical chronicle, a clinical study. The narrator follows the events as they unfold: in the stairways, in the gutters, rats die "with a little blossom of blood on their pointed muzzles." Then men are attacked, ganglions appear in the armpit or in the groin, the rhythm of the infection's spread is studied in the light of statistics, the symptoms of the sickness, its variations, described with method and in the even tone of the expert. The same concern for objectivity appears in the presentation of the emergency-aid teams, in the announcement of the prescribed mandatory regulations. The funeral pyres of Athens, the charnel houses of Marseilles, "the carts full of corpses in terrified London," and a number of other sinister evocations have long nourished the lyricism of painters and historians. Method and the spirit of organization henceforth deprives the scourge of every spectacular—if not to say literary—aspect. Each chapter is headed by an incisive reflection in the manner of Thucydides. In one place it serves as a frame for the episode which follows, in another as an anticipated commentary; and it is one of the book's primary paradoxes that the blind onrush of the plague furnishes through its effects the material for an equally pitiless, lucid analysis.

On a higher level, Oran bursts out of its own limits. We have France and all of Europe under the Nazi boot, a vast concentration camp. All forms of mass repression in modern times stand accused, from the gigantic California farms where the "grapes of wrath" ripened to the Siberian labor camps, from the colonial countries to Spain. All the manifestations of incipient or institutionalized totalitarianism, of social injustice and tyranny, whether they be hidden under the mask of technol-

[3] In 1944 Oran suffered a typhus epidemic, which Camus used as a source of information. However, at that period, the first manuscript of *La Peste* was already one year old.

ogy or ideology, are cast in relief by the Plague. If it were otherwise, it would be difficult to understand the importance attached to the black market, to separation for loved ones, to fear, to the inhumanity gangrenously eating away at thoughts and feelings. The attempts to escape illegally remind us of so many evasions, or the simple passage beyond lines of demarcation. We recognize the various interdicts and the multiple regulations of wartime, the thin wisp of smoke from the crematory ovens and, last but not least, the street celebrations in which the enthusiasm of the Liberation was given free course. The Plague has "as its obvious content the struggle of the European resistance movement against Nazism."[4]

But the myth has still yet a higher meaning. What matter that Oran might have known the plague or not? Oran, an ugly neuter city, is valued for its very insignificance; a city which is everywhere and nowhere, as African as it is foreign to Africa. In it a mediocre crowd circulates, entirely plunged into an unrelieved existence: work, cinema, visits to the beach. We would hardly suspect that any other values could exist there except those of money and agitation for its own sake. A city "without soul and without recourse,"[5] and without love also—love is indeed encountered there in the form of a burning passion or as a habit, but in general human tenderness is absent. In brief, a city that had lost the meaning of true life. But had it ever had it? Is true life anything else but a mirage? In any case, Oran, which turns its back to the sea, seems to be condemned to frivolity.

The myth, then, encircles and covers all forms of evil. The Plague is an old acquaintance. At Djemila in the wind it had still fallen short of scandal; we had seen it resurface under Caligula's grimacing mask: "I am the Plague." Meursault's shots had unleashed it; it was again the cause of the "misunderstanding" in *Le Malentendu*. Its incarnations are diverse: moral, social, and metaphysical. It insinuates itself in hearts, dons the ermine of judges, guides the assassin's dagger, the executioner's movements, the revolutionary's gunshot; and lastly it is insidious and unfathomable death which crushes human breasts "with an invisible weight," disconcerting in its appearances and its retreats, in the respites it grants as

---

[4] "Lettre à Roland Barthes," *Club* (February, 1955); reprinted in *Théâtre, récits, nouvelles,* pp. 1965–67.

[5] "Le Minotaure ou la halte d'Oran," in *L'Été;* on Oran, see also "Petit Guide pour des villes sans passé," in *L'Été.*

the cat does with the mouse, through its arbitrariness. While Cottard prospers, the Othon child writhes in agony.

It is also necessity, the inevitable "anagke." The threat is as terrifying as the fact itself: "they thought themselves free and no one will ever be free as long as there shall be scourges." Supplications, prayers, sacrifices and wealth, nothing can stop it from doing its work, inexorably. Every hope, every undertaking is condemned in advance. Each instant is turned in upon itself. "The city resembled a waiting room" in the Saint-Lazare prison refectory during the Reign of Terror as Vigny has described it for us in *Stello*. All exits are locked. With its guards and its lookout towers, Oran is a continual present. The sea on one side, the city gates on the other—a tragic locale par excellence—the city finds itself sealed off like a concentration camp, absolutely delimited and ringed in, ready for the symbol and ready for exile.

Strange exile, lived on the spot that one thought was one's homeland, in the very middle of formerly familiar objects, with long-cherished faces. Oran is only a vast prison in which each one stumbles up against the walls before stumbling up against himself. The plague forces some into complicity with it. To some—Cottard for example—it offers a number of advantages. Others, in order to fight it, are forced to play its game: assign numbers to individuals, organize quarantines, snatch the sick away from their families, speed up burials. Abstraction imposes abstraction, violence attracts violence. Father Paneloux in his first sermon had claimed to borrow a few arguments from the plague. He did not suspect that at the same time he was underwriting the most outrageous of scandals. Henceforth, no one any longer has clean hands.

So it is in life. "What does that mean, the plague? It's life and that's all." Life with its inevitable degradation, its eternal starting all over again: to take up unendingly the same old routine, to listen every day to the same old recording, to go round and round. Sisyphus' monotonous stone never stops rolling down the slope of Hell. The day following the city's deliverance from the plague, looking down over Oran, peaceful at last, Rieux "knew however that this chronicle could not be that of definitive victory: the bacillus of the plague neither dies nor disappears, ever." There is in every man a mixture of the concrete and the abstract, of creation and destruction, of being and nothingness. Life carries with it the strange mixture of human and inhuman. "The old man was right: men are always the same." As long as the balance is kept equal between the human and the inhuman—that is between what men accept and what they impugn—that is called life; the plague begins with a break in the equilibrium with the insertion of arithmetic into the calculation of suffering. Its triumph is rapid; it appears total; but its very excesses condemn it. It is what the military calls the duel of the cannon and the breast plate. Revealing to men their solitude, the plague constrains them to join together; plunging them into shame and necessity, it awakens them to honor and freedom; its cold cruelty elicits revolt, and as soon as men of resolve, brought together from different horizons after many detours, have united their efforts and defined the limits beyond which life loses all meaning, equilibrium is not far from being established. Surcease succeeds revolt and, for those who have not lost too much, happiness takes again its rightful place. Temporarily.

This confrontation of men and Destiny has as its effect the stylization of the characters: "In order to struggle against abstraction one has to resemble it a little." We know nothing of them before the plague begins its ravages; we only know them by their acts and the words that a narrator, who attempts to be impartial, has been able to retain (with the exception of Tarrou, whose diaries enlighten us at the same time that they confer on Rieux's account a second degree of objectivity). About Rieux we know his demeanor, not his past. By a roundabout remark we learn that he is the son of a worker and owes his understanding of the scourge to deprivation. But nothing will be added to sharpen these fleeting notations. On first sight one might think of a kind of psychology of behavior, if Camus had not vigorously condemned it in *L'Homme révolté,* and if, especially, each gesture did not implicitly affirm or indict some value. If one is willing to admit that epic and immensity are not necessarily synonyms, the stylization of *La Peste* would be of rather an epic nature, but an epic of banality.[6]

The characters are revealed to us as the scourge comes to them or as they go to meet it. *L'Étranger* already had offered us, in its second part, a

---

[6] Mauriac applied this phrase to Hugo, who possessed the art of enlarging the most ordinary sentiments. Camus, on the other hand, reduces to the ordinary the most scandalous of events. This, too, is the source of his humor.

similar tête-à-tête with evil. But it is from the linear character of the story, from the presence of a single victim from which, as the title indicates, the earlier book draws its unity. The plague constitutes the unity of the later work and reveals about each character only what it wishes to reveal—and finally his personality less than his greatness and his wretchedness. As in the medieval *danses macabres,* rich and poor, high society and low, undergo each in his turn the curious examination of the moralist, skillful in distinguishing common attitudes from group or class reactions.

The great discovery of *La Peste* is that of the existence of a human nature. Society, like the earth, "lets rise to the surface boils and pus which until now had been working upon it internally." Fear scours habits clean, breaks conventions, exposes for us in its nakedness our condition as Pascalian prisoners. Condemned to idleness, "reduced to going in circles in the dreary city and yielded up to the deceptive fires of memory for day after day," the Oranais become abruptly aware of the emptiness of their existence and of their solitude. Yet however, just as Meursault wound up by becoming accustomed to the walls of his prison and stubbornly reread the same shred of newspaper, Oran accommodates itself to exile. Superstition responds to terror; "sterile and stubborn monologues, arid conversations with a wall" strive to break the silence. The inadequacy of imagination and the sparseness of memory imperceptibly soften the harshness of separation. Lust, once scorned, manifests itself insolently, betraying the passion for life. Love affairs erupt into graveside orgies. Unbridled egotism, the instinct for self-preservation burst their bounds. It is not conventions alone that surge forth anew. Words, which seemed purified, charged with a new life, fail to break the barriers of solitude. At last, it is necessary to come back to trite formulas. Oran yields to "diversion."

But with the appearance of the plague's accomplices, the tone changes and attains, completely without violence, the tone of a pamphlet. Administrative institutions, in particular, are subjected once again to the fires of satire. When imagination is needed, it knows only "orders"; when it becomes imperative to make the population fully aware of the danger, it has posters pasted up in the most obscure corners of the city; in the midst of the epidemic, the military and the police pursue among themselves Byzantine discussions on the choice of decorations. Camus's cold and measured irony comes into play at the expense of the prefect who is filled with a derisory satisfaction by the sound organization of burials or of official medical services. "The plague's progress chart with its incessant rise, then the long leveling off that succeeded it," seems entirely reassuring to Doctor Richard, for example. "It's a good chart, an excellent one," he said. He estimated that the disease had reached a plateau . . . Doctor Richard, too, was carried off by the plague, and precisely during the disease's "plateau." These men played with abstractions as children play with fire.

There were also the profiteers, devoted wholly to that other fetish, money: newspaper headlines, greedy to exploit sensationalism; competition for customers led them to juggle statistics, to publish prophecies. Finally came the speculators of all kinds: moving-picture houses and cafés filled by the general idleness, black marketeers, skillful or half-skillful con men, raincoat merchants exploiting the myth of immunity due to rubberized fabrics in order to unload their unsalable goods, wine wholesalers launching this model of advertising phraseology: "Good wine kills bad germs."

But the crowd in the streets, the movie houses, the cafés form a sea of banality out of which several exceptional figures arise. The crowd defines the zero point, the normal behavior of average humanity. We are at the antipodes of those studies of the masses for which Zola gave us the model in *Germinal.* Movement is subordinated to analysis here and irony masks conviction. Is it not that, for Camus as for Tacitus, for example, great collective tragedies provide the measure of everyone's solitude?

Already with Cottard, the prototype of the profiteer, irony no longer fits. He is a character who lives a secret drama. We re-enter the world of men. Let us immediately set aside one temptation; we are not seeking an authorized spokesman for Camus himself. Did he not write: "it is possible for the novelist to be all his characters at the same time" (*HR*)? Successively or concurrently. If we ignore this caution, we run the risk of finding in Tarrou the hero of the book and of then being surprised that *L'Homme revolté* does not continue the theme of saintliness. Perhaps behind each of them there is the face of some Resistance comrade, Leynaud, for example. I would see rather a fragmentation of Meursault's character: Grand would have his humility, Rieux his lucidity, and Tarrou his desire for insignificance. But this would be to simplify to excess. Each character, however, does have his logic. All things being equal, each of them represents a temptation of the average man: security, wealth, and speculation in Cottard, purity in Tarrou, decency and determination in Grand, respectability in Othon—the examining magistrate straight out of *L'Étranger*—sensual life in Rambert.

Two lines are most often enough for Camus to depict a character for us. Depict is not exactly the term; rather, Camus characterizes. No seeking after the picturesque and the sharp silhouette. Before Rambert, short, thick, massive, and self-collected, we sense right off that the man is full of decision, stubborn and concrete. He is one of those who insists upon "caressing their too real chimeras and on pursuing with all their strength the images of an earth where a certain light, two or three hillsides, the favorite tree, and women's faces make up for them an irreplaceable climate." He will be the most exiled of all.[7] Prompt to commit himself, he took part in the Spanish Civil War and no longer believes in heroism, which is too easy and too murderous for his taste. In the Oranais necropolis, Rambert feels out of place: "I do not belong here," he repeats with hostility. Three times he will try to flee to rejoin the woman he loves, his springtime and his flesh. Two failures, two long detours in search of lost time will finally implant him firmly in the midst of the Plague: "I know that I belong here whether I like it or not," he will admit with a sort of bitter rancor. For him, the entire business remains absurd. However, he will struggle without reasons and without joy, motivated by a sort of negative solidarity: "There can be shame in being happy all alone."

Rambert is perhaps, along with Grand, Camus's preferred character (I do not say his spokesman). They have the same simplicity, Rambert in his grumpy refusal, Grand in his consent. Grand possesses the quiet humility of the truly poor; he has the rare "courage of his feelings," that is to say "of feelings that are neither ostensibly bad nor exalting in the shabby way that a spectacle is." He escapes effortlessly from the deceit of words; it even seems to him that each word might be a world in itself, and this is the entire meaning of that single and banal sentence he constantly reworks over and over again. If Grand had been more self-centered he would have sung, while Oran rotted, of the chestnut mare's trot and her elegant rider; he would speak of beauty, or pure form among the corpses. But without any rationalization or speeches, this nobody, this

---

[7] I have in mind Camus after he had become a Parisian. He himself told me one day that Rambert was the character to whom he felt closest.

weakling, committed himself to the struggle against the plague in spite of, or rather because of those few lines. Each evening after leaving a tiring job, he would devote to them patient and delightful hours, thus giving a meaning to the dreariest of existences by the most insignificant of activities: "let a single thing in this world find its form and that thing will be reconciled." That is why Grand cannot die. He is a kind of innocence—that of inventors who compete in the Lépine Competition or of poets who enter the Floral Games,[8] which the plague can never conquer.

Practically speaking, all the characters in *La Peste* join the Resistance without fanfare. Their paths differ, all more or less winding, but never rhetorical. Rambert yields to shame as much as to his two failures to escape; Othon, the judge, feels less far away from his stricken child. Grand and Rieux take part quite naturally, almost by profession. As for Tarrou and Paneloux, their conversion is born of a shock: they are the mystics. Father Paneloux, an erudite Jesuit, a brilliant preacher, has an apocalyptic conception of the plague: "My brethren, you are in the midst of misfortune; my brethren, you have deserved it." Just as Bossuet saw in Cromwell the scourge of God fallen upon England in apostasy, as Joseph de Maistre hailed in the Revolution of 1789 the punishment of a society prostituted to Voltairian liberalism, Father Paneloux discerns in the plague the finger of God, purifying evil. His God is the God of vengeance, the terrible Yahweh of Exodus and Leviticus. Paneloux borrows his maledictions and his style from Jeremiah. Then comes the day when, bent over the small convulsed body of the Othon child, he encounters death in the child's eyes. Strange revelation of the flesh in revolt! Then, this kind of intransigent Jansenist, henceforth launched into the mainstream of the Plague (from the first to the second sermon does he not pass from "you" to "we"?), caught between scandal and the desire to justify it, will offer himself up to God's blows. Just as the "scrupulous murderers" (*HR,* pp. 571–79) meant to follow their victims to the grave, Paneloux, "having to lose faith or accept having his face bashed in to keep it," chooses martyrdom. Attached to the crucifix by that "tragic hopefulness" that Camus attributed to Pascal and Saint Augustine, rejecting all human

---

[8] The *Concours Lépine* is an annual competition open to minor inventors. The Floral Games (Jeux Floraux) is a competition held annually in Toulouse, open to poets writing in the Provençal language [trans. note].

therapeutic efforts, he painfully affirms his confidence in the impenetrable designs of God.[9]

All this makes of Paneloux the most controversial of the characters in *La Peste*. Aimé Patri and Pierre de Boisdeffre, to mention but two, are surprised that the author appeared to consider as illogical the concrete struggle of a Christian against evil. Camus always had a tendency to consider Christianity "a doctrine of injustice." He had also retained the memory of those episcopal letters to the faithful that saw in the occupation the punishment that had to be accepted as a Vichyssoise penance. Furthermore, he is a victim in this case of the stylization that he imposed on his characters and even more so of that which the reader additionally brings to them. It is certain that the early version of Paneloux, a spiritual profiteer of evil, is a product of the pamphleteering tradition. But Camus could not hold to an oversimplified vision of the Christian who belongs to the category of secular Pharisaism that he denounced in 1946 and 1948. The Church, he knew, counted in its ranks the murderous chaplain of the *Lettres à un ami allemand* as well as a Leynaud or a Paneloux. It seems that, having arrived at this conception, he developed his character in the direction of a certain Christian logic: the acceptance of creation such as it is can only be joined with the "virtue of revolt and indignation that once belonged to [Christianity]" through sacrifice and martyrdom. Paneloux's attitude is not that of *the* Christian—but more exactly that of a Christian who desires to be entirely consistent,[10] if not excessive. That logic, whose heretical character Rieux senses (*LP*, p. 1400) reveals "perhaps more anxiety than strength" (*LP*, p. 1404). Moreover, Paneloux will not be understood by anyone.[11]

Tarrou is another intransigent, and the most attractive of the characters in *La Peste*. A curious and skeptical ease of manner, a vaguely disillusioned irony mask a determined, hypersensitive, and exacting temperament. We had met Tarrou in an earlier encounter: he was the young man who gazed fixedly at Meursault during his trial with fraternal looks.

[9] In the manuscript version, he seemed to lose his faith: "His face however expressed the opposite of serenity." There was no mention of a crucifix as there is in the published version.

[10] "Paneloux does not want to lose his faith, he will go all the way" (p. 1404).

[11] "Paneloux's behavior appeared incomprehensible to those who surrounded him" (p. 1404).

Like him, he loves all pleasures—and particularly swimming—detests having to talk when he has nothing to say, cultivates insignificance to the point of seeming intellectually barren. And, however, that day when his father, a public prosecutor, had obtained the head of an accused, the rug seemed to have been pulled from beneath his feet. He was to reject that murderous society; renounce the easy life, the certainties of a fine future; and throw himself passionately into poverty and politics. The same spiritual itinerary followed by Simone Weil of whom he reminds us in more than one way and with whom, on the morning after crossing over to join the revolutionary armies, he might have agreed in saying: "One departs as a volunteer with ideas of sacrifice and one falls into a war that resembles one waged by mercenaries, with many great acts of cruelty and the least sense of consideration owed to enemies."[12]

He was suddenly penetrated by the awareness of the manifest evidence on which all the reflection of *L'Homme révolté* is founded: "Today it's just a matter of who will kill the most. They are all consumed by a rage for murder and they cannot do otherwise." Revolt which had up to then motivated opposition to bourgeois murder now impels him to act against revolutionary murder. That double experience places him outside the stream of history: "I shall refuse to give any justification, you hear me, not a single one, to that disgusting slaughter." He knows what an exhausting undertaking it is "to do the least harm possible and even sometimes a little good." He knows that this means irreversible exile and a continual tension of the will, for the microbe alone is natural. But in defiance of that solitude and that pessimism, as if he were quietly redeeming the honor of man, he has chosen sainthood without God. An approximation of sainthood, since after all we all carry the Plague within us. From his bourgeois and Christian education, Tarrou has retained the nostalgia for the absolute and the virtues of charity and humility, an absurd chivalry that forces him "to be always ready to change sides as does justice, that fugitive from the camps of conquerors."[13] Finally, "Tarrou had found that difficult peace of which he had spoken, but he had found it only in death, at the hour when it was no longer of any use to him." At least he had sustained his wager to the end, disappearing only

[12] Simone Weil, *Lettre à Georges Bernanos.*
[13] Simone Weil, *La Pésanteur et la Grâce.* (We must make clear that Camus did not discover Weil's work until after having written *La Peste.*)

with the last spasms of the plague whose complement he had been. For he was one of those who never find equilibrium, but who form a counterweight to evil.

It would seem that the physician, Rieux, who is the connecting link between all these characters, ought to dominate the book with his personality. With his strong shoulders, his jutting chin and his burly, Sicilian peasant's build, he is not a man given to complexities: "Nothing is worth turning away from what one loves, and yet, I also turn away from it without being able to know why." He is a man of flesh and blood who knows the complete importance of the body, by nature and by profession. A certain heaviness, a very earthly patience gives him assurance as well as gravity to his demeanor. One senses that he is determined, impervious to discouragement in spite of that weariness which seems to follow in his wake. As equal as the attitudes of each and everyone seem to him, his comprehensiveness masks a Jacobin exactitude: "I accept only testimony given without reservations." However Rieux retains something undefinable. At the end of the book, it seems to us that we have seen him only from the back or against the light like the reporter in *Citizen Kane.* He stands out in our memories like a thick silhouette against a window recess looking out over the morning and evening of Oran. For the rest, he blends in most often with his ways of seeing things and his action, and escapes from us into a kind of two-sided objectivity. And doubtless he is the reason that readers and critics have tended to seek in *La Peste* a message rather than a confession.

In fact, we know nothing of the narrator until the epilogue. Throughout the work he effaces himself in an anonymity which sets the entire tone. Like Caesar in his war accounts, he, apparently at least, lets objects and events speak. This procedure is the inverse of that utilized in *L'Étranger.* Meursault spoke in the first person of events that seemed in no way to concern him; Rieux in the third person recalls days in which his personality blends entirely into the struggle against the plague. The result is not far from being identical—setting novelty aside. Meursault saw himself transformed into an exemplary victim to the exact extent that he had remained a stranger to himself; Rieux is the perfect witness, as disengaged from the narrative as he was engaged in the action. He maintains that balance between familiarity and exile which characterized Camus's art from his earliest works.

One must not then fall dupe to the story's apparent objectivity. Doubtless the narrator's thought has something circuitous about it, even in its clarity. Each of his remarks is cut by a restrictive phrase: "These few indications give *perhaps* a sufficient idea. In any case, *one should not exaggerate anything.*" A precaution which is revealed in the multiplicity of expressions such as "in sum," "to some extent." Numerous logical connectives slow down the progression of sentences: "*What had to be emphasized,* was the banal aspect of the city and its life. . . . *From that vantage point, doubtless,* life is not very exciting. *At least,* we no longer know disorder among us." A flat style in which digressions are added to meanderings: "One can only regret that . . . At that point, one will easily admit . . . These facts will seem quite evident to certain people." The frequent and intentional use of indirect style accentuates this quality of false impersonality. "In the evening, Rieux telegraphed his wife that she was to continue to take care of herself and that he was thinking of her." There is no longer even any trace of that mechanical aggressiveness found in the telegram Meursault received. Feelings are condensed, muffled: "Rieux thought to himself it was the hour of his letting go . . . he added only . . ." The charm of a woman is summed up in "that smile which obviated all the rest" and the scene that marks Rieux's eternal separation from his wife, whose first name we do not know, is completely understated: "He saw that her face was covered with tears: 'No,' he said softly." As a result of approaching objects and persons only with infinite precautions, Camus finally is caught in his own game: "Rieux," he writes, "*seemed* to become gloomy." Would Rieux be so self-detached? And yet, "it is not difficult to make out the ardent memories compressed underneath these so disinterested sentences."[14]

In striving to maintain the greatest distance between the initial idea and the final expression, Camus not only had recourse to the rules of French Classicism in general and of Valéry in particular; this style is a complete moral program in itself. And that he should hold this in common with many others does not prevent Camus's most personal thoughts and reactions from being expressed through it. In spite of that persistent illusion of Camus as a philosopher who makes us pay more attention to the symbol or to the exhortation than to life itself, we will

[14] "L'intelligence et l'échafaud" (a reflection based on *La Princesse de Clèves*); see *Théâtre, récits, nouvelles,* p. 1891.

one day have to let the following evidence sink in: *"La Peste* is a confession, and everything in it is calculated so that this confession might be as complete as its form is indirect" (*A, II,* p. 758). Considering these circumstances, it is not unimportant that the conception of *La Peste* goes back to the very early days of the war. The very day that he notes in his *Carnets* his new project for a tragedy, *Budejovice* (the future *Le Malentendu*), he writes: "Plague or adventure (novel)" (*CN, I,* p. 229). Its long years of gestation made of it a book consubstantial to its author, one of those books that react on the thought and the conduct of their creator and vice-versa. His earliest characters are passive and resist only through the use of irony, like that philosopher who was to write "an anthology of insignificant action," or that professor of Latin and Greek who "understood that he had not until then understood Thucydides or Lucretius" (*CN, I,* p. 230). Each of the deaths, that of the bourgeois judge, of the lover, takes on a mocking quality which blends into the general satire (of the government, advertising) of a world reduced to its true uselessness.

At this stage, *La Peste* sought to be the description of an absurd world which generalized death revealed to itself. *"L'Étranger* describes the nakedness of man in face of the Absurd. *La Peste,* the profound equality of all points of view in face of the same Absurd. It is a progression which will be elaborated in other works. But, still more, *La Peste* demonstrates that the Absurd learns nothing. That is the ultimate progress" (*CN, II,* p. 36). A pedagogy of pedagogical impotence.

In the original manuscript, Grand and Rambert did not exist. But Stephan, the professor, embodied their naive way of struggling against the event by fleeing from it into the act of writing. But Stephan disappeared in 1945, to be replaced by "a man separated from loved ones, an exile who does everything to get out of the city and who cannot," a *résistant* in spite of himself. Behind this character, still without a name, as often is the case with Camus, all the "separated ones" sweep in. The notations on insecurity, the isolation camps increase. "Make thus the theme of separation the great theme of the novel" (*CN, II,* p. 80). It is then that the configuration of Orpheus becomes the summit of the tragedy.

In short, with time, Camus discovered better what the war meant in terms of suffering for everyone. The work takes on a social sense that penetrates through events and chronicles, a moral sense (in terms of observation of human behavior) that penetrates through the characters. The conversation between Rieux and Tarrou reveals to us the anguish of an era dedicated to barbarism and murder. The contrast between Rieux and Paneloux emphasizes the struggle of the powers of relativity against the powers of the absolute. "It is the relative which triumphs, or more precisely, which does not lose" (*CN, II,* p. 69). Finally, except for Cottard, destined to collaborate with the scourge and to die with it, all the characters, in their own way, join in the resistance. The "we" of the narrator then takes on its entire meaning. "The narrator is persuaded that he can write in the name of all, what he himself experienced then, since he experienced it at the same time as many of our fellow-citizens." The plague is a personal adventure lived little by little in communion with an entire people. *La Peste* conceals a progression, not towards the infinite and the sacred, but on the path of a morality based on relativity.

If we needed a word to characterize that morality, honesty could provide us with it. In it, each of the principal characters would recognize himself in his own way. Honesty is first of all lucidity, no longer brutal and vehement as before, but comprehensive. To look things in the face, the world and men such as they are, to avoid all overestimation as well as all denigration. There are circumstances in which we must not fear a word, but call a cat a cat and the plague a scourge; on the other hand, so that words retain their force, we must use them with modesty and reject all boastfulness, even if it is sincere: "From this point of view . . . the narrator considers that Grand was the true representative of that calm virtue that animated the sanitary squads." Hence, Rieux's impatience with "the epic or honors-day tone" of the press or the radio. Words are powerless against the Plague; it demands action. Not spectacular action with brilliant victories, but modest efforts, tirelessly repeated from day to day. Old Castel continues to search for his serum although the first trial only succeeded in prolonging the suffering of the Othon child; Rieux continues to take care of his patients, even when he can do nothing for them; Rambert also renews his attempts at escape, and Grand reworks his sentence about the lady horseback rider. All of them, without actually formulating it, think that "it is not necessary to hope in order to undertake, nor to succeed in order to persevere." Honesty implies patience, composed less of spectacular efforts to overcome oneself than of flexibility in the face of events.

Basically Camus was searching for a kind of average morality; good will rather than heroism, health rather than salvation, humanity rather than saintliness. Paneloux and Tarrou are extreme cases. In deeds, this morality can go hand-in-hand with Christianity. In spirit it is radically opposed to it: pessimistic with regard to destiny, Camus is optimistic with regard to men.[15] One day, "the plague will reawaken its rats and send them to die in a happy city": but the plague's passage will have revealed the existence of men. The book takes the form of a balance-sheet; but, in the final analysis, the balance is reckoned on Rieux's scale. Had Rieux set himself up more or less as a hero we would now only have to invoke mediocrity's claims. But Rieux only did his job, and his actions, whether he likes it or not, resound like appeals. "One does not congratulate a school teacher for teaching that two and two make four." The comparison is significant. The task of the schoolteacher, like that of the true physician, is humble and without luster. There is demanded of him less a spirit of sacrifice than of patience, genius less than comprehension. From one year to the other, from one generation to another, ignorance is always there to combat. Measured against the scale of centuries progress remains imperceptible at the individual level. But what does it matter: "The plague: that consists in beginning all over again." In the same way, Grand understood his wife, Jeanne, who wrote him before her departure: "one does not have to be happy to begin all over again." And Grand himself endlessly begins anew his sentence as the doctor begins anew to care for mortals, and the schoolteacher to teach what the pupil will nonetheless forget.

The last form of honesty is finally comprehension. If humanity is cursed, or rather abandoned and forgotten, since for Camus there are no accursed, the various characters of *La Peste* do not hide their curious sympathy for the criminal, Cottard. Whatever the temptations may be, each one makes an effort to understand his fellow man. Rambert's attempts to flee meet, if not with Rieux's accord, at least with his consent. To appreciate fully the humanity in each one of these countenances is what counts: Camus's humanism does not lie in his conception of the world, but in his moral viewpoint.

That sympathy for the living preserves the preoccupation with

[15] "*La Peste* is the most anti-Christian of my books," and again: "The physician is the enemy of God, he struggles against death."

happiness in the absence of happiness itself. There is not one of the characters who does not seek his own solace in one way or another and who does not fight for some memory. The friendships born of the plague give evidence that men wish neither to die nor to betray. Is it not in the name of friendship that Tarrou and Rieux transgress the official regulations for the first time and swim in unison together in the sea? When Tarrou in his turn is infected, Rieux will once again sidestep his own proscriptions: "You will be better off here," he tells Tarrou, permitting him to spend his last days in Rieux's apartment rather than in one of the isolation camps. Exacting men must possess modesty in order to let life bite into their principles. One has to have admitted that neither any definitive nor absolute truth exists and that it is a blindness of good will whose effects are revealed to be damaging to experience.

It will seem paradoxical that such a morality can stem from the work of one whom a number of critics have disdainfully called a "pure soul." The world of *La Peste* is however exclusively a world of men, of organizers and combatants, whose dominant virtue does not at first sight appear to be sentimentality. One must of course take into account the instinctive horror of the French intelligentsia for everything which from near or far recalls virtue. Honesty among us has not been doing very well lately, since the time when high temporal and spiritual authorities appropriated it and prostituted it to mediocre ends. We support it only all decked out *à la Corneille* or in bizarre and disturbing forms. Camus, by instinct, had little fondness for virtue. He had been able at one time to denounce Pharisaism and mystification through those honest and pure murderers, Caligula and Meursault. But from the moment when he strives to give a countenance to clandestine combat, to incarnate his anxieties and his distaste for injustice, finally, to imprint upon necessary virtue the banal and insignificant aura of great collective adventures, Gide's anathema comes to mind: "Good sentiments make bad literature."

It is true that, upon reflection, sentiment and generosity of soul hold the same place in Camus's moral viewpoint as they do in the common man's reactions and that, on the other hand, hatred and violence are banished from it. But it is no less true that the very notion of duty is rejected from it as abusive and unsuited to represent the simplicity of personal commitments. In fact, the misunderstanding lies elsewhere, and Roland Barthes has sensed it; the choice of an epidemic evil as a symbol for an inexplicable war deprived that war of its violence. The *résistant* took on the countenance of a physician and the effort devoted to killing is changed into a struggle for life. But do not the heroes of the plague carry on their fight in the manner of the clandestine journalist that Camus was, constantly threatened but never touched? Is it not the direct experience of an anonymous scourge undergone as such by the immense majority of combatants in modern-day wars, launched without knowing why into battles they did not want and in which they had difficulty in hating an adversary about whom they knew nothing? "What would the combatants of the Plague do in face of the too human countenance of which it is supposed to be the general and undifferentiated symbol?"[16] Barthes ingenuously asked. Camus had no difficulty in replying to him that the question had "already received its response, which was a positive one. What those combatants whose experience I have somewhat translated did, they did precisely against men, and at a price that you know. They will do it again, undoubtedly, in face of every terror, whatever its face, for terror has several of them, which further justifies my having named none of them precisely in order better to be able to strike at all of them" (*PL, I,* p. 1966).

To be sure, one can maintain that *La Peste* offers us a world without causes and without consequences, entirely one dimensional, almost without past. One can also see in it a crisis of a tragic nature with its progression, its eruption, and its passage. And it is precisely one of the book's riches that in it the plague appears both as a banal incident and as a state of crisis. Like the war in one sense. For if all of life is combat, struggle of men, of classes, or of nations, war then takes on the appearance of concentrated life. One will argue against me that "the function of History is to organize the progressive revelation of facts in function of an epicenter exterior to the crisis itself, it is to substitute for the idea of time that of structure."[17] I note the capital "H" and a definition that smells to high heaven of its Marxism. It is as good as others assuredly. But why does one insist that Camus, who was not a Marxist, borrow from it his point of view. Henri Barbusse's soldiers, in his novel, *Le Feu,* did not have any explanation for the crisis and did not see too well how it could be

[16] "*La Peste,* annales d'une épidémie ou roman de de la solitude," *Club* (February, 1955), p. 6.
[17] Barthes, "*La Peste* . . ."

"recuperated in some way, by transference, within the whole of humanity." Let us say that *La Peste* is war seen by a Curiace and not by a
Horace. Beneath the objectivity of tone appears in filigree the longing for
peace or the dream of a just and nonviolent combat in which we would
more gladly kill microbes than men—in this sense, the book is a "confession."

Perhaps it is so on another level as well. It would only be seemingly
paradoxical to say that *La Peste* is a love novel. Woman, physically
absent from the work, is constantly present. I am not talking about old
women, whose place in Camus's work we already know: Rieux's mother,
discreet and understanding, or Rambert's elderly hostess, a naive Catholic.
Neither am I talking about those anonymous women who people the
crowds of Oran, but of those shadows who are Rieux's wife and Rambert's mistress. The former, we scarcely catch a glimpse of; of the second,
we know nothing except that she is Rambert's beloved. She remains for
us a "form" who ran to meet her lover, a face buried in the hollow of his
shoulder. The gates of Oran were swung shut upon the prisoners; and, as
in every prison and in every *stalag*, women are henceforth more "present"
than ever. "Perhaps I was brought into the world in order to live with a
woman."

At first sight they are only *objects* of love. We know of them no
more than the effects of their absence on their lovers. Rambert and Rieux
—especially Rambert—suffer from this separation as they suffer from
being deprived of the sun and the sea. Landscapes disappear[18] and woman
is effaced along with them. But she rises up in the background like a
carnal and living reason for dying, one of those reasons whose weight and
warmth everyone knows. In that abstract universe of the warring plague,
woman speaks of peace and the flesh.[19]

However she is something besides the warrior's dream. The couple
does appear in Camus's work. Caesonia and Caligula were accomplices;
Meursault and Marie do not form a firm relationship. The couple comes
to the fore with Jan and Maria, but without real conviction. The Castels,

---

[18] "It is not by chance that one does not find landscapes in great European
literature since Dostoevski." *Actuelles, I*, p. 403.

[19] This way of seeing the woman at times as an object and at times as a
symbol rather than a person explains how Simone de Beauvoir may have
discerned a certain misogynism in Camus.

along with Rieux and his wife, introduce us for the first time to tenderness, tenderness effaced by daily preoccupations and discreet to that very extent, the troubled and gruff tenderness of busy people that is not without some remorse at not being able to grant more to the loved one. This is why, at the instant of separation, Rieux abruptly asks his wife's pardon. "To speak at last of lovers," he writes further on, *"who are the most interesting,* and of whom the narrator is perhaps in a better position to speak, they found themselves further tormented by other causes of anguish among which we must mention remorse." Love then takes over everything and becomes, by preterition, the source of all joys. Memory deepens tenderness, rids it of mediocrity in which it bogs down and returns it to its purity as well as to its original exigency: "The great desire of a troubled heart is to possess interminably the being that it loves."[20]

La Peste, to the extent that is truly a novel, is then the novel of separation and exile.[21] Not enough attention has been paid to the story Tarrou tells of an evening at the municipal opera. "This story reconstructs somewhat the difficult atmosphere of that period and this is why the narrator attaches some importance to it." It was a Friday and they were giving what was to become a weekly performance of *Orpheus.* In the course of the great duet, at the very moment when Eurydice leaves her lover, Orpheus collapses in a grotesque position. The plague had played its role even on the stage. Eurydice eludes Orpheus for all time. Oran joined forever the sad Carousel from which Baudelaire's swan[22] tirelessly unleashes toward the heavens the exiles' plaint.

It seems moreover that Camus rarely had so little taste for solitude as he did at the time he was writing *La Peste.* Thus the book is a protest against forced solitude. All self-complacency, every inclination toward retreat is excluded from it. If it is true that solitude was always one of Camus's temptations and a source of anguish for him, the very difficult experience of clandestine activity seems to have momentarily developed in him the taste for solidarity and happiness. Despite all the menaces and

[20] See also *L'Homme révolté,* p. 665, and the entire analysis of the desire for possession, and, notably, this remark: "on the cruel earth where lovers sometimes die separated, where they are born apart, total possession of a being, absolute communion during the entire lifetime is an impossible demand."

[21] Exile and separation were Camus's own lot from 1942 to 1944. (See Biography.)

[22] See *Les Fleurs du mal,* "Le Cygne," LXXXIX.

all the anxieties, exile in *La Peste* is charged with promise. "They knew now that if there is something that one can desire always and obtain occasionally, it is human tenderness . . . And Rieux . . . thought that it was only right that from time to time at least, joy should come to reward those who find sufficiency in man and his poor and awesome love."

Poor love, indeed, subject to so many eclipses, worn out by habit, stifled by conformity, cowardice or Pharisaism. Poor love which yields so easily to mechanical routine, to hypocrisy, to force of power. Awesome love as well, capable of jealousy, of murder and tyranny. For the Plague is equally the province of men (do we not talk of bacteriological warfare!) carried away by insane love, the love on which Camus's German friend is intoxicated, the blind love of race and the nation of overlords, the love that in the past inebriated many servants of God and which Camus bitterly denounced in contemporary Spain. Terrible love, finally, like that of the *Montagnard* terrorists of 1793 or the Russian revolutionaries of 1917, who, starting from the most generous of ambitions, arrived, according to Camus, at nothing but the Reign of Terror whose history *L'Homme révolté* precisely sketches.

Against the abstractions of the totalitarian state, whether it be Russian, German, or Spanish, Camus resolutely took "the part of the individual, of the flesh in all that it has that is most noble, of earthly love, in fact," delivered of all excess. Inviting us to join the struggle against evil in all its forms, *La Peste* appears thereafter as an appeal to tolerance and modesty, the most despairing vice being that of ignorance which thinks it knows all and which authorizes itself to kill.

In the light of these notions of tolerance, modesty, and rigor, one better understands why all Camus's art tended toward unobtrusiveness. The most classical conception of novelistic composition was thus the nearest to the testimonial. In reality, nothing is more painstakingly designed than such a narrative. From the manuscript to the definitive text, Camus strove for unity of tone through the indirect style or ordinary speech of the clandestine narrator. He blended the various diaries into a single one—that of Tarrou. Especially, he orchestrated his theme in five parts: the first, which is that of discovery, concludes with the declaration of the state of plague; the second treats of the reaction of individuals in face of the scourge—attempts at adaptation, then resistance; the third analyzes the state of plague; the fourth presents the battle in its relativity, up to Grand's victory over death; finally, the fifth evokes the reflux of evil. This development is the movement of a classical tragedy.

But Camus made an effort to break this movement by alternating the appearances of his characters (Grand, Cottard, in the first part) or by interweaving specific remarks and generalities of a moral nature. Finally, he interlaced the different levels: historical or metaphysical, realistic notations and symbols. Without actually being able to speak of a system, it clearly appears that the book's structure is founded on somewhat regular alternances. By this very means, the author makes of his book a summation: an absurd décor, a tragedy, men come to grips with their destiny, and the eye of the narrator who records and judges without appearing to do so, either through a sort of cold irony or through the very indifference that he affects. Many details only become apparent on second reading, so many are the intentions and so discreetly are they expressed. Quite naturally the book lends itself to anthologizing.

Some have reproached it for this reason, seeing in it a weakness. In reality its ambiguity lies elsewhere: in the fact that "absurd (and gratuitous) thought is the expulsion of all value judgments to the advantage of judgments of fact. Now, we know that there are inevitable value judgments."[23] In *La Peste*, hither and thither, Camus superimposed judgments of fact—neuter in tone—and value judgments. Insignificance (the insignificant characters are grouped in Book Two) rubs shoulders with important dialogues. The blank language of neutrality, the corrosive humor stands next to categorically stated positions. The whole book purports to be written in a tone of reserve, but the pretended author accepts "only unreserved testimony." Between the observer and the combatant is established a kind of hiatus that the unity of testimony does not suffice to overcome.[24] One balances between lucidity and the loneliness of detachment on the one hand and the ethics of collective involvement on the other. But one does not always find the warmth of solidarity nor the barrenness of lucidity. And that intimate dichotomy prohibits the characters from being anything other than the symbols of an attitude.

[23] Letter to Pierre Bonnel on *Le Mythe de Sisyphe*.
[24] See pp. 112–13 on Camus and the difficulties of language.

If, beyond this torn century, *La Peste* claims the attention of posterity, it will assuredly be owing less to the consistency of its characters than to the ever-unresolved debate between rigor and formal indifference on the one hand and, on the other, the most demanding and most quivering sensibility that has ever been.

9

From Apocalypse to Martyrdom

L'État de siège and *Les Justes* make up the second panel of the triptych of revolt. These two plays represent, on the theatrical level, an effort of renewal in different directions. They experienced opposite fates.

The critical failure of *L'État de siège* is a known fact. The public was cold toward the play after the critics indicated their reservations. An explanation for this lack of success was necessary; Barrault was the scapegoat. Had he not misfortunately led Camus on to his own personal terrain of the mime and "spectacle"? If Barrault provided a temptation, we must suppose that Camus desired nothing less than letting himself be tempted. He never regretted any part of that adventure; ever since *La Révolte dans les Asturies,* he had always retained a fondness for team undertakings, notably in the theatre where every performance derives inevitably from a collective act of creation.

It is manifestly evident that *L'État de siège* is more than an adaptation; that the work carried the stamp of the author of *La Peste* is equally evident. Treating the same myth, the same writer cannot radically modify its spirit and the play recalls the novel in more than one detail. As proof I need offer no more than the curé's brief sermon, which differs from Father Paneloux's first sermon in its tone and brevity, not in its spirit. And, just as Orpheus died on the stage of the *Opéra,* an actor collapses on the boards. But it must be recognized that, if irony and the spirit of analysis presided over the construction of the novel, the play attempted to be as impassioned as it was polemic.

Let us take *L'État de siège* for what it claimed to be, a spectacle; I would further say a "play" (*jeu*) in the medieval sense of the term, the representation of man and nothingness.[1] Camus had tried certain of its

---

[1] Camus told me of having had in mind the technique of the medieval morality plays and of the Spanish *autos sacramentales* (did he not later adapt Calderon's *La Dévotion à la croix?*).

techniques earlier in *La Révolte dans les Asturies:* café or crowd scenes, pantomimes and even radio broadcasts. Two actions unfold simultaneously on the same stage and the actors had in mind to make of the entire theatre a place of action. As for Barrault, one is aware of his fondness for spectacle in the fullest sense of the word. Thus one is not too surprised at this definition of the play: "There is no question of a traditionally structured play but rather of a spectacle whose ambition is to intermingle all forms of dramatic expression from the lyric monologue to the collective theatre by way of the mime, simple dialogue, farce, and the chorus." Moreover, simply reading Paul Claudel's *Christophe Colomb* would have suggested to them the essentials of these techniques.

The first act is an apocalypse. We are in Cadiz,[2] whose walls stand out silhouetted against the background, as though they had had to be snatched from out of space. In the city itself the stage is everywhere and nowhere. We move from one corner to the other of the marketplace, from beggars to the fishing area, then to young Victoria's windows; from the governmental palace to the church and vice versa. The stage unites all these places like so many "mansions."* This is because the entire city is concerned, or, better still, because the catastrophe is universal.

There is no question of date; the spectacle is timeless, outside of time, if not at the end of time. Doubtless the first act has something of the medieval about it. The choice of a Spanish city would suffice, it is true, to give us that impression. Cadiz has its crenellations, its *alcaldes;* plays are still performed on the public square; a king still reigns over Aragon and Castile. The language of the poor and of the players is not without analogy to that of the medieval mystery plays: "good governor, gracious ladies, lords." In the marketplace presses a raucous and willingly superstitious crowd: shopkeepers with catchy slogans, drunks with facile jokes, thieving beggars, not to mention the astrologer and the aptly named Nada, who is as much buffoon as town crier: "Nada, you must know. What does that mean?" "I've already told you, son, we are already up against it. Hope for nothing. The comedy is going to begin."

---

[2] The play was almost given the title *L'Inquisition à Cadiz* [The Inquisition at Cadiz]. Earlier, *Le Fléau* [The Scourge] and *Le Vent se lève* [The Wind is Rising] had been envisaged as titles.

* In the medieval theater, the particular location in which a given scene took place [trans. note].

Why these collective scenes? We have already sensed it; an entire people is involved, from the beggar to the judge, from the shopkeeper to the *alcaldes,* from the gypsies to the parish priest. The drunkenness of some, the love of others, credulity, thievery and goodnaturedness, innocence and art (the actor is the first to be struck down), *joie de vivre* and the summertime of which the chorus of fishermen sings to us, all are going to be infected by the plague. Good and evil, spontaneity as well as cunning, in short, all of life in its anarchical movement and its tumultuous gaiety are conjointly menaced by a mysterious evil.

A musical overture with a "call to arms" theme creates the aura of expectation. The slow apparition of the comet, an inverse symbol to the dove so dear to Claudel, the constant buzzing growing more and more intense, the two enormous dull thuds, the death knell that rings at full peal, all rhythmically follow the mounting inquietude of the people. All these techniques are aimed more at the body than the mind of the spectator, a fact that is confirmed by the continual use of pantomime. The stage is prey to a kind of enormous fear, as blind as it is instinctive.

But the plague appears and, as it cruelly states: "when I arrive, the pathetic flees." At this precise point, the play breaks. The entire problem would have been to render, if not pathetic, at least picturesque the mythical representation of an evil whose manifestations are characterized by monotony and bareness. A dreary terror is not of necessity without mystery. In this case, we no longer feel anything. And how could we, when the Plague hides nothing of its character from us and willingly lends itself to a kind of reconstruction of the crime. In a certain manner, Camus had attempted to remain too closely faithful to the idea he had formulated of reality and that he expressed elsewhere: "what is astonishing is that these henceforth deaf and blind silhouettes, terrorized, nourished by food-stamps, and whose entire lives are summed up on an official registration card, can be treated like anonymous abstractions."[3] Up to that point in the play we participated with our eyes and our bodies in a spectacle in which the fantastic dominated, and suddenly there surges forth, scarcely concealed, a kind of allegorical skeleton. To be sure, allegory is a proven theatrical element, quite particularly in medieval

[3] "Le Témoin de la liberté," an address delivered at the *Salle Pleyel* before an international writers' meeting in November, 1948. (See *Actuelles, I,* p. 402.)

drama and mystery plays. But most often its role was secondary (as in the case of "Imagination" in Lope de Vega's *Christophe Colomb*). What can be tolerated in the character Nada can be accepted only with difficulty in the central character.

I do not know if myths are imposed from the outside or if they are not rather carried within the collective imagination: Christopher Columbus had his legend before Claudel took it and made use of it; for the spectator of the medieval *Jeu d'Adam,* the story of the temptation already had a familiar reality. Joan of Arc and Moses are first of all definable and chronologically fixed characters which mythology utilized as a framework and which it fills with an enlarged timeless significance. Now, the plague in Camus's play is only the mythical representation of an abstraction. The plague, at least in the way in which it is presented to us, has no history, no roots. It is less timeless than ideal, or as our philosophers would say, abstract. It attempts to put down roots through a process which is inverse to the one we have just analyzed above. Its implantation itself is curious, since we are led to define it step by step by way of a series of abstract terms: occupation, revolution, bureaucratism, state control, organization, planification. If we try to clarify these notions we stir up, all in one movement, Nazism, Falangism, and Communism; or, if you prefer, red tape, state police, and bureaucracy. These are without any doubt hard realities whose substance we all know, whether they be concentration camps, mass executions, food-rationing stamps, graphs of salaries or of the electoral system. In addition, instead of our rising from history or legend to the eternal, and from the particular to the general, we rather descend from the general to the particular and from the eternal to history by means of a cascade of abstractions which finally find their incarnation in a series of sketches of narrowly contemporary and subjective scope.

It seems even that there may have been confusion over the very notion of myth and that dramatic myth and explanatory or satirical myth may have been superimposed, the former being Dionysian in its principle, the other Platonic. At one moment, the plague in Cadiz obscurely represented the most eternal and most subtle forces of evil; at another it is no longer anything but the garment tossed to cover the desiccated nudity of contemporary evils. It systematizes them and gives them an arguable homogeneity. Let us say it quite frankly, Camus gives the impression of using the Plague and of not believing in it. As he approaches its different aspects, the tone changes. Considered individually, a particular scene of Nada-bureaucrat is good in its Courtelinesque movement (minus the frankness). In one place we meet with the *canular,* the tongue-in-cheek satires of the music-hall *chansonniers* on the subject of the bureaucracy or the housing shortage, evidenced by the variations and stylistic plays on the words *convoquer* [call together] and *ravitailler* [reprovision]. In another place the interplay becomes sinister, the satire hard-bitten, "hysterical" even, as directed. "I have concentrated them. Up to now they lived amid dispersion and frivolity, thinned out, so to speak! Now they are more solid, they are concentrating themselves." We balance between a somewhat facile anarchism and eternal and tragic satire of which Nada's next-to-last tirade, charged with bitter vehemence, furnishes us the best example: "There they are! The old guard is arriving, the 'before' crowd, the 'all-time' boys, the petrified, the reassuring, the comfortable, the dead-enders, the prim-and-propers, in other words, tradition . . . Here are the little tailors of nothingness, my friends, you're going to be custom-fitted . . . They are going to concern themselves with the heroes. They are going to put them in a cool place, under the paving stones . . . Let's watch them. What do you think they are already doing? They are conferring medals on themselves." Here is the tone of Hugo's *Les Tragiques* and *Les Châtiments.* We return at this moment to the first act in which the Governor, the village priest, the judge, and the entire crowd seemed destined to the pillory (in the manner of the bourgeois, priests and tradesmen in Ghelderode's *Mademoiselle Jaïre*). But in the meantime, we have abandoned men for institutions.

Fundamentally, in order to be able to render us sensitive to this tragedy of monotony and maintain a climate of indignation in the manner of Hugo or d'Aubigné, Camus lacked one quality—or one fault: hatred. Camus was without hatred; he loved to unburden men of all responsibility and transfer to that allegorical figure, the plague, all his power of rebellion. For him there were hardly any accomplices and no guilty parties. But with them the adversary vanishes at the same time. Fundamentally, Camus did not believe in hell. One scene makes this quite obvious: the judge, his wife, and his children are condemned to live in the midst of truth; all masks fall off. It seems that we are on the road toward a kind of "no exit" in which all these solitudes will henceforth be stripped bare. But Camus depicts cowardice and deceit only from the exterior; he caricatures them. The characters reach the level of insults and vocal outburst without even the least of their words ever attaining the cruelty of Racine's gentle Iphigénie. Had he succeeded, this scene would have been no less inserted like a foreign body into the second act's satire. It seems as though someone might have wanted to tell us: the Plague is this, too. The authors did not know how to choose and the play finally is as much recital as spectacle.

If Camus did not choose between the diabolical mystery play (with the eternal satire that it permits) and contemporary satire, it is because he intended to maintain a parallel between his metaphysical and social preoccupations. It is also because the play corresponds to a certain propaganda concern. The schema is familiar: the arrival of misfortune, the reign of misfortune, and rebellions against the plague.[4] The satire marked the first stage of the struggle against evil: it must be brought into disrepute. For, as the secretary explains to Diégo, one needs only to understand and to cease being afraid, after which the counterattack is possible. It becomes clear at this point that the play is founded on a paradox: create fear in order to reduce it to its exact proportions and destroy it. But is not to destroy fear also to kill in the spectator the sense of the pathetic?

The picture of collective cowardice ("there are no men left in this city"), the degradation of life ("living and dying are two forms of dishonor"), the plague's percussive slogans ("deport, torture, something always will remain") are supposed to provoke Diégo's sudden awakening, which is Corneillian in spirit and melodramatic in its expression.[5] We can find the corresponding commentary in "Le Témoin de la liberté" (*A, I*, pp. 399–406): "In the world of the death sentence which is ours, artists bear witness for that in man which refuses to die." Moreover, there is yet another play that begins with the third tableau. We follow Diégo in his attempt at flight (similar to Rambert's), in his fight against the mindless violence of the people who snatched the secretary's notebook from her

---

[4] Reflected in the two earlier projected titles, *Le Fléau* and *Le Vent se lève*, which hesitate between two aspects of the work.

[5] Equally melodramatic (does one not find an example of it in Hugo's *Les Burgraves?*) is the bargain that Death proposes to Diégo; Victoria's resurrection and happiness in exchange for Cadiz delivered over without recourse to the Plague.

and set about hurriedly to settle old accounts through a summary purge, and in the final sacrifice which is the sign of deliverance. The bizarre love of the allegorical secretary for the human Diégo does not manage to conceal its meaning. *L'État de siège* is, then, an appeal to resistance in all its forms: resistance to the temptation of the ivory tower, the temptation of violence; resistance to totalitarian tyranny in the manner of the Spanish exiles, since, indeed, the book is dedicated to suffering Republican Spain.[6]

In counterpoint: the love of Diégo and Victoria with its fears, is upward surges and its retreats, its jealousy. The two characters portray personalities less than they represent love in the midst of the debacle. They speak of its necessity, its strength, and its hope. Victoria with simplicity and spontaneous self-sacrifice, Diégo with curiosity and, in a certain manner of speaking, in solitude. We find here again the opposition of Jan and Maria from *Le Malentendu*. Here again, Camus yields to the urge to tell everything. This intrigue would finally be without great scope if a few lyrical duets, whose fervor and luxuriance sometimes recall Claudel, did not bring bursting into that meager universe love's true promise. These are incontestably, along with the warm sensuality of the choruses that carry us back to the poetry of *Noces,* the best moments of a play which, because it could not rid itself of a certain number of uncertainties, was unable to find anywhere either its climate or its movement.

Overall, the play doubtless suffered from the celebrity of the group that created it: text by Camus, direction by Barrault, music by Honegger, settings by Balthus, Pierre Brasseur and Maria Casarès in the lead roles; a masterpiece was expected; a composite work was the result. In a certain sense it was a Camus festival, a review of all his themes: at a given moment Caligula's philosophy of loss—that which brings salvation "by way of the greatest of evils"—comes to the fore; at another, "the evil from which we must save ourselves."[7] In the play one discovers scorn of the powerful (the *Alcalde,* the Governor), of judges, hostility toward all churches, defiance of every consecrated institution. And Diégo, the prototype of those chasers after shadows who "prefer the idea. They flee their

---

[6] See also "Pourquoi l'Espagne? Réponse è Gabriel Marcel": *"L'État de siège* represents a rupture" (*A, I,* p. 392).

[7] Jean-Louis Barrault, *La Table ronde* (February, 1960).

mothers, they break away from their beloveds, and there they are, running off after adventure," like Jan; and women who have the weight of living flesh, the taste for happiness, like Victoria, Maria's sister.

But the spectacle itself, now Aristophanic, near to absurd buffoonery, now lyric and ardent, does not find its point of equilibrium. It is true that Barrault brought to it a scenic conception borrowed from Daniel Defoe; while Camus, who had just finished work on *La Peste,* dreamt of escaping from the even-toned language of the chronicler. At least the common memory of Antonin Artaud united them in the search for a form of exaltation and a paroxysm in which our repressions might "come to life." "All the conflicts that sleep within us, [the theatre] gives back to us with all their powers."[8]

But he added dangerously, "it gives to these powers names that we hail as symbols. As a result, there takes place before us a *battle of symbols,* piled one upon another in an impossible stampede." *L'État de siège* borrowed the allegories of the Spanish *autos sacramentales,* their mixture of tones and styles, and it owes to Artaud its battles of symbols. Is it because of a deformity of our taste, an excess of intellectuality? Whatever it may be, this apocalypse, like Diégo's martyrdom, inspires in us neither terror nor admiration.

Deep within himself Camus accepted the play's failure with difficulty. He envisioned a kind of revenge in Athens, in an open air production.[9] He was ready, in order to achieve this, to rework the play.[10] Perhaps one day, in spite of its weaknesses or because of them, *L'État de siège* will find a naive and passionate public, ready to applaud in a natural setting, this myth-ballet situated halfway between farce and review and between dance and opera.

Apart from different techniques and opposing climates, *L'État de siège* and *Les Justes* [The Just Assassins], are subject to common preoccupations. The final tableau of *L'État de siège* retraced the stages of revolt

---

[8] Artaud, *Le Théâtre et son double.*

[9] In a 1956 interview in *Combat.*

[10] In a 1957 interview in *Paris-Théâtre;* reprinted in *Théâtre, récits, nouvelles,* pp. 1711–17 (the date of the interview is given here as 1958 [trans. note]).

in acts beyond time and place. Diégo symbolized that handful of combatants that humanity unleashes from time to time in an assault against tyrannies. For a time, Diégo has transformed himself into a terrorist in far-off Holy Russia delivered up to the Tsarist plague. Moscow and Saint Petersburg are in a state of siege; the icy room in which the terrorists shut themselves up and even the terrorist's fleshless hearts are no less so.

It was in poring over the Rebel's genealogy, while preparing *L'Homme révolté,* that Camus discovered the Social Revolutionary Party. In January 1948, an article, "Les Meurtriers delicats," which he published in *La Table ronde,* recalled those innocent faces of which history had retained only a pale and frightened memory. Later, an entire chapter of *L'Homme révolté* again took up the same elements in order to integrate them into this vast fresco of European revolt. The two texts bring deliberately into focus the historical character of the situations and the authenticity of some of the most striking remarks the author lends to the characters of *Les Justes.* These are, moreover, based on actual terrorists. I am not speaking of Kaliayev alone, whose name was retained in homage to the 1905 martyr, but as well of Dora Doublebov, Boris Annenkov, and Voinov, who are doubtless not unrelated to Dora Brillant, Boris Savinkov, and Voinarovsky, all members of the Combat Organization of the S.R.P. But why mention the 1905 movement alone? There is no doubt but that Dora Doublebov owes more than one of her traits to the so surprisingly grave and gentle features of Sophie Peroskaia, Vera Zassoulitch, Lebedeva, and Kovalevskaia, all of whom participated at different periods in the assassination attempts of what one is pleased to call "la belle époque." As for Stépan, he resembles all in one the cynicism of the early Bakunin, the scorn of Netchaiev, and the pitiless realism "of the *grands seigneurs* of the Revolution."[11]

When, on February 2, 1905, Kaliayev had refused to throw his bomb at the Grand Duke Serge out of regard for the life of the latter's niece and nephew, Marie and Dmitri, and when on May 10, of the same year he had mounted the scaffold without having made any effort to save his life, he had already won an eminent place in the long revolutionary martyrology. Moreover, the play, which takes these two dates and steals them away from history, is not entitled "Kaliayev" but *Les Justes,* with

[11] At the outset he is "the realist" who wants to enter the Okhrana (political police) as Klekovchinkov had.

everything this word suggests not only of collective action but of sharpness and purity as well. Polyeucte, in Corneille's play of the same name, surpasses the third century Armenian martyr and provides the pretext for a tragedy of Christian grace and humanity. Similarly fixed in time, the Just Assassins escape from time in order to animate the tragedy of purity and history. Sartre's *Les Mains sales* [Red Gloves] had already posed the question; here it becomes more precise and more limited: can the revolutionary kill? Under what conditions and up to what point? The Just Assassins in the answers they bring forward commit all their strength and their very lives. "The greatest homage we can render them is to say that we are unable in 1947 to put to them a single question that they have not already asked themselves and to which in their lives or by their deaths they have not answered in part" (*HR*).

Nothing, however, seemed to destine them to the role of executioners. Voinov, for his part, admits as much: "I was not made for terrorism." He is afraid of seeing others die. Annenkov retains a delightful memory of his brilliant and facile former life: "Yes, I loved women, wine, those nights that never ended." Dora is only a child grown up too fast who does not hide her longing for a now demolished innocence and irresponsibility: "I remember the time when I was a student. I laughed, I was beautiful then. I used to spend hours walking and dreaming." Intoxicated for an instant by the unshakable breath of a destroyed adolescence, she will try to escape from the hell of the present and be a girl like so many others, called to something "above this world poisoned with injustice." Is not what she loves in Kaliayev his exaltation, his fervor, his weakness even: "too extraordinary to be a revolutionary." One finds him "a little mad, too spontaneous," whimsical to put it bluntly. Always ready to seize the most simple pleasures that life offers him, he derives naive enjoyment from his peddler's disguise. Incapable of doing anything as others do, deliberately facetious, he modifies the agreed upon signal. They call him "The Poet"; he sings of gaiety, beauty, joy. He wants to endow even his death with poetry. Of a romantic imagination, he proposes to throw himself under the horses' hooves or considers committing hara-kiri. Thus between him and Stépan no sympathy is possible. Stépan is the only one who seems at ease in the midst of murder, the only one who truly knows how to hate. He is a brother to Martha, an ageless puritan. Was he perhaps different once? He has come too far since; for him, three years in prison have amounted to a baptism by blood.

Hatred, humiliation, and desire for vengeance have introduced Stépan to terrorism by way of the narrow path. The others have come to it by the most direct and simple way. "I love life," Kaliayev says, "I am not bored. I joined the revolution because I love life . . . I love beauty, happiness. For that reason I hate despotism. Revolution, to be sure; but the revolution for life, to give life a chance, you understand." Russia is only a great leafless tree in the silence of an interminable winter. Such a vision is intolerable; the Just Assassins have turned away from themselves, their families, their futures, to give back to their homeland its true face and its health; it is a question of honor. In the atmosphere of the time, in face of the resignation of the masses, murder is the unique means of awakening the oppressed to rebellious consciousness. In other places—in India, for example—Gandhi's nonviolence could work. But in Christian Europe respect for life is hardly more than a memory. Scandal and fear are indispensable arms, since every other form of predication hurtles up against skepticism or force. Justice then will borrow from evil its own arms. Given this state of affairs, Kaliayev asks himself: "Can one speak of terrorist action without taking part in it?" To bear witness from a condition of deprivation and the most irrevocable form of involvement is again a question of honor. In choosing the bomb, the Just Assassins enter into the realm of religion.

To act? But how? To kill? But who and how many? Some are tempted to shrug their shoulders. The question is however of the kind that the resistants sometimes had to ask themselves. Killing is not easy in itself, but to kill a defenseless man, whether he be cheerful or worried, a man of flesh and blood, whose last thought is of dying . . . For these mystics of life, even a tyrant's life is precious. Even now they must play tricks with words: "It's not he I'm killing. I'm killing despotism." With the least thing, a kind of intoxication, a sudden gust of hatred, they will be able to restore to their victim his tyrant's mask. Kaliayev, then, can leave calmly; no not calmly—the Just are never calm—but rather joyous, exalted, in a kind of second state. Until the moment when, in the grand-ducal carriage, his eyes light upon two children "lost in their fancy-dress clothes, their hands resting on their thighs, sitting stiffly on either side of the carriage door . . . Those two serious little faces, and in my hand that terrible weight." Kaliayev did not throw the bomb. He cannot explain why not. As if by reflex, his energies vacillated: "My arm became weak, my legs trembled." As once before in the Ukraine, he experienced a nauseous sensation at the idea of running down a child: "I imagined the shock, that frail head striking the pavement in full flight."

From what was only a reflex, a failure of the imagination, doubtless, the Just will draw a principle and a rule. The instinctive refusal to kill has created a problem of conscience. When the carriage returns will they throw the bomb in spite of the children's presence? For Stépan there is but one duty: to strike, to effect without false scruples the organization's decision, to carry out a verdict. A puerile gesture threatens to render useless months of trailing the Grand Duke's movements. He imposes an implacable logic against so many arguments borrowed from popular sentimentality: "Children! You can't talk about anything else. Don't you understand anything? Because Yanek did not kill those two, thousands of Russian children will die of hunger for years to come." A mathematical problem that has nothing to do with the requirements of a scrupulous heart? It is not so simple: "Have you seen children die of hunger? I have." Stépan's expression is heavy with horrors he has seen or been subjected to. It is necessary to choose between two cases of suffering: "Do you live only in the present moment? Then choose charity and cure only each day's evil, and not revolution which seeks to cure all evils, now and to come."

The Just could reply, and they do so briefly, that efficacity requires also not offending public opinion needlessly: "Destroy . . . Demolish . . . ," wrote Gapone, "only do not touch private citizens or private dwellings."[12] Terrorism's effects are a function of its purity. But the essential does not lie therein; efficacity is not a good criterion. The dialogue between scrupulousness and cynicism, of which Thierry Maulnier's *La Maison de la nuit* has since furnished us another example, is pursued on another level. Kaliayev's hesitation calls into question an entire hierarchy of passion and honor. The Just do not want to choose between justice and life, virtue and love, for the demands of each are borne upon the shoulders of the other. In an earlier time, in the name of

[12] *Tribune russe* (1905).

"this miserable and dried-up substitute for love which we call morality" (*A, I,* p. 403), they had to set life off in parentheses and consent to murder; just as in Corneille's *Le Cid,* Rodrigue, in order to strike down Don Gomèz, must forget for a moment that he is Chimène's father. But let no one come to them afterwards and demand more:

> L'infamie est pareille, et suit également
> Le Guerrier sans courage et le perfide amant [III, vi].[13]

It is very difficult in fact to distinguish whether the horror of murder alone opposed itself to the terrorist's duty or whether a certain intuition of the permissible limits did not rather destroy the passion for vengeance and sacrifice. For what is honor if not the sense of limits, of what is intolerable? On the basis of pure logic, Stépan is right as is the Grand Duchess, who will contrast the Grand Duke's good-naturedness with the meanness of the two children. But what does it matter to Rodrigue whether his father, Don Diègue, was justified in his complaint against Don Gomèz? The Corneillian sense of honor took for its mission to preserve a capital of glory acquired by generations past. Revolutionary honor demands the passing on of a capital of hope to generations to come —the passing it on to them untainted. The suffering of an entire people in chains called forth revolt, but two threatened children's faces turned revolt against itself. Justice balances off life, but life balances off the exesses of justice. In entering the terrorist movement, Kaliayev had no other hope than that of creating a world in which children would no longer die of violence or hunger. He refuses to strike out of conformity to that principle. In truth, he intends to save everything; the choice between violence and life to which he consents is only exceptional and limited: "and if one day—and I am still living—the revolution were to become separated from honor, I would turn my back on it." Devious means are enough to save a reputation but not a sense of honor.

Make no mistake, in fact, about the meaning of terrorist violence. It is not a means of destruction in the usual sense of the word. What progress is likely to come from the death of a single tsar or a single grand duke? Its material usefulness is nil. It is a sign, a cry of alarm in a world

---

[13] The infamy is the same, and pursues with equal fury
The warrior without courage and the perfidious lover
[trans. note].

of silence and ice. Its value is mystical, pedagogical, like Caligula's killings, and not practical: to smash idols, to return to the people an awareness of the frailty of tyrannies. The colossus has feet of clay and barely remains erect except by its own weight. Like the prophets, the Just oppose to the arid old law, drained of its human content, that feeble hope which they nourish with their blood. In a universe from which prophecy is banished, the bomb is substituted for the sermon. Each explosion is similar to those stars that guide the progress of the magi toward the rebirth. The Just are blood-stained apostles.

The revolt of the Just is in essence "religious, if not metaphysical" (*HR*). The Just are least of all economists or technicians, not even professional revolutionaries. If the revolution came into being suddenly, the present would become cumbersome for them: "for Dora Brillant, questions of program did not count" (*HR*). Their undertaking "aims at re-creating a community of justice and love and at resuming thus the mission that the Church has betrayed. The Terrorists in reality want to create a Church out of which a new God will spring forth" (*HR*). Their acts are situated midway between the crusades and martyrdom. And it was doubtless not by chance that, among so many atheistic characters, Kaliayev was precisely the one that Camus elected as the central figure in his drama. Kaliayev is a believer; he does not practice, but "he has a religious soul."[14] With him and his comrades, everything exhales faith— the word is pronounced. The bare room in which the conspirators meet resembled the catacombs and the austere temple of justice. In spite of the inevitable interpersonal clashes provoked by this sealed chamber, the conspirators are united by a kind of communion of the living and the dead: "remember what we are: brothers, welded one to the other . . . we kill together and nothing can separate us." And again: "there is us, the organization. Beyond that there is nothing. It is a brotherhood of knights." When Voinov is led to confess his fear and asks to be reassigned to the rank of propagandist, each of them senses what a similar admission would cost him: "He told me there was no happiness for him outside our organization." And one thinks of the terrors of Blanche de la Force,

---

[14] Mauriac, citing Saint Augustine, called Camus "anima christiana naturaliter" [a naturally Christian soul]. Questioned by Viggiani concerning this affirmation, Camus replied that he was "not so naturally, but rather by osmosis."

rejected from a community which alone could bring her peace and a sense of pride.[15]

For these beings consumed by a mad love, there is no escape from their torment except martyrdom; it alone is capable of redeeming murder. In a certain sense, one can call it an exchange. Undoubtedly we are far removed from that exchange of souls founded on the communion of saints which creates the mystery of the *Dialogue des Carmélites*. We remain on the human level, life against life. But there is something strange and fascinating sometimes in the fervent march toward torture of these martyrs without certainties. And if there were no other eternity than that composed of the days that lie between the act of murder and the scaffold! One might with reason speak of a morbid temptation to suicide (an equally constant and just a bit histrionic temptation for the Corneillian hero). "For a year I have thought of nothing else. It is for that moment I've lived up to now." Dora, too, in a breath, lets escape a fearful word: "There is a greater happiness . . . the scaffold." For them martyrdom is not only the supreme justification, but happiness as well. The happiness of the task accomplished and of peace recaptured once more in that reconciliation of the entire being that had already obsessed Tarrou. The scaffold is the baptism of blood: "to kill and die," the two summits of the terrorist's life are joined in a unique protest of the twice-wounded flesh, in a double sacrifice upon which the liberated city of tomorrow can be built.

The three temptations of the fourth act are so many steps the martyr must mount in his movement of purification. There is an evident similarity between Yanek's temptations and those of Polyeucte. However so adroitly that ascension may be carried out, here it takes on a somewhat rhetorical character. Foka, the man of the people, a drunkard and a murderer, who can barely conceive that someone could be mad enough to die in his name, cruelly emphasizes the romantic naiveté of Kaliayev. His cruel presence is ironic. This superstitious, blind, and finally mistrusting character drains revolutionary lyricism of any meaning whatsoever. "All that's not normal. You don't think of getting yourself thrown in prison on account of stories about saints and carts stuck in the mud." There is

[15] See Georges Bernanos, *Dialogue des Carmélites*.

something pathetic in Kaliayev's effort to salvage some one of his reasons for dying. One thinks one hears the hoarse voice of Anouilh's Antigone when the mystery of the corpse exposed before the gates of Thebes was revealed and she murmured with a desperate softness: "Me, I believed." This could be for Yanek the worst of temptations, that of solitude, the collapse of a whole universe.

In reality, the Just's faith is too deeply rooted for it to happen thus. They are more fearful of the face of their crimes than of the breakdown of logic. Unmoved by either the offer of a deal or the threats of the grossly Machiavellian police agent Skouratov—for whom Zoubakov, the tsarist chief of police, served as a model—Yanek weakens before the Grand Duchess. As long as they tried to judge him in the name of traditional laws or popular norms, he could reply with the pride of the hero: "my person is above you and your masters. You can kill me, but you cannot judge me." But it is more difficult to bear up under the sorrowful and deranged smile of his victim. "I was wearing a white dress . . . He was sleeping . . ." Each of her words in its simplicity strikes hard at Kaliayev. While her appeal to charity finds him reticent—and us along with him—the Grand Duchess' very presence in her mourning veils attains a certain pathos. She is there, immobile, charged with memories and enshrouded in her wounded tenderness as by a heavy perfume. Vainly, he becomes curt, opposing justice to charity. He is trapped. She re-endows flesh with its weight, blood with its color, suffering with its outcry. She resuscitates the Grand Duke, his voice, his idiosyncrasies, and Kaliayev meets his victim. He is dead, and his niece and nephew, despite their meanness, have been spared out of sentimentality and principle. Why? This "why?" echoes endlessly beneath the cell's vaulted ceiling. "Certainly you, too, are unjust." Most fortunately for Kaliayev she returns to the question of charity.[16] She attempts to convince him to pray with her, for her. That attempt at conversion, in its rhetoric, permits Yanek to defend himself by retreating and separating himself from this living image of sorrow, this woman who is his sister in spite of everything. He is still left with the terrible fear of being condemned to live in the name of an implacable charity.

[16] The scene is taken from the actual incident. But Camus had a great deal of difficulty in treating the matter of charity, as the final scene of *Réquiem pour une nonne* [Requiem for a Nun] further attests.

In the end, he will have to surmount the final shame, the last temptation, and die in a state of suspicion and doubt. Skouratov has conceived of the idea of spreading the false news of the condemned man's request for a commutation.[17] This has the effect of forcing the community of the Just, all of them, to rise to Kaliayev's level. Dora is forced to wish his death so that his loyalty can be proved: "Oh, yes! let him die, but let him die quickly . . . Your love costs dearly." Harking to the hero's appeal, Voinov returns to the organization to assume on his part the challenge Kaliayev had hurled to society from the prisoner's box. The condemned man's appeal resounds miraculously in his comrades' minds. Passing beyond solitude, with a kind of glacial fervor they resolve henceforth to follow him into death.

Death alone could reconcile the terrible love that Kaliayev bore the earth and the tenderness he bestowed on Dora. Death alone could reunite them. *Les Justes* contains without doubt the most beautiful love scene, the only love scene—since, moreover, Diégo's and Victoria's dialogues are more lyrical than dramatic—that Camus ever wrote. Yanek and Dora are bound together by the passion for justice and purity that leads them to the organization. They share the same faith, and that seems to suffice them. During all of Act I, love is latent; Dora's voice becomes gentler and more caressing when she speaks of Kaliayev, but always they return to "professional" problems. Until the moment when, within Dora, the proud "straight-necked" revolutionary, the flesh rebels. She is seized by the desire to give herself up to tenderness, to abandon for an instant that rigidity that grips her whole body, the tension that grips her spirit. "One single little hour of selfishness; can you think of that?" One time, one more time, Dora desires to be loved for herself and more than anything in the world. She waits avidly for an avowal; may the severe love of humanity yield for an instant to the woman's desire? Supreme and naive coquetry? A sign of weariness? Whatever it may be, the need for action presses upon them. They will set out side by side "from the same somewhat rigid love, for justice and prisons." They will only rejoin one another in a rendezvous of sorrow, united by the same cord. Dora, henceforth cut off from her own flesh, will soon mount the scaffold: "Am I a woman, now?"

[17] Maria Kolougaia, in similar circumstances, was accused of betraying her cause.

The final perspective, which almost gave the play a more sinister title—*La Corde* [The Rope][18]—is enough of an indication, despite a similar ascending movement, of how far removed we are from Corneille. The Just do not have—far from it—the optimistic radiance of the Corneillian hero. The grandeur of soul, the nobility of character, the tension of will and the fondness for the difficult are the same, but the atmosphere in which they are expressed is radically different. This is discernible from the beginning. The room into which we step is cold and bare. Fear is in the air. Each ring of the doorbell is greeted with a tightening of the heart. The rhythm of the action follows less the stages of martyrdom than it does the interminable periods of waiting: three acts of waiting. The atmosphere belongs to the world of clandestine operations. Prisons are everywhere, outside as well as inside. "It was with a joyous heart that I chose this, and it is with a sad heart that I stay with it. There is the difference. We are prisoners."

The air which the Just breathe is imbued with the oppressive lightness of alpine altitudes. Despite their ardor, they are surrounded by cold. All the last act, which takes place in the full flowering of springtime, is punctuated by Dora's "How cold I am." The Just live an eternal winter. "For three years I've been afraid," Dora says. Fear of the present or of the future, fear of weakening or of betraying, fear of being entrapped by that injustice which "clings to us like glue." This fear is enough, for brief instants, to corrupt friendship itself. "What a frightful taste brotherhood sometimes has." Dora's eyes are sad, Kaliayev becomes afflicted with that stabbing sadness of nightmares. Each of them seems to bear on his forehead the sacred oils of death. And this makes them at moments as alien to us as Lazarus resurrected. By dent of bending all their energies to the service of a single passion, the Just have separated themselves from the living world. They have something abstract about them, with their fixed, dry eyes, their heads held straight like a flagstaff. They no longer live according to the world's rhythm, but hurried, too hurried to really know themselves. Thus, silences insert themselves between their speeches as if to prolong them. They have unlearned how to talk and their deepest thoughts, never reached, are revealed to us in flashes. One could say that they are simultaneously exhausted and tireless,

[18] It was almost called *Les Innocents,* also; a title that Jean Grenier advised against.

carried along on nerves. The world for them is only a desert, covered by a "fearful silence" as by a great cope. What do they know of the world? They have reconstructed it in their own fashion. Their only knowledge of people is an *image d'Epinal*,[19] colored by their own nostalgia, and the dialogue between Foka and Kaliayev bitterly emphasizes the misery and loneliness of these beings for whom the present and the future are only abstractions.

Their naive faith masks, then, a profound inner anguish. Each of the Just "bears his life at arm's length." The day after the first assassination attempt, Voinov, overcome with fear, is incapable of regaining his nervous equilibrium; life fails to return. In the face of Voinov's faltering, Kaliayev experiences a morbid feeling of responsibility: "I have hurt him, hurt him very much." Annenkov, walled off behind his role as leader, suffers from the comfort his position requires him to have. All, or nearly all, of them are hypersensitive, scrupulous people gnawed at by their concern for purity: "justice itself is full of despair." And it is these insurmountable contradictions, this absurdity with which they are unable to nourish themselves, that bears them to final martyrdom with a sort of bitter joy or, if one prefers, exalted bitterness.

All this turns the Just into solitary beings, living corpses. Cut off from the people to whom they are unknown, cut off from them even at the moment when the bomb burst brilliantly spotlights them, they are proscribed in this rarefied atmosphere from sharing any feeling of tenderness. Between Dora and Kaliayev, murder has opened an abyss. They look at each other, come near to one another, their arms pasted to their own bodies, without touching one another. Once, however, Dora holds out her hand, then changes her mind, as if gestures of welcome were not for them. They take their places in a kind of majestic immobility among the heroes of tragedy. Even in their knightly order, in the fraternity of combat, they remain alone. What Stépan has suffered, Kaliayev has not yet experienced. And when Kaliayev walks toward the waiting rope, no one can do anything for him. None of these beings belong to one another; they are dedicated to death, the death they inflict and the death they receive. Though they are barely adolescents, their summertime is behind

[19] Epinal is a town southeast of Paris, known primarily for the manufacture of brightly colored, often sentimental prints of scenes of country life, regional costumes, military figures, etc. [trans. note].

them, swept away by premature old age. And the dawning spring is incapable of bringing warmth to bodies which are nonetheless consumed by the pure and arid flame of the absolute.

Les Justes therefore resumes the great tradition of the heroic theatre, but time has obscured the meaning of its heroism and poisoned its sources. The anguish of the Corneillian heroes was only relative and short-lived. Deep within them, they hold to a clear conscience, not to mention the certainty of success. The contradiction in the midst of which the Just struggle can only be resolved on the scaffold. Perhaps, as Dora suspects, this means they are not on the right path. These remorseless beings are not liberated from doubt.

If the play teaches us something about Camus, it would be his nostalgia, his solitude, and his weariness. *L'État de siège* has already told of his temptation to escape from the new forms of modern society and to reject their constraints. Doubtless, upon reflection, Camus always professes himself to be firmly involved in our epoch (he did so many times), but his solidarity is instinctive. He could not help but cry out his weariness, if not his scorn. *Les Justes* embodies another dream, the dream of a time when combat was not impossible for the pure, for revolutionaries who refuse intentional cynicism. But what would the Just do today when rebels repent and confess their treason? What bright tomorrows could they still hope for?

"Russia will be beautiful . . ." However, the work is in no way depressing. A play for the young, said the actress-critic Béatrix Dussane, in which one senses the author's nostalgic admiration for his two heroes. A play of revolt, against the suffering of poverty, against resigned acceptance, but also against excess; man comes to grips with the eternal necessities of history, with violence and revolution, and with that dream of purity or happiness that dwells within him. All of this, set forth in a classical progression, in a chaste style as heavy with ellipses and silences as with words, in which the dialogues, it seems, have no other object than to give greater force to the silences.

10

On the Proper Use of Maladies

"One must first accept
a lot of things if one wants
to try to change a few
of them."—J.-P. SARTRE[1]

It is rather bizarre that *L'Homme révolté* [The Rebel],
which, all things considered, is the statement of one of Albert Camus's
clearest historical positions, should have earned him the accusation of
social disengagement. Some expressed their pleasure that a pen so devoted
to order in writing seemed to consent to order in the land. Others,
scandalized, denounced in the very fondness for style the symptoms of an
objective betrayal. These various reactions merit an analysis of the disor-
dered minds to which they attest. Let us be content with seeing in them a
further manifestation of the Cold War and conclude from them that a
book cannot give rise to such professions of faith if it does not in itself
constitute a kind of political act in the broadest sense of the word.

The solicitations of which it was the object would be proof enough
of this, just as the sarcasms that were heaped upon it. After all, for years
Camus had not ceased to aggravate both politicians and newspaper
columnists inclined to hold the public domain as a private preserve. One
is further astonished that certain pundits, after having long embraced
Camus as a colleague, with the competence which this word presupposes,
should henceforth, with an indulgent smile, relegate him to the category
of infantile dreamers, who at that time were conventionally called "left-
wing intellectuals." But the latter, equally dissatisfied, rejected him on the
charge of "bourgeois deviationism."[2]

[1] "Réponse á Albert Camus," *Les Temps Modernes*. The whole question lies
evidently in knowing what should be accepted. And the question is not even near
to being decided.

[2] It would be interesting for a sociologist to follow the subsequent evolution
of certain of these "attorneys for the prosecution."

What I am saying about this question goes far beyond the case of *L'Homme révolté* and concerns the relationships between the intellectual and the public administration. There was a time when the protests of a Voltaire against royal arbitrariness were credited with having somewhat re-oriented the course of history, in which Montesquieu's *L'Esprit des lois,* Rousseau's *Contrat social,* and Voltaire's *Traité sur la tolérance* figured among the presumed ancestors of the French Revolution. Have, then, the times of arbitrariness passed away and false idols been forever overturned? It is true that today, and thanks to the efforts of intellectuals such as Marx, Engels, or Lenin, we can expect more from sociological or economic studies with reference to the direction of public affairs; and, all things considered, ten good monographs are worth the best of ideological works. Doubtlessly on the day when politics shall have become a matter of pure technology, we will be permitted to smile indulgently at artists who go astray and become entangled in it. But who then will not be astray in it? Until such time it is well that the laborers of thought oppose more general and more human points of view to the immediate and technical preoccupations of politicians, and that they preserve, finally, those capital reserves of hope that others are condemned to fritter away at high interest.

It is in this spirit that one must approach *L'Homme révolté.* With what is it in fact concerned? Certainly not with balanced budgets or the choice between inflation and deflation, between heavy and light industry, the essential problems of the economy whether it be capitalistic or revolutionary, but with revolution itself, with its necessity, its limits and its laws. It is concerned, in short, with taking cognizance of the confusion of a world in which each man proclaims himself a revolutionary without attaching the same meaning to the same word; an effort to impart to action some principles in a time in which opportunism and cynicism triumph simultaneously, indistinguishably intermingled with lamentations, permanent indignation, and moral pretensions alike. "Now is the moment to transfigure our experience and not to be satisfied with it. It is to this that I wish, not without some inner struggles, to contribute . . ."

This exercise in demystification merits examination only in the light of being the effort of a man "who never used failure as a pretext for condemning the undertaking."[3] In matters of revolution, neither the

[3] Preface to *Moscou au temps de Lénine* (Paris, 1953). The citation is applied to the book's author, Alfred Rosmer.

renegades nor the conservatives are valid witnesses. "If *L'Homme révolté* judges anyone, it is first of all its author."[4] In one sense, the book is a kind of self-critique without any pretense of being definitive or exhaustive. Camus felt he had lived, in his time and within his place in society, the temptation to revolt that has shaken the European world for almost two centuries now and whose effects are being extended today all across South America, Asia, and Africa: "I have lived nihilism, contradiction, violence, and the vertigo of destruction. But at the same time I have hailed the power to create and the honor of living." It is not necessary to restate the story of that personal temptation toward nihilism and violence whose mark Camus's works prior to 1945 bear more or less. For a long time yet, Camus was to waver between God and history; and, in moments when he most passionately affirmed his rejection of violence, he was not certain that he had not retained some nostalgia for it.

In a text published through my efforts, Camus traced as far back as 1940 the perturbation from which *L'Homme révolté* was born: "I did not understand how it was that men could torture others of their own kind without ceasing to look straight at them."[5] One had to struggle against these men, these Caligulas. "But at the same time that I recognized the necessity of this struggle, I become aware that . . . we were almost completely lacking in justifications drawn from a tested moral code . . . For me, I had at my disposal no more than a sense of revolt that was sure of itself but which was still unaware of its reasons for being." The failure of bourgeois morality, exploited for commercial ends ("the Merchant Europe"), and of communist morality, cynically reduced by Stalin and his admirers to the values of efficiency and power, become flagrantly apparent first with Munich and then with the German-Soviet pact—"strange epoch in which the great Jacobin principles tyrannize the colonies, in which Christ would be showed at the teller's cage of a bank, and in which oil from socialist refineries brought over our cities the planes of their no doubt temporary but equally very efficient allies . . . we knew clearly wherein lay the lie without being able to say wherein lay the truth."

L'Homme révolté was born of ten years and more of experience: Spain, the *Anschluss,* Munich, the war, the Resistance, the postwar purge, the Nazi camps, the Soviet camps, and the dubious enlightenment

[4] Letter to the review, *Libération* (May, 1952), in response to Gaston Laval.
[5] "Défense de *L'Homme révolté,*" *Essais,* pp. 1702–16.

they threw upon the Moscow trials of 1936 and on those which the communist regimes of the East were to know,[6] the cold war with its procession of barely restrained acts of violence, its underhand struggles, the nuclear threat. "Can one, without recourse to absolute principles, escape from a logic of destruction, and rediscover a promise of fecundity and pride on the level of humiliation? Ten years after the discovery of which I spoke, I felt I had the right to answer *yes* on condition that it be shown that this *yes* was never to be divorced from the original refusal, and that it supposed an incessant struggle against the mystifications that our own weakness and the dogmatism of others proffered us."

Once again, Camus experienced the need to take stock and to endow his thought as well as his actions with a coherence that life and events had compromised. There is no good political program that does not rest on moral health. But moral health, like physical health, is only the search for a precarious equilibrium. With *L'Homme révolté,* Camus undertook a work aimed at restoration of good health. He reassures his previous views and furnishes the theoretical justification for his public positions which they lacked. But Camus's utterances appear ambiguous. On the one hand they resume the reflection at the point where he had left off in *Le Mythe de Sisyphe,* and strive to introduce value into a world that seemed dedicated to surface experiences. In brief, he intends to arrive at the attitude of the logical agnostic confronted with the world's absurdity. On the other hand, the rejection of murder appeared to him intuitively necessary at the present juncture. Therefore, he tried to find this instinctive attitude in right and reason and to draw consequences from it suited to the level of thought and action. He tries to reconsider old objects of admiration, to settle for once and all certain equivocal sympathies, and to proceed finally to a sort of reorganization of values. A difficult effort of coordination which could avoid neither reservations nor internal strug-

---

[6] "The day when the liberation of the worker is accompanied by hideous trials, when a woman presents her children before the bar to heap abuse upon their father [allusion to the Slansky trial in Czechoslovakia in which the wife of one of the accused, André Simone, and her son came to call for the condemnation of their husband and father (R. Q.)] and ask for a terrible punishment for him, on that day the cupidity and cowardice of bourgeois society might well pale, and the society of exploitation is no longer sustained by its vanished virtues but by the spectacular vices of revolutionary society" ("Défense de *L'Homme révolté*").

gles, but which Camus pursued with the implacable and restrained rigor that, with him, was undoubtedly always the surest mark of the rebellious spirit.

An epigraph suffices to put us back into a framework of unchanged thought. In opposition to heaven, the author chooses "one more time" the grave and suffering earth with its inevitable occurrences, its enigmas, and, in the end, death. This sort of invocation to Cybele once accomplished, he again confronts the problem of life. How to conduct oneself in a world deprived of meaning?

The absurd equation which confronts human needs and the realities of the world could be resolved in different ways: suicide, which eliminates man; mystical submission, which stifles his desires or transposes them on to another plane; the postulation of a rational world, another solution based on faith, camouflaged beneath the mask of intellectuality. Camus was somewhat subject to all these temptations. It was the aim of *Le Mythe de Sisyphe* to denounce all these forms of accommodation to the Absurd which range from everything to nothing. The refusal to abolish the Absurd, to checkmate it or to tame it through an essentially individual effort, left us faced with a cleared field. Everything was not permitted, but indifference remained the rule. But to experience, a mode of conduct founded on universal equivalence had to appear precarious: to live is to choose. Quite naturally, Camus abandons nihilism, which he had already sacrificed by renouncing suicide. "Beyond suicide, man's reaction is instinctive revolt."[7]

To consent to live was, then, to accept intellectually the world for what it is and to reject it through action. In this sense, every form of life is more or less a form of revolt and every man more or less a rebel. Scarcely has one become conscious when one immediately protests. It could also be said that every act of revolt (as instinctive as the protest may appear to be) is a coming to consciousness; it is not a matter of sequential acts but of concomitant ones, as *L'Étranger* and *Les Justes* were to prove. It was the simultaneity, constantly observed and preserved, of these two phenomena, revolt and coming to a consciousness of human

[7] Discussion at "La Maison des Lettres" (June 13, 1945).

limits, which constituted in Camus's essays the nature of man. He did not deny, properly speaking, that man alone "makes himself," to use Sartrian terms. He does impose natural limits on man's self-creation. Human nature is not for him an immutable reality, an essence, but the permanence of a contradiction. Man is not this or that, a being consecrated to a given psychological behavior, bound to a given economic and social structure, but a perpetual effort in the direction of a total freedom which is denied him in advance, which in no way means that a relative freedom may not be immediately accessible to him. In short, Camus identifies the existence of a force of resistance, a weightiness of things and men which, variable as it may be, is still not indefinitely reducible. And if philosophers must be satisfied, we could say that essence and existence march side by side.

In truth, the movement of revolt is rather negative at the outset. When, at the end of a period of submissiveness, ignorance, or blindness, man awakens suddenly (a coming to consciousness that the apostle arouses in the slave and Marx in the proletariat), his abrupt start marks the extreme limit of his concessions and his malleability. (Still another way of approaching human nature is to discover it in acts of refusal.) Each of his acts of refusal supposes the secret hope that unbearable oppression "can cease," and soon the certainty that it "must cease." To go from refusal to the will to change the order of things or to reverse roles, there is but a single step, and it is quickly taken.

It is here that Sartre reveals his interest in the concrete totality of revolt, in the hatred it arouses as well as the love. Camus, on the other hand, ignores resentment in order to fix upon pure—Kantian, one might say—protest alone and on the ideal that it engenders. From the individual revolt of a given slave against a given master, he sifts out an obscure protest in favor of all men or, if one prefers, the affirmation of a henceforth irreducible human reality. Revolt eludes the individual realm in order to sketch in the contours of a community. It is not Man, the general idea, that revolt brings to light (on the contrary, it energetically fights against excesses committed in his name), but the solidarity of men of flesh and blood, the solidarity of victims just as much as that of executioners: "I rebel, therefore we are."

It goes without saying that this revolt is developed on a double plane: metaphysical insurrection, with which we are all associated at one time or another, against an ill-defined destiny, and of which the art of medicine could very well be considered one of the spontaneous manifestations; and political insurrection, which pushes men into conflict with one another, the victim against the executioners, and which finds its consecration in so many revolutionary movements. But the two planes are not so easily distinguished from one another. It very much seems that the weight of men, of their interests, their prejudices, have many times retarded the progress of medicine (Rieux and Tarrou are the first to recognize this fact). Many examples of misery which can be explained by stupidity or human selfishness are imputed to destiny. Inversely, failures amply justified by the resistance of natural phenomena, the most ordinary deaths, and bad harvests become suspect. Lacking any "evil eye," we suspect the ill will of some or the sabotage of others. This confusion, long exploited by conservatives of all times, solidly associated with destiny, is equally exploited—but in an inverse way—by modern revolutionaries, willingly inclined to believe that the resistance of phenomena is only a mystification to which their techniques will inevitably bring an end. To the conservatives, Camus replies that revolt is, in whatever form, legitimate; to the others, that modesty is the necessary condition of its efficacy, if efficacy there is at all.

The economic evolution of the modern world, and in particular the development of industry in the European countries, has made of revolt no longer only a human reality, but "our historical reality." The ancient democracies, founded on slavery and political segregation, yielded to feudal systems which, through the complementary processes of armed competition and monopoly, bloomed into absolute monarchies. The ultimate forms of theocracy, divine-right monarchies, yielded little by little under the attacks of the industrial and mercantile bourgeoisie, which, in order to arrive at its ends, exalted the popular desire for freedom and equality. But the theory of freedom, as it is spelled out in our constitutions and our holiday orations, and the practice of freedom are without a common yardstick. Revolt against this bourgeois mystification, which Camus bitterly denounces, is therefore no longer bound to natural phenomena (famines) or episodic ones (wars and oppressive demands of all kinds); today it has become permanent.

Now, revolt cannot remain indefinitely defensive. There comes a time when people grow tired of tracing the limits of oppression in blood and when, ceding to the invincible need for eternity and stability, they begin to dream of a world purged of all tyranny and responding at last to those values of justice and freedom which revolt exalted. Then difficulties arise.

How can we transform into reality freedom negatively defined through the forms of oppression that deny it—this justice that we know only from the injustices that flout it? How can a need, no less confused for its being a fundamental one, be inserted into the stream of day-to-day history? To be sure, "the most elementary kind of rebellion paradoxically expresses aspiration toward an order." But that new order, in its turn, denies revolt, domesticates or channelizes it. Similarly, the act of creation, the manifestation of pure freedom, is barely any longer discernible in creation, which has become fixed in an immutable collection of phenomena, forever closed in upon themselves. No more than the artist can accept being closed up entirely within his latest work can revolt recognize itself completely in the order that it has created. This is to say that revolt is permanent, that the rebel's vigilance, even if it should be so with regard to his own creations, must not contradict itself. This is to say also that, in return, he must renounce eternity as well as perfection in his undertakings. Such are the limits of our condition which condemns us to create freely an order which more or less denies our freedom and which our freedom will inevitably put back into question.

If it happens that the rebel lacks modesty and lays claim to absolute freedom, absolute order lies in wait for him. Paradoxically, the doctrinaires of perpetual refusal reach the point of demanding of others the most complete submissiveness. Having set out to remake life, they wind up exalting murder. Whether it be Sade, claiming the most total sexual freedom and striving to make of sexuality the explosive that will disintegrate all human order, or Romanticism—or its substitute, dandyism—intoning out of spite Satan's litanies; whether it be Stirner or Nietzsche, literature as well as history, from the end of the eighteenth century on, has opened itself up to the pride and boundlessness of the all-or-nothing attitude from which nihilism has formulated its theory. The nostalgia for the absolute ends, through a logical process, in the enslavement of the majority in the name of the most complete of individual or collective freedoms. Camus poses in unequivocal terms the problem of pious murder, murder out of idealism. "It is a question of knowing whether innocence, from the moment it comes into play, can avoid killing."

Lenin in his time studied the childhood sickness of Communism. Camus applies himself to what he considers a now chronic morbid state. For it is indeed Communism with which the book deals in the final analysis, and everyone realized it. In order to formulate a diagnosis and to recommend a course of therapy, he tries to discover the sick man's antecedents, to study his heredity. Under these circumstances, he undertook to record the various forms revolt has taken from 1789 up to our time and to emphasize their continuity. Then, noting that the same upward surge of freedom plunged regularly into terror or negativism, he formulates an explanation of that repeated failure which recalls, in its own way, Sisyphus and his rock. The most baffling aspect of this enterprise is that it does not fall into any of the major currents that have set up stalls, if one may speak thus, in the ideological marketplace. Camus once again re-enters the ideological game only in order to condemn its excesses.[8] But it seems that this iconoclast takes out after idol-smashing sects, that the conformism against which he rebels has not entirely ceased being anti-conformist, that the tyrannies that he cleaves asunder sustain throughout the world, and principally in those places where they have not come to power, the cause of freedom. His position is analogous, all things being equal, to that of Rousseau ransacking the encyclopedists' chapels: the Genevan priests' engaging smiles and Voltaire's progressist sarcasms earned him for a time a reputation as a retrograde spirit which history has since justified on more than one point.

Camus vainly pointed out that this was all in the family, that the spirit of revolt was not being called into question, but its outrages were. There was no little naiveté, in a time when deviationist doctrines were chronic and intentions were measured in partisan terms, in supposing that an entire past could serve as a guarantee of purity. Camus did not think it necessary to resume in detail Marx's pertinent analyses of capitalist society, considering it enough to agree with them. He had repeatedly said of the bourgeois order that "its crime was not so much in having held

---

[8] "I believe that it makes no difference to me if I am contradictory. I have no desire to be a philosophical genius. I have no desire to be a genius at all, having already enough difficulty being a man" (*Carnets,* 1946).

power as in having exploited it to the ends of a mediocre society lacking in true nobility . . . which derives its pleasures from the work of millions of dead souls." The vocabulary was suspect. Only a mass execution of the minions of order would have put the reader completely and finally at ease.

In truth, Camus's method, which consisted in treating the history of concepts of revolt rather than of historical revolts, lends itself to dispute. He was vehemently reproached for it, as though he were implying that ideas run the world. Doubtless, Camus had a tendency to consider ideas as acts. However, in strict Marxist orthodoxy, it is not absurd to maintain that the study of ideological superstructures considered in their evolution reflects rather precisely the contradictions of the epoch. One might object now that each of these attempts was developed in a given social and economic milieu, in an original context; Camus willingly admits as much —perhaps his error was in believing that this went without saying. Camus admits that the revolutionary movement, incessantly renewed during the past one hundred and fifty years, is explained by the development and the febrile activities of capitalism, that the excesses and the desire for revenge of this same capitalism provides us with the key to more than one deviation from revolt. So firmly does he admit it that he retains almost integrally the severest critiques that have been made of it.[9] But the problem does not lie here; its most precise formulation might be: is there a vice of form or constitution which inevitably drives philosophical, political, or literary revolutions which have for their object the total liberation of man from philosophical, political, or literary terrorism?

The philosophical terrorism of a Nietzsche constitutes a key example of this slippage from absolute revolt to absolute submission. Finding "God dead" in men's minds, ascertaining that the world, as though knocked off its axis, "is marching off helter-skelter," he proclaims full freedom. A more difficult freedom, however, than one often thinks (and Camus brilliantly demonstrates that he is capable, whatever one may say,

[9] "If one gathered together the significant passages from *L'Homme révolté* on this subject, instead of falsifying them, their meaning would leave no room for doubt. The class against which all the great artists have labored for the past century, the one which has bequeathed us vaudeville and the *métro* style of architecture, has today revealed virtues which attain the level of these fine inventions and which make them unworthy, in our country, of their leadership role" ("Défense de *L'Homme révolté*").

of grasping texts and taking hold of them in their nuances): it requires an exhausting struggle, it forces whoever has placed himself above traditional laws to create new responsibilities for himself: "revolt flows directly into asceticism." But, through a curious evolution, Nietzschean heroism fortifies itself with an unreserved submission to natural forces: "total adhesion to a total necessity, such is the paradoxical definition of freedom." Let each man be what he is, let him consent, and he will participate at once in the universal omnipotence. The Christian God once dead, the Sacred reappears beneath the most implacable traits of a natural fatality. In proving himself inexorably egotistical and tough, the superman will be paying his tribute of homage to nature rendered divine in its might and its will for power. At least Nietzsche demanded of the superman that he have a soul far above the ordinary; a bastard descendancy was to retain from him only the spirit of domination. It is nonetheless true that his logic ended in a world of overlords and slaves as well as in the glorification of murder. Accepting everything inherent in the universe, he consented to the lie as well as to truth, and "to the most fearful means" provided "the ends were great"—and each one sees greatness wherever it pleases him.

The Nietzschean adventure in its principle remained essentially individual or exclusive. Surrealism, however, attempted to reconcile the subjective requirements of language and of dreams with the objective preoccupations of justice; that is to say, freedom for all. It first sought some constructive rule in madness and subversion. Insult and blasphemy, already dear to Baudelaire, became the puerile manifestations of a sincere revolt. The deliberate choice of the irrational, the plunge into the dream world, the frenetic attacks on literary pundits and their honors, the more or less forced flirtations with the communist revolution are all evidence of the desire to "remake life." But, curiously enough, "this gospel of disorder found itself in the position of having to create a new order." These fervid apostles of the Absurd, these systematically impatient men, contemptuous of every form of morality, chose a leader, regulations, a code. Interdicts multiplied, succeeded one another as though handed down from some ecclesiastical tribunal. Contradiction? Camus thought not. Pride and intransigence "suppose a moral code" that is rigorous. Their purity, in one sense, led them to violence (at least verbally) against a morality of compromise and corruption, against a language atrophied through daily familiarity. And this new, rebellious morality soon became accuser, then judge. It was lacking in temperance and in love of something real, whether it be the Earth or men. Surrealistic revolt was aimed less at chaos and the Absurd than at the carnal necessity of existing; it involved, to a certain extent, a kind of angelism. And finally, for Camus, surrealism remains an authentic spiritual adventure, too long gone astray in political paths, a sort of stormy and northern mysticism which was never to know ecstasy.

In any case, it declared itself (following Nietzsche) as a rival of the Creator, at one moment elevating desire to the level of the divine, at another striving to bring to light new rules of language and living which owed nothing to existing ones. Violence grew out of magnification of these efforts, and order was reinforced to the point of dictatorship. New pontiffs officiated over the ruins of temples and the debris of idols. Doctrines of discomfort momentarily chose, in spite of themselves, "the comfort of tyranny and servitude."

It can be seen at what point literature, philosophy, and politics join together: philosophy is always more preoccupied with the transformation of men and the world (psychoanalysis, sociology, philosophy of work). Literature avoids social preoccupations only at the risk of artificiality, and, most often, accords them an important place. Doubtless, it is not by chance that the last one hundred and fifty years have breathed the same sense of revolt into all of them. History in effect more or less emphasizes the Absurd. On the one hand, it develops human demands to the maximum (the technical progress which produced the scientific illusion still marks certain aspects of Marxism and inspires naive American optimism as well); on another, it deepens the opaqueness and the resistance of phenomena, it increases injustices and facilitates oppression (bourgeois capitalism furnishes the best known example). These two effects are sometimes concurrent; scientism and capitalism have had no trouble coexisting. History, therefore, can excite or calm revolt, modify the scope of its application or its conditions. It cannot distort its basic characteristics, which literature and philosophy reveal to us under the same auspices as politics.

In fact, literature and philosophy hardly any longer offer us ideas —in the Platonic meaning of the term. Here too, ideas are only signs of an active attitude,[10] the motifs and, still more, the motives by which every human force that stirs needs to justify itself. The dialectic of a Nietzsche or a Stirner interests us only for its anecdotal value. But the will for power of the one and the nihilism of the other touch us through any number of acts that they have aroused or foreshadowed. What shall we say of Marx's writings? Are they not acts rather than a collection of words and ideas, almost in the same way as the speeches and reports of a Saint-Just: long-range acts or, if one prefers, delayed actions? For this reason, it matters little whether Camus read or did not read Marx's complete works (have the majority of Marxist leaders read them?). On the contrary, it is essential that he knew what citations from Marx his faithful use most regularly to justify their actions.

Some will say that it is useless to compare one and another attitude, that Revolt does not exist, that there are revolts: that of 1789, that of the Commune in 1871, or that of 1917. They have to have something in common, however, since revolutionaries place them all in the same Pantheon and meditate over one or another of them in order better to assure the success of the next one. If it is permissible to study their strategy, to dwell over the economic or tactical reasons for their failure, why would it not also be permissible to seek their causes—not the metaphysical causes, as some would have us believe, nor even their ideological ones, but the physical causes, in the sense of an essential physics of human action? This line of approach, this explanatory hypothesis, is as valid as any other. For Camus, it dominates all others more or less directly; it seemed to him preferable for a revolutionary to know man, his needs and his limits, rather than economics or revolutionary strategy. Assuredly, everything should be known. This being impossible, it is certainly necessary that a few moralists counterbalance the mass of strategists and economists.

Now, if revolt found its source in individual experience, with its sufferings and its resentment, in order to arrive at a general and equally obscure protestation which does not yet involve either system or reason, but the community of the living, then revolution (every revolution was

[10] "If every action is truly symbolic, then books are, in their own way, actions . . .": Merleau-Ponty, *Les Aventures de la dialectique* (Paris: Gallimard, 1955).

first of all revolt) interprets the wishes of the rebels, abstracts and organizes them. It intends from this point on to fashion the world in the image of a certain conception it has formed of it; in this sense, it dehumanizes it. Attentive to the complaint of the concrete man, to his thirst for unity and eternity, it judges him on the basis of what he would like to be and neglects what he is. Having thus modeled him according to his nostalgic longings, it postulates that institutions by their own weight or history by its very direction favors this re-creation: "Revolution even, and especially that which claims to be materialistic, is only a boundless metaphysical crusade." And the principle of the history of the ideas of revolt for this reason is, *a posteriori,* justified.

Such angelism, such confusion between the political and the sacred, inevitably falsifies the perspectives of revolt. The entire drama of revolution resides in these relationships. Formerly a political philosophy took cover beneath the mantle of the local gods, as currencies derive value and protection from a more or less fictitious gold supply. With absolute monarchy, even Christianity came to play the role of guarantor. But if the Church seriously compromised itself thereby, at least the sacred and the profane were not inseparably joined. The powerful, who did not take care to live and act according to the laws of Heaven, had difficulty in imposing their political acts as divine decrees. In this sense, religion guaranteed their divine derivation and cheaply satisfied our need for totality (as long, at least, as it abstained from assuring the salvation, by iron and by fire, of heretics and unbelievers).

With the French Revolution, a new faith arose opposite the old one. (It is to Camus's credit that he freed this historical period from the superstitious respect of which it is the object and placed its defenders—of whom he is one, in the main—face to face with their responsibilities.) The Carmelites' chaplain in Bernanos' *Dialogue des Carmélites* rightly replies to the Chevalier de la Force: "It is you they fear but us they hate . . . every civil war turns into a war of religion." We now have a new type of religious war which takes its inspiration from *Le Contrat social* and from Montagnard intransigence. A political system that directs its efforts precisely toward the liberation of men substitutes the decrees of an absolute justice for grace. Popular sovereignty borrows the attributes of divinity; and, at the time of Louis XVI's trial, two transcendencies confronted one another: an unjust and corrupt political system guaranteed by established religion is battered by a politics of austerity and virtue that would willingly make of freedom the object of a new sect. Louis XVI's head carried away with it temporal Christianity and inaugurated the anointing of the new administration—or of its image. Saint-Just was to be the Joad of that political faith. His hatred of Christian formalism and of the mystifications which it maintained led him to erect a no less formal morality, in which the immutable principles, permanently fixed in the law, would no longer have to be lived but submitted to: "the French Revolution, in claiming to construct history on a principle of absolute purity, opened the modern period and, at the same time, the era of formal —and purely objective—morality."

If the law embodies absolute good, it must be obeyed at no matter what price, and revolt is dead from that time on. If the plans for the future state correspond to the canons of perfection, it must be realized, if necessary, by way of the most implacable terror. From the living thing that it was, freedom is transformed into an idol worshipped from a distance. In its name an empire is organized; in its name, decisions are made and imposed by all means including the scaffold. The logic of absolute good becomes synonymous with the logic of evil. And just as Sartre pointed out strange similarities between the language of Theresa of Avila and Jean Genêt, it is permissible for Camus to stress the common fury of a Torquemada, a Saint-Just, or of some other modern tyrant. At least, Saint-Just paid without protesting, dying "from an impossible love that is the opposite of love"; the latter being concrete and carnal, a love of men more than of humanity, of life more than of the idea of life, of humming beehives rather than of great cemeteries beneath the moon.

Saint-Just had calculated without the Absurd. He postulated an impossible conformity between institutions and men, between principles and life, and—faced with the resistance of the latter two—he turned to purifying murder. The communist revolution, noting his failure and the "discouraging hypocrisy" of a bourgeoisie which made use of Jacobin values only "as an alibi, practicing on every occasion the opposite values," turned away from institutions in order to devote its attention to structures. It points the way to the edification of the new city of man. The rapidity with which worlds come apart, concomitant with the evolution of technology and the tenor of life, gives birth to the idea of a history that carries man along in its forward movement which, at the end of a logical

process of purification, must bring him to the state of total freedom. If
the present betrays us, the future is ours. "After the Jacobin revolution
which attempted to institute the religion of virtue in order to find unity
within it, there will come cynical revolutions, whether they be of the
right or of the left, which will try to conquer the unity of the world in
order finally to find the religion of man."

To be sure, Camus did not deceive himself. He does not confuse the
egotistical religion of the Aryan overlords who exalt race and sacrifice
millions of victims to it in extermination camps with that other equally
cynical, but in this case, altruistic religion, which sings the praises of labor
and claims to re-educate the asocial in the Siberian steppes. These two
revolutions are of quite different quality. Because the first is momentarily
subdued, he dwells at length on the second, with which he would have
liked, deep inside himself, to be more often in agreement. The tone is all
the more bitter from being one of disappointment: "in order to draw the
necessary lessons from the decadence of revolutions, one must suffer because of it, not rejoice in it."[11] But once again the crime is commensurate
with the ambition: the necessary struggle against capitalist oppression has
been carried on with the arms and in the name of a dangerous ideology.
Scientific in its critique, Marxism is prophetic in its construction: if from
the depths of history a miraculous future calls us, each of the revolutionary's gestures, as contradictory as they may be, mark a progress on the
way toward salvation. This is what Camus, citing Plekhanov, calls the
"active fatalism" which consecrates the triumph of the principle of
authority and the dictatorship of the accomplished fact. Moreover, the
Marxists gladly recognize that the working class interests them less
because of its grievances than because of the force for the future that it
represents. If capitalism is wrong, it is above all because it is "an outworn
order."

Such faith in history, whose "ends would be revealed as moral and
rational," justifies the most brutal of surgical operations: "one hundred
years of pain are fleeting in the view of him who affirms, for the hundred
and first year, the ultimate city of man." Some will say that if the Kulaks
had not resisted in the thirties, many deportations would have been
avoided; this fails to account for man and his habits, which are not all

---

[11] Preface to *Moscou au temps de Lénine.*

criminal. Doubtless the agricultural slowdown threatened to create a bottleneck. If so many men had to be deported,[12] it was perhaps because they had been forgotten in the evaluations of the plan and because everything was not always equally possible. "The new church is once more face-to-face with Galileo; to preserve its faith, it is going to deny the sun and humiliate the free man."

The Communist revolution here culminates in a kind of atheistic theocracy. It has the theocracy's imperialism; it condemns all neutrality: whoever is not with me is against me. Marx, Engels, and Lenin are so many prophets whose declarations nourish a vast scholasticism: establishment leaders are so many potential priests—and apostates. In this de-Christianized order, in which the Party constitutes the church militant and trials are veritable ceremonies of exorcism, sin resumes its place: "Marxism, under one of its aspects, is a doctrine of guilt with regard to man and of innocence with regard to history." And step by step, "at the end of that long insurrection in the name of human innocence, through a fundamental perversion, the affirmation of general guilt surges forth."

The search for totality has been imperceptibly substituted for the quest for unity; or rather, the revolutionaries have wrongly imagined that "the path to unity passed by way of totality," that freedom could not be obtained except through the momentary renunciation of freedom. Rather than living freedom, they have raised it up and adored it, as though all revolt were not already freedom. However, "suffering is never temporary for the one who cannot believe in the future." Many human lives and energies have been thus wasted.

Now, the faith that inspires such sacrifices and justifies similar purges "is no more founded in pure reason than earlier faiths." Its predictions have only been very relatively verified. (There would, however, be something to say on the subject of the peremptory criticism Camus makes of the Marxist law of concentration in agriculture.) The most solid of revolutionary certainties stems from the apocalyptic spirit. What matters, however, is to save the revolt which is hidden at the very heart of the Stalinist ideology (and Camus would readily agree with Sartre that the struggles of the Communist worker in capitalist regimes

[12] Camus remarked in a letter (1952) to the author: "Socialism today is devoted to constructing society at the expense of the rural element. That is why it is terroristic."

participate in revolt). The role of the thinker, in isolating a nefarious logic and in denouncing it, is to save the revolutionary spirit from an irremediable downfall. "One is not justified by just any heroism or just any hope."

An analysis of just which ones do provide justification raises several remarks. It is certain, to stick to only the essential points, that Camus's vocabulary is not always without ambiguity. To speak of perversion of revolt leads one to suppose that healthy forms of revolt exist. Camus's technique is, in effect, analogous to Rousseau's in the two *Discours:* establishing the morbid evolution of society and describing what might be called "the fall" from natural man up to the contemporary period. There is no arguing against the fact that a certain nostalgia emanates from these works. Rousseau imagined a fable which gathered together all that longing in a sort of prehistoric era. We are now past these childish games. Where, however, are we to place the moment of healthiness in this history of European pride? At the zero point of Christ's birth? Under the Girondin Convention? In the time of Camus's Just Assassins? Perhaps there has never been any healthy revolt. To tell the truth, the question smacks a little of its nihilism. To pose it is to recognize that we have not yet gone past the all-or-nothing attitude. In politics, as elsewhere, health is a relative thing, a point of equilibrium, not a state of perfection. It is with revolt as it is with peace; history has never truly known peace. This does not prevent anyone from talking about it, nor from knowing what he is talking about, nor especially from doing battle in its name.

Camus contented himself with isolating a virus. It is perhaps neither the real or the only one. At least it is (in the same way as the natural man) a working hypothesis which the texts illustrate. It is therefore not reasonable to reproach him with having fallen into the inquisitorial bad habits he denounces. Did revolution appear to him as a "deviation" of revolt? And if so? Did he ever call for liquidation of the deviationists, or strike out at them in any way? On the contrary, he intervened, in favor of Henri Martin.[13] At no time did he consider them from the exterior as pure monstrosities. There was practically no attitude which did not appear to him to be valid in some aspect and with which he was not at least par-

[13] "Défense de la liberté," *Franc-Tireur* (December, 1952). See also Grenier's remarks.

tially in agreement. His objective is less to judge or condemn than to avoid doing so by creating a "moderate demoralization" (*CN*). Was this not already his method in *Le Mythe de Sisyphe?* "To say to consciences that they are not spotless and to reasons that they are lacking in something" (*CN*). Some will express their astonishment at this appeal to consciences. But was not Marxism itself, at the beginning, a vast enterprise of debunking and demystification? Here again, to be sure, Camus, in an equivocal manner, makes use of a moralizing vocabulary. The Marxist, in his hopefulness as in sacrifice, in no way seeks to justify himself and it matters little to him whether he is personally spotless. But, precisely, one of the subjects of the debate is to know if revolution can be moral in its effects when revolutionaries are cynics. Lenin doubtless did not think so when he wrote: "The conscience of the working class cannot be a true political conscience if the workers are not accustomed to react to all abuses, all manifestations of arbitrariness, whatever may be the classes that are their victims. . . ."

Camus, who thought so even less, could not believe that cynicism was the necessary condition of efficacy. He did, however, have some doubts on the matter and wondered, along with Alfred Rosmer, if the repression of Kronstadt were not necessary. "When one sees with what struggles certain lives were filled, one can wonder what those who, like us, have not had the good fortune and the pain of living in a time of hope, could profess to do but listen and understand." It is certain that *L'Homme révolté* only skims the difficult problem of the relationships between the revolutionary mystique on the one hand and the political system and the economy on the other. Whatever the regime, the industrialization of new countries imposes heavy sacrifices, of which one is not sure, in the final analysis, whether the burden is increased or lightened by the mystique. Anyway, neither the electrification which Lenin for a time saw as the foundation of socialism nor any other form of transformation of nature by man could justify, in Camus's eyes, the systematic scorn for individual lives.

Whatever the case, he refused to despair. His work is a wager in favor of a renaissance, a base for new departures: "if there were something to preserve in our society, I would see no dishonor in being a conservative. Unfortunately, there is nothing. Our political and philosophical credos have brought us to an impasse where everything must be

resubmitted to questioning, from property rights to revolutionary ortho-
doxies."[14] The Rebel will no more tolerate the bloody mystifications of
the revolutionary order than the disguised oppression of a tired capitalism. Moreover, the fate of the world is not theirs to decide; Camus repeats
after Léon Blum:[15] "Their ends will be the same; it will be decided
between the forces of revolt and those of the Caesarian revolution."

Is what is needed, then, to escape revolutionary totalitarianism, the
re-establishment of the distinction between the profane and the sacred,
and the return to the people of that share of mysticism they are lacking?
Camus might undoubtedly have been touched on occasion by this aristocratic temptation to which Vigny ended by yielding, but the chances of
Camus's doing so were practically nil. He called more simply for "remak-
ing and recreating Greek reflection as a revolt against the sacred";[16] that
is to say, bring politics back down from the missionary heights to which it
has risen and return it to the modest rank of a vocation; a vocation like
medicine in which mechanical knowledge and good will are conjoined.

But first a few fixed rules: human nature exists, or rather its plastic-
ity is not infinite. Thus, the mirage of the total man evaporates. This
amounts to saying that dialectic, for all that it might suppose a solution to
human contradiction, is close to the existential leap. Authentic dialectic,
"pure movement which aims at denying everything that is not itself . . .
is not and cannot be revolutionary." Every synthesis is provisional; every
society decomposes in its own way to be reborn out of its own ashes. The
radio which yesterday was a luxury has become a necessity; and, as high
as one might raise the standard of living, human dissatisfaction will find
in it no fewer reasons for revolt. One can speak of progress in terms of
centuries and history; in terms of generations and men, progress is
imperceptible and prosperity is never anything but a memory.

At this point, let us posit that, in the continual upheaval of values,
there is one at least which escapes the agitation of history: freedom,
which is put to the proof daily in action and in revolt. Its legal or
material conditions are variable. Its permanence bears witness "to the
refusal of the being to be treated as an object and to be reduced to simple

---

[14] Letter to the editor-in-chief of *Arts* (October, 1951), *Actuelles*, I, p.
39.

[15] Preface to Burnham's *L'Ère des Organisateurs.*

[16] Unpublished document.

history." Camus protests, then, against the condemnation that revolutionary movements inflict upon freedom in order to punish it for the deceptive use to which bourgeois society puts it. "There is no ideal freedom that will be given us all of a sudden one day, the way one collects one's pension at the end of one's life. There are freedoms to conquer, one by one, painfully, and those we still have are insufficient steps in that direction, but steps, meanwhile, on the road to a concrete liberation."[17] It is up to the oppressed to pursue this struggle, everywhere and always. Therefore, Camus, at the time, hailed the East Berlin workers' revolt, as well as those of Poznan and Budapest (*A, II,* pp. 1771–78). Can it be said that to choose freedom is to renounce justice? Such an antinomy has no meaning except in totalitarian thought. "It is indeed true that there is no freedom possible for a man who is chained all day to a lathe and who, in the evening, is crammed with his family into a single room (*A, II,* p. 794). That man is not free and nothing is more unjust. The interrelationship of justice and freedom then is close, provided one deals with it in moderate form.[18] Absolute freedom culminates in disorder and the oppression of the weak. Total justice stifles all freedom. Both are madness.

These modest and elementary principles make of the rebel, not simply man, as Pierre de Boisdeffre would like, but a being profoundly conscious of historical solidarity and resolved to preserve it to the limits of his abilities. "We cannot turn our faces away from our hell . . . The longing for repose and peace itself must be rejected; it is one with acceptance of inequity. . . . On the contrary, may we praise the time in which misery cries out and delays the sleep of those whose bellies are full! Maistre already spoke of the terrible sermon which the revolution preached to kings. It preaches the same sermon today, and more urgently to the dishonored elite of our times. They must hear this sermon." The struggle against tyranny and injustice is only one form of combat against the Absurd, and it must be carried on in the spirit of Sisyphus. Lucidity constrains every man to involvement, not to enlistment. There is no power, even if it were proletarian in origin, which, through a natural

---

[17] "Le Pain et la liberté," a speech given in Saint-Etienne, on May 10, 1953 (*A, II,* pp. 792–99).

[18] "That justice may be the collective form of freedom . . . shows well enough, it seems to me, the dupery there can be in separating these two notions as many wrongly do." (Letter of April 5, 1952, to R. Quilliot.)

inclination, would not wind up by weighing upon those whom it intended to serve. One cannot reign innocently."[19] Camus here joins in a certain anarcho-syndicalist current for which the powers that be are a necessary evil.[20] To the predictions and prophesies which derive from nostalgia, he opposed reasonable probabilities, the relative to the absolute, the consideration of means to the reign of ends, for, as one libertarian essayist has said, "if socialism is an eternal becoming, its means are its end."

The rebel thus will try to liberate himself without killing. Disdaining ideological quarrels, he will exercise concrete action within the framework of his profession, according to the traditions of revolutionary syndicalism. Professional education and culture will furnish "the new cadres which a world without honor cried out for and still cries out for." At the same time he will take his inspiration from the practical and moderate examples of Scandinavian and British socialism. Whatever the regime, the great problem of the modern world is that of the worker's enslavement by the machine and, soon, by technology and technicians: "any philosophy that does not advance the solution of this problem barely even begins to touch working-class misery." Let our industrial society discover and organize the sense of proportion that it for certain carries within it, despite its present outrages, and man, delivered from the exclusive concern with production, will once more begin to think of creating, in keeping with his deepest vocation. But this is another matter altogether . . . Camus, who proceeds in this area only with tentative probes, does not adventure further on to the terrain of economists and sociologists.

Hold on! some will say. The clean sweep that Camus has initiated favors a new conformism: it is not for nothing that the conservative "center" has long since appropriated to itself the title of "moderate." It is true that moderation, like good sense, is often no more than the screen for already acquired privileges. However, people could write of the Jacobins that they are, "with passion and revolutionary fervor, holders of a moder-

---

[19] Saint-Just, *Idem.* See also Varlet, cited by Merleau-Ponty: "For every creature who reasons, government and revolution are incompatible."

[20] Camus remained closely associated with libertarian and anarcho-syndicalist groups, particularly those represented by two reviews, *Témoins* and *Révolution prolétarienne,* to which he contributed occasionally.

ate political viewpoint. They imposed by extreme means perfectly reasonable solutions."[21] There was a bit of the Jacobin in Camus that the terror would have disgusted. The man who in 1936 approved of Marshall Toukachevsky's execution has now joined a sense of limits to the intransigence of principles. Moderation is nothing more than a revolt against the very excesses of revolt. All his effort tends toward keeping us from falling into the lyrical illusion and in bringing us back to a realistic view of human possibilities.

Thus, it is not surprising that *L'Homme révolté* was the target of a double criticism. Some, recalling Tolstoi or Péguy, reproached him for introducing romanticism and mysticism into politics. The origin of this complaint is obvious. Camus compromises on the question of aims, resigns himself to approximations, but remains intractable with regard to the means, out of a visceral and sentimental reaction. He said and reiterated that he no longer consented to murder in a time when people are not far from believing that the hangman's noose is the first condition of efficacy. In brief, to the revolutionary romanticism of the "great twilight," he would oppose the romanticism of clean hands.

With respect to *L'Homme révolté* itself, the reproach is hardly tenable. If he tirelessly repeats that "the economy of blood should be the first imperative of a common doctrine, today,"[22] it is precisely because he radically divorces himself from the prophetic spirit and the romantic sense of mission, in which he saw one of the sources of modern nihilism. Esthetically and philosophically speaking, *L'Homme révolté* is an anti-romantic work, but written by a man tempted by romanticism because of its dreams, its conquering spirituality, its absolutism. The book is a charge against the nihilist trap of all or nothing, of which *Caligula* was the fascinating incarnation. "I have described an evil from which I did not exclude myself. Far from wanting to acquit, I wanted to understand the kind of guilt in which we find ourselves, and I did not think it possible to reduce it, but merely to accept it while placing limits upon it."[23]

He found its practical limits in the revolutionary syndicalists[24] and

[21] Gaston Martin, *Les Jacobins.*
[22] Letter to R. Quilliot.
[23] "Défense de *L'Homme révolté*."
[24] "The effort and the successes of free syndicalism, like the permanence of libertarian and communitarian movements, in Europe and in France, are reference points to which I have referred in order to show, on the contrary, the fecundity of a tension between revolt and revolution."

the English or Scandinavian Laborites. The former have never passed for choir-boys nor the latter for moonstruck dreamers. They have this in common, that they represent the two political poles of an attitude that Camus wanted to be both modest and intransigent: the pragmatism of the Laborite movement and the intransigence of revolutionary syndicalism. Between anarchy and reform, between mistrust of the constituted powers and moderate utilization of them toward reformist ends, Camus did not choose. He judged them to be historically complementary, for he does not believe in the direction of history, but in an undefined evolution in which freedom at one moment is frozen in institutions and at another exhausts itself in disorder. Thus in one place it was suitable to guide men back to the limits of the human condition, in another to shatter unfailingly oppressive institutions. It could be said today that such is the utility of a "contestation" continually on guard against abuses and capable of constraining the powers that be to take popular aspirations into account.

Thus, Camus refrained from appearing as the knight-defender of lost causes. Doubtless, if he had yielded to his natural inclinations, the conqueror of *Le Mythe de Sisyphe* would have easily consented to such an extremity. "After all, one has to do something for the vanquished." But, he protests, "one of my constant themes has, on the contrary, been the condemnation of a certain romanticism of failure and inefficacy."[25] Revolt is not revolution that fails. The two notions are both contradictory and complementary. "It is not possible to raise up absolute revolt in face of every historical reality in an attitude of superb sterility, nor to suppress in a revolutionary orthodoxy the spirit of revolt to the sole advantage of historical efficacy . . . I have simply said that revolt without revolution terminates logically in a delirium of destructions and that revolt, if it does not rebel for everybody, winds up by attaining an extremity of solitude in which everything would be permitted it. Inversely, I have tried to demonstrate that revolution deprived of the spirit of revolt's constant supervision ends with plunging itself into a nihilism of despair and resurfaces in the midst of terror."[26]

If these justifications can be accepted, one finds that the work is much more modern than it appeared. Written in 1951, it justifies in advance the student revolts against an essentially materialistic society, as

[25] "Défense de *L'Homme révolté*."
[26] "Défense de *L'Homme révolté*."

well as the Czechoslovakian effort to free itself from the iron yolk of Soviet domination. The de-Stalinization process, a moderate reaction against a tyranny, confirms what we have indeed to call Camus's optimism. Sartre, in 1952, pronounced Camus's position untenable and condemned in advance by history. This was to admit that millions of men in all countries who aspire to a politics of progress, delivered from prophecies and concentration camps, had also renounced history as well. It was to enclose us in a series of apparent dilemmas: the antinomies of God and History, Justice and Liberty, Violence and Nonviolence exist only in the absolute. Empires are not eternal. Already in 1956, the Khrushchev report provided Camus an initial satisfaction. The horrors of the Stalin era were denounced, insufficiently no doubt, but no one would henceforth be able to justify them. The military equilibrium between military powers in confrontation and the extraordinary powers of modern engines of destruction impose peaceful coexistence on the world's peoples. The two superpowers are drawing closer together in their structures and their methods through a slow dilution of what is most virulent in their principles.

L'Homme révolté aroused so much ire only because it shook so many consciences. Merleau-Ponty, in *Les Aventures de la Dialectique,* arrived at very similar conclusions: there is no end to history, every revolution is always a failure in relation to its initial ambitions, every institution atrophies. "The fact that all known revolutions have degenerated is not a matter of chance . . . revolutions are true as movements and false as regimes." Vercors abandoned a certain Machiavellianism; Louis de Villefoire admitted having complacently let himself be mystified; Edgar Morin discovered the extent to which the collectivist mystique degenerated into a permanent inquisition. Since 1951, a fecund disturbance has not ceased to overtake many minds which slumbered in revolutionary conventions or which hid their torment.

Why then, at the time, was the exact significance of the book overlooked? Let us quickly pass over various minor aspects: some critics fixed upon each particular analysis proposed in the book; the historian of revolution pronounced the study of regicides to be either incomplete or partial; the Marxist and the surrealist made similar criticisms of the treatment of state terrorism and the poetry of rebellion. Each could cer-

tainly find lacunae in the book. Camus on this occasion was a victim of
his own application. He had been sensitive to the reproaches made to *Le
Mythe de Sisyphe* of having been inspired from secondhand sources.
Therefore, he approached his reading with the zeal of a conscientious
student, which gives *L'Homme révolté* a massive and sometimes heavy
aspect. While his talent lay in clarity of expression and taut firmness of
line, the book suffers from overdeveloped commentary, as though he had
wanted to defend himself from criticism, protect his rear, and prove his
ability to gloss expertly. All the documentary apparatus with which he
clothes his ideas blurred their contours, softening the work's shock effect
and exposing its flank to criticism of details. Camus was unable to choose
between a history of revolt, the analysis of its perversions, and the sum of
his own experience.

The book is founded on "a historical experience . . . perhaps too
strange, too particular to be generalized"[27]—that of modern totalitarianism. Camus could not resist the desire to reestablish a coherence in the
history of the world whose thread he found in that recent experience.
However interesting and legitimate it may have been, the hypothesis of
such a continuity was nonetheless audacious. It did not take sufficient
account of history's complexity and its sudden changes of direction. It
isolated intellectual history from history in general with its contradictions
and its miscarriages. Embracing too much, Camus doomed himself to an
imperfect grasp of his subject, to multiplying the number of impasses, to
merely basting together a history of the philosophy of revolt which it
would have taken a whole lifetime to conceive.

Camus, lastly, could not resist his own myths: "Nothing is pure,
nothing is pure; that is the cry that has poisoned this century" (*CN*)—
the same cry that Caligula in his own time had uttered. Camus, desiring
to infuse some balance into this desire for purity, turned back toward
ancient thought. *Summum jus, summa injuria,* said the Romans, for
whom justice was the force of equilibrium which assured balance. Revolt
and moderation must be reconciled; or, more exactly, permanent revolt
must limit revolutionary ambitions and purify its methods. A bridge must
be thrown up between the modern notion of the just order and the
ancient one of the just man.

[27] Preface to *Moscou au temps de Lénine.*

It was this which he called, with a reverent longing, "Mediterranean thought." For him, the idea was not new. He had already made use of it, as we know, in 1936 when he was playing a militant role in the communist movement. But who was there to remember that in 1951? The qualifying adjective was an unfortunate choice. Some denounced its chauvinism, others its anachronistic aspects. People did not hesitate to recall Hellenic upheavals, the Roman will for power, the violence of Spain, or the then current revolt in North Africa. Some pointed out, not without justification, that moderation and respect for man seemed to have taken refuge in more northerly regions: in Great Britain, with its concept of *habeas corpus,* or in Scandinavia.

However, geography is of little importance here. Camus chose the word moderation; he could just as well have spoken of confrontation or of contradiction. And the expression "pensée de midi" is clarified for whoever knows that the sun at its zenith symbolized for Camus a vehement extremity. But a too emphatic reference to Greece inclined many readers to find wisdom in what was an uncomfortably maintained state of balance. "Every human undertaking thus meets a limit beyond which it changes into its opposite, just as disgust follows prolonged pleasure. To say then that we must hold to that limit comes down to saying in reality that we must take our stand at the extreme frontier of the struggle where anguish is not separated from lucidity."[28]

Is *L'Homme révolté* the turning point that too many contemporaries strove to discover in Camus's work? Even before *La Chute* appeared, I questioned the likelihood of such a reversal. Camus had not waited until 1951 to condemn historicism; he had already done so in *Caligula.* The first chapter of *L'Homme révolté* is, except for a few nuances, nothing more than the essay *La Remarque sur la revolte* written between 1943 and 1945. Had not Camus noted that, if the rebel says "no," he also says "yes"? As for this refusal, it already meant "there are things I cannot do," equally well as "there are things you cannot do." How was it that no one saw that the traditional idea of revolution was questioned in statements such as these: "if there were ever *one time* a revolution there would be no more history . . . Thus, rather than an emancipation, it would be truer to speak of a progressive and ever unachieved affirmation of man by man."

[28] "Remarque sur la révolte," *Essais,* pp. 1682–97.

Need more be said? "There is in every revolution a stage at which it calls forth a movement of revolt opposed to it which indicates its possibilities of failure . . . An examination of the great historical attempts at definitive revolutions such as that of Christianity, of great modern metaphysical revolutions (even when they seem to deny metaphysics), the Nietzschean revolution, should show clearly that opposition between the movement of revolt and the attainments of every revolution."

It would be easy to multiply the examples, borrowing them for the prewar as well as from the postwar period. The sense of the relative was a constant with Camus from the moment he began to think, just as the sense of the absolute formed the bedrock of his instinct. "Every revolution must take into account the limited character of human experience, give free reign to every utterance, accept approximations." But what else had certain readers of *Combat* thought they read? Here one touches on one of the difficult problems of writing. Even when the author reiterated his criticisms of existentialism, no one heard. He repeated in vain that the Absurd is only a point of departure and that revolt is the first step of a "mind seized by strangeness." Would it have sufficed, then, that Chapter I of *L'Homme révolté* be headed with an introduction which would situate the book within the scope of the author's permanent preoccupations—suicide and murder—for people to be able to conclude that he repudiated them?

The moralist was victim of the artist, creator of myths, and of the conjuncture which caused him to tend toward oversimplified positions. It was the time when each of the hostile camps called upon us to take its side, in which one was anticommunist if one refused to see in the Soviet labor camps the most well elaborated forms of reeducation. At the height of the Cold War, intellectuals were hot-headed and quick to hate.

L'Homme révolté rejected this delirium. If its author had indeed been tempted by moral comfort, this painfully elaborated book would have only plunged him anew into anguish. But could he ever have ceded to such a temptation, he who wrote at the time: "The value which keeps him going is never given to him for once and for all; he must always maintain it unceasingly."[29] A proud and painful isolation would be the price he would pay for it. One does not with impunity try to provide

[29] Letter to René Char (1954).

oneself with reasons for action and to define for oneself a line of conduct. In so doing, one runs the risk of letting oneself be caught up in the games of abstraction against which one rises up and of slipping from revolt to judgment. Camus lived this drama of a book of reconciliation which turned into an act of rupture, of an open work on dialogue which leads one back to silence.

"Eaten up by doubt," he remained no less firm in his positions: "If I had it to do I would write my work all over again just as it is."[30] Sisyphus could have said no more.

[30] Letter to René Char (1954).

11

Pilgrimage to the Wellsprings

"My soul is a three-masted ship
seeking its Ikaria."
—BAUDELAIRE

L'Été defies all classification. In it, the initial elements of an ironical guide to Algeria, meditations on existence, ethical stances, and literary self-criticism exist side by side with veritable prose poems. On the first reading, the book seems heterogeneous, put together from bits and pieces. However, despite differences of genre, tone, and periods of composition (the first essay dates from 1939, and the last from 1953), the book is not without unity.

It is valuable first of all for the historian. "Le Minotaure" belongs to the lineage of ironic works. In 1939, Camus had planned to treat the theme of the plague in this same mode, as evidenced by the essay begun at the same period, *Les Archives de la Peste* (*PL, I*, pp. 1959–65). "Les Amandiers" confirms that, in 1940, Camus was in no way a complete "absurdist," but a man already prepared for the coming struggle. "The first thing is not to despair . . . It is useless to weep over [the defeat of] the mind, we must work for it . . . In any case, let us not forget strength of character . . . it is that which, in the wintertime of the world, will prepare the fruit." *L'Été*, then, constitutes a mine of documents for whoever is interested in the genesis of Camus's work. It permits the curious reader to dissipate those legends of which "L'Enigme" speaks to us.

More profoundly, *L'Été* marks the line of resistance to history. It gives us access to that secret garden in which Camus never ceased to tend, like so many rare flowers, his concepts of love and innocence. It was there that he found courage in adversity and rested at the end of the day's weariness. *L'Été* reveals to us the permanence of an inner life, not in the

Christian sense of one in which scruples and remorse unfold, in which problems of conscience struggle (Camus also knew these from experience), but a haven for memories. There, he cultivated the innocence of the nuptial feasts of Tipasa in which morality was resumed in carnal fulfillment and in which it was not necessary to will or to choose, but simply to love. All that which is withheld from society and from history is won for silence and the natural life.

It is a Greek world, the cyclic world in which summer is being prepared for in the very heart of winter, in which flowers and buds reappear with the springtime—the world of natural history, freed from the harassing march of progress and the unfurling of conquering humanity on the paths to salvation. We are poised between noon and midnight, between meaning and meaninglessness, between yes and no. The cycle of the hours and days, despite the years that pile up and the wrinkles that mark both faces and works, leads us back to the times of *L'Envers et l'endroit.*

There, in that eternity maintained in the very midst of time's swell, Camus built for himself two worlds, one carnal, the other spiritual. Algeria, which had already been celebrated in *Noces,* inspires successively "Le Petit Guide pour les villes sans passé" and "Retour à Tipasa." "I have thus a long liaison with Algeria which, doubtless, will never end and prevents my being entirely clear-sighted with regard to it." There is indeed a certain fetishism or, if one prefers, a lyrical chauvinism in the love Camus bore his native land.

Camus defends himself against this tendency by the use of irony. He affectionately pokes fun at the youth of Oran, whose games he shared, concerning their two essential pleasures: "having their shoes shined and taking those same shoes on a walk along the boulevards." The rivalry between Algiers and Oran, concretized in the Homeric duel between the boxers Perez and Amar, provides us, in "Le Minotaure," with a picturesque scene which skirts the burlesque. We can sense the author attracted by that unleashing of brute force; attracted but nonetheless distant. A period of withdrawal, a margin of indifference, reveals to him the crowd's contradictions, the mechanical and naive aspects of the spectacle. His curiosity leads him straight through and beyond the artifices and the shadow effects, to the eternal significance of the event. But this detachment does not last. To joke about Algeria, its childish games and its blemishes, one must live there. With exile, the irony becomes weary (as in "L'Enigme") or acid and polemical. The smile fades, and quickened passion carries us to the "grave and blind hymn" of "Retour à Tipasa."

If Camus, for the first time, felt the need to explain himself in direct terms in his preface to *L'Envers et l'endroit,* it is because he doubted. Had not people raised enough questions about the exhaustion, the stagnation of his inspiration! Had they not laughed enough in scorn over his successes, as though failure were the guarantee of talent and integrity! Camus, they whispered, had bogged down in moralizing and conformity, and they envisioned, joyfully or spitefully, the columns of *Le Figaro* being opened to him.[1] They depicted him for us as sure of himself, they described his pure and, finally, comfortable state of spirit, while he himself worried and took himself to task for wanting people to legitimize "the hesitant confidence that an author has in himself and which needs ceaselessly to be reassured, for true grandeur does not go without an underlay of doubt and modesty."[2]

Is not Algeria an entire childhood, the presence of a mother as far away as she is dear, and, all things said, a kind of alma mater, in the real sense of the term, where Antaeus renews his courage and strength? Tipasa, to be sure, beset with the gangrene of morality, had become regimented and barbed-wire encircled; civilization had brought its ravages even there, and innocence saw itself threatened by thunderbolts of virtue in its last refuges. But the sun continues stubbornly to shine, the sea dances upon the beaches, and the heliotrope spatters the ruins with its colors.

As Italy and Florence had been once before, Greece is now the soul's homeland. Already in that summer of 1939, when the beautiful dream of a leisurely Hellenic tour had evaporated, inaccessible Greece had conquered a preeminent place in Camus's heart. It symbolized the conjunc-

[1] The columns of *Le Figaro* are frequented by a number of *Académiciens.* I thought I was being original in using the phrase, but I must render to Francis Jeanson what is his; in his article on *L'Homme révolté* and its author in *Les Temps modernes* ("Pour tout vous dire" [August, 1952], pp. 354–83), he writes: "a new outlook on *Le Figaro,* easy conscience, we didn't want the Indo-Chinese war, and moreover the Vietminh is communist . . ." and so on for thirty pages written in the same ink.

[2] Preface to Roger Martin du Gard, *Œuvres complètes,* 2 vols. (Paris: Editions de la Pléiade, 1955.)

tion of nature and beauty, of beauty and the intellect. Helen, the so often disparaged Helen, was resplendent there with her conquering charms; the Greeks had done battle for beauty. Empedocles the obscure is side by side there with Socrates; and, even in revolt, Prometheus bound defined human limits, the threshold which cannot be crossed without peril: "The Greeks never said that the limit could not be passed. They said that it exists and that he who dared go beyond it was struck down without mercy. Nothing in the history of today is able to contradict this." Camus's Greece has the dazzling beauty of Aphrodite and the wisdom of Athena.

These spiritual homelands are all the more pure for their being inaccessible. *Noces* was a present lived; *L'Été* is only a hope or a memory. Adulterated as it may be, Tipasa, with all its colors, its light, its natural exuberance, still stands opposed to modern cities. Paris, as Prague, Lyon, and Saint-Etienne had once done, forced Camus to live his life on the surface. He lived there as a stranger, imprisoned behind rain-drenched windowpanes, oppressed by the grey skies. Would the child of Belcourt turn to the Parisian social "world"? "What can be more trying than a very Parisian dinner party?" Nothing irritated him more than that "expenditure of the soul" and those whispered confidences whose waters "trickle with a subdued sound interminably among the fountains, the statues, and the gardens." Paris superabounds in intellect and finally turns up lacking in heart. The working-class quarters on the outskirts, the factories? In a certain manner, he would feel more at ease there; there they have more modesty and fewer artifices. But without sunshine, everything is too cold, too ugly, too miserable. From whatever aspect one considers it, "Paris is an admirable cavern, and its dwellers, seeing their own shadows moving on the back wall, take them to be the only reality. But we have learned, far from Paris, that there is a light at our back. . . ."

Paris is the image of all of Europe, mechanized and convulsed. The great cities in which Hegel saw the crucible of tomorrow's civilizations are for Camus the negation of a true humanism. "We are living the era of great cities. The world has been deliberately amputated from what comprises its permanence: nature, the sea, hillsides, the meditativeness of evenings. Heir simultaneously of Christianity and Marxism, Europe has plunged into an interminable adventure. It has gambled on salvation, ensconced itself in history, turned its back on everything eternal the Earth entails. "In its madness, it pushes aside the eternal limits, and immediately shadowy Furies swoop down upon it and tear it to ribbons. Nemesis, the goddess of moderation and not of vengeance, watches."

Algeria and Greece, modern cities, and Europe are so many myths that Camus charges with his longing and his hopes. Each of them bears a judgment on our epoch and our way of life. The large city is thousands of men cut off from their share of pure air, from the peacefulness of forests and the joyousness of springtimes; it is the indefinitely extended walls behind which Camus languishes, a prisoner. A willing prisoner, moreover, since no other but himself forces him to live there, if not the desire to maintain, through regular work, the independence necessary to creation. His presence in the heart of Paris is a symbol: once again Camus deliberately chose exile.

Exile was Caligula's lot on the morrow of Drusilla's death; Martha's lot, lost in Slavic coldness. In order to escape from it, each imagined nothing other than burrowing themselves deeper into it. But Jan and Rambert, both of whom knew happiness, chose on the one hand to remain in Oran at the plague's height, and on the other to return to Bohemia. Exile has become the law of the world, the very condition of human solidarity. Nature and love are, in fact, more precarious than ever. "What a little thing! Dry like a plant growing in rock, but holding on in the same way. It endures humbly. From time to time a downpour causes it to flower, or rather, simply to breathe, to suffuse a faint perfume. And then it shrivels up again immediately." What Jacques Rivière said of the love of God,[3] Camus could have written of love of the world. He even had to tolerate his work's being desiccated by contact with morality, gnawed at by the cancer of cities and civilizations. "Am I yielding to the miserly times, to bare trees, to the winter of the human world?" Human faces have obliterated landscapes; poetic verve, rigorously channeled, crops up only in rare instances. *L'Été* claims to return to the wellspring.

It is a difficult and often artificial effort. One does not re-create Tipasa, one regrets it longingly: "We sometimes remember regretfully the timeless grass, the olive leaf we will no more go to see for itself, and the grapes of freedom! Man is everywhere—everywhere his cries, his sorrow, and his threats. Among so many assembled human creatures there is no longer any space for crickets." But perhaps exile is more profound

[3] See *À la trace de Dieu.*

than a certain determined optimism would allow us to believe. Would it come to an end on the soil of Algiers? There was already reason to doubt it. Men there had changed a great deal, too. In 1952, Camus discovered the reflection of his era on the faces of his former friends. Africa, in its turn, had entered into the upheavals of the times.

At certain moments—and "L'Enigme" cannot hide the fact from us —it seems that weariness dominates; bitterness is even greater following controversies. Could art itself be a prison? One day a man launches a phrase, he inaugurates the Absurd (the word, not the reality) and he is stuck with being absurd forever after. Most often he refuses to come to any conclusion, but the critics, the press and the readers gladly jump to the task. What took years to write is judged in a moment. Words become fixed or they degenerate slowly. What was only a temporary anguish is immobilized into despair. The legend is stronger than the facts. If an attempt is made to re-establish exact intentions, to protest against abusive deformations, immediately voices are raised, friendships break apart; and, for having aspired to an exchange of dialogue, one finds oneself once more all alone. Is every truth no longer fit to be heard or said?

Moreover, what use does this battle serve? At the same time that Camus defended himself against the charge of being the absurd man, the Absurd takes its revenge: a trip to South America, the bouts of weariness reawaken the dormant illness. For at least two years, he will have to moderate his activities and slow down his literary production. Misfortune, as *La Peste* had let it be foreseen, resurged, breaking the painfully constructed moral dikes, and everything is left to be done over in silence. To be sure, Camus drew himself up and strove "to be equal to the best as to the worst." With the aid of memory he preserved "in the midst of winter . . . an invincible summer." But under these conditions, existence seems like an indefinite expectation. Expectation of the return to light and sunshine, expectation of the sea, expectation of a pacified history in which nature would have resumed its rights; expectation of solitude amid the demanding mob, expectation of love in the midst of solitude. "There is why I suffer, with dry eyes, from exile." All that *La Peste* enclosed within it of restrained suffering bursts forth in "La Mer au plus près." Separation is for all time.

"La Mer au plus près" is a poem in prose, the only one Camus gave us after *Noces.* These pages were written in a fevered state, sketched out upon his return from South America. A ship's log, we are told, a symbolic log of the grand tour of existence. The first part is heavy with bridled impatience. In one place the phraseology is filled with delight: "I await the returning ships, the house of the waters, the limpid daylight." In another, it languishes and becomes charged with indifference: "Someone praises me, I dream a little; someone offends me, I am scarcely surprised." Soon irony comes into play and denounces this blind and deaf stranger who brings nothing but his presence: "It is at funerals that I outdo myself. I truly excel." The poet goes his way, distracted, inhabited by a single image. Mechanical gestures take his place. "It is not I who speak." How could he, this man who is "not yet anything"?[4]

Suddenly the tone swells. An odor of the sea envelops us. It was only a dream. "Besides, I do not possess enough of my art to hide my distress or to deck it out in the latest style." However, as bitter as the illusion may be, it overlays a certain reality. "Thus I, who possess nothing, who have given away my fortune, who pitch my camp beside all my dwellings, I am nonetheless satisfied when I want to be; I set sail at any moment, despair knows me not." The power of imagination, dreams, memories can calm certain forms of impatience. To be separated is not to be entirely alone. True life is absent from our "outlying districts blossoming with scrap-iron . . . planted with cement trees" and our skies redstained like bandages; but the sea beats tirelessly against the beaches and the rocks. "Finally a day comes . . ."

The poem of expectation mingles weariness with modernism. ("Paris changes! but nothing in my melancholy has stirred!") The voyage, by contrast, is a kind of vision, a feverish one like Rimbaud's *Bateau ivre*. The rhythm becomes light; the wind is vigorous, the sails snap. All the senses are awake: here the waters bloom into camellias, there they spread out "heavy, scaly, covered with fresh foam," elsewhere the foam is "unctuous, the spittle of the gods." Camus seizes upon it with vehemence. He makes it crackle, burn, smoke under the sun. In a kind of hallucination, we follow the rapid course of the moon and the sun in the sky; we pass an iceberg in the Tropics, then a herd of stags swimming in the frothy water. On taking leave of the land, we renounced our tradi-

---

[4] In the Preface to *L'Envers et l'endroit,* the same theme, by way of which the author expresses the dissatisfaction he feels concerning the already written work, can be found.

tional ways of seeing and feeling. We have gained a savage world, freed from the laws of gravity, in which the sea, rocked by an invisible and familiar song, covered itself with "strange yellow flowers." Even the impossible has ceased to be foreign to us.

This succession of images, now strange, now familiar, is in no way gratuitous. The sun at the bottom of the sea, the waves installed in the heavens, as on the morning after some kind of cosmic upheaval, emphasize the fraternity of men and their incomprehension at the same time. The buildings "cracked under the growth of the virgin forest," which crumble amid the laughter of the monkeys of La Tijuca, are like our proud civilizations and, like them, mortal. The sea, finally, is a model of faithful and fleeting love, the "long journey, never begun, never achieved."

> Elle est retrouvée
> Quoi? —L'Eternité
> C'est la mer allée
> Avec le soleil.[5]

It justifies existence: "Great sea, always furrowed, ever virgin, my religion with the night! It washes us and fills us with its sterile waters, it liberates us and it keeps us upright." It alone can pardon death. It is ultimate peace despite storms, immobility in movement, silence beyond the slapping of the waters. "O bitter bed, princely couch, the crown lies at the bottom of the waters."

Suicide and nothingness are an old temptation for Camus. Already in "Le Minotaure," Buddha in the desert beckoned us to sleep. Annihilation is the ultimate refuge against the vain wispy substance of fame: "yes, all this noise . . . when peace would be to live and create in silence. But we must know how to be patient. Another moment yet, the sun will seal mouths." In the desert of the cities, he was seized with the desire "to go stretch out in the valley under the same light" and there find repose. Before the sea, he abandoned himself to fascination with the waters: "a day comes which accomplishes everything; we must let ourselves be carried by the current, then, like those who swim to the point of exhaustion." In mid-ocean, he yielded to that "intolerable anxiety, paralleled by an irresistible attraction . . . is to live, then, to rush to our destruction?

---

[5] It is rediscovered/What? —Eternity/It is the sea gone/With the sun.

Once again let us rush without respite to our destruction." Carried away as if by a kind of morbid mysticism, he took pleasure in a voluptuous anguish in which the ardor of life and the sweetness of death were confusedly commingled, along with the seeking for equilibrium and pride in facing danger. "I always have the impression of living, threatened, on the high seas at the heart of a royal happiness."

Let us be careful, however, not to accord an excessive importance to such temptations. All literature, whether it be creative or critical, unavoidably exaggerates sentiments which, in daily reality, play only an episodic role. Poetry more particularly heightens emotions and passing anxieties. In order to be objective, we would have to insist equally on what the various essays enfold in the way of determination to live and sensual enjoyment. But was it not proper rather to extract the dominant tonalities, of which certain ones, judging by the title of the collection, escaped the author himself? Unless he intentionally put us on the wrong scent.

Can one in fact speak of a true expression of love in the sense that was intended in *Noces?* Here love is more a memory or a longing than a reality. We were waiting for a song of maturity; it was not given us. Camus was obsessed by *Noces.* Returning to Tipasa, he ran the risk of finding there nothing but shadows and of chasing after memories, in brief, of repeating himself with less brilliance. One has only to compare the final pages of "Le Minotaure," proud and shimmering, to the studied flights of "Retour à Tipasa." Sometimes Camus failed to consent to growing old.

This could lead us to fear a certain drying up of poetic production. It is certain that most of the pieces collected here teach us little that is new, nothing at least that was not developed elsewhere in another mode. Most often the poetry can be reduced to nothing and the logical commentary constitutes the essential material, without one's finding that overlapping of poetic themes and reflection which comprised the originality of *Noces.* Alone, "La Mer au plus près" opens up perspectives of renewal in spite of its exceptional character. The visionary mixture of the real and the surreal endows the myth with all its depth and its mystery. The author's obsessions are expressed directly in it, without the support of commentaries. And they are the obsessions of a man of forty years. The poetry, less vehement and more glacial, takes into its province the ugliness of the modern world, the cry of machines, the weariness of the exile, and the hallucinations of the sick man.[6] In it, images are renewed in relation to another stage in life: fewer adjectives perhaps, certainly fewer colors, more verbal images which are drier, more active, and more unpredictable. The brevity of each of the poems and their relative independence offered Camus important possibilities. In any case the poetic vein was not dead within him. Perhaps, even, as the last part of *L'Homme révolté* leaves us to suppose, that poetic vein might one day have taken its revenge on the discursive essay, invading the domain of reflection in order to give back to it its suppleness and its complexity.

But finally, it was once more the *récit,* the mocking narrative tale, through which the renascence would come to pass. Between "La Mer au plus près" and *La Chute,* there are few common points, were it not for a certain figure . . .

[6] Already expressed in "Pluies de New York," *Essais,* pp. 1829–33.

12

The Anguish of Algeria

One could not end a study on Camus without recalling what was the final drama of his existence: the Algerian war which he considered a case of fratricide, and which he had wanted to prevent with all his energies. There is no doubting—and I can attest to it—that from 1955 until his death it was at the heart of his preoccupations and that it sometimes took him away from his creative work. Who can honestly be surprised that this is the case? One tried to be a part of one's times; one did everything to understand history and was swamped by it. There are few men who have not known such bitterness.

Algeria is scattered somewhere in all his books, or in nearly all. It represents something greater than a reality: a myth.

Essays, novellas, novels: all of Camus's works are related to Algeria and are rooted there: *La Peste, L'Étranger, L'Envers et l'endroit,* as well as *Noces, L'Été,* and *L'Exil et le royaume.* There are three illuminating exceptions: Camus situated *La Chute,* that novella expanded to book length, in the grey mists of Amsterdam. Clamence, lost in the canals of the Dutch inferno, secretes his bad faith—that of a "judge-penitent" who, in the act of saying his *mea culpa,* strikes the breast of another. In contrast, Algeria, or rather the Mediterranean of which it is only a boundary, may represent unconsciousness or lucidity, but never hypocrisy. When Camus again wished to express the jealous desire for life, he created Martha, a Slav, who—living in cold Czechoslovakia, which is untouched by any sea—dreams of waves dancing in the sunlight. Martha is one of the living dead, as are the Just, exiled in frozen Russia, cut off from happiness by a thirst for justice, and cut off from their own people by their unrelenting obsession. The latter have renounced youth and love; they kill so that Russia may be beautiful. Martha, who has renounced nothing, kills so that she may one day come to know life and beauty on the shores of the Mediterranean. As opposed to the lands of ice and death, Algeria is the incarnation of love of life, natural beauty, and the splendor of the world.

Beautiful like the sea, Algeria is sterile like the sea: alive like the sun; like the sun, it is murderous. From *L'Envers et l'endroit* to *L'Exil et le royaume,* Camus discovered in Algeria the pendulum swing from yes to no, from life to death, from abundance to sterility. These poverty, Belcourt, and his mother's small apartment taught him. But a few kilometers away, the beach offered him its treasures. Not far from Algiers, the Roman ruins at Tipasa, buried under exuberant and richly colored vegetation, sang of the victory of life over death, of ever-renascent nature over the ephemeral constructions of man. But farther south, Djemila, eroded by the wind, spoke of the permanence of death and the annihilation of stone under the sun. For the sun is life-giving, but the sun kills. It rides high in the sky, it dazzles Meursault's eyes, and it triggers the murderous shot—the sun is the real murderer. It strikes down oppressively on the day of the trial, similar in its cruel and blinding relentlessness to the prosecutor's accusations; its brutal flash is like the blade of the guillotine. The desert at the edge of the wheatfields, the red of the hibiscus and the dull sand, the odor of flowers and the smell of human misery, the starving Kabylia and the modern buildings of Algiers—Algeria is full of contradictions, a land of men and an inhuman land.

Men there also carry within them their contradictions: indolence and brazenness of bodies stretched out on the beaches, the naive cult of the body and latent mysticism, aloofness and familiarity, amiability and violence, the concomitant taste for exhibition and mystery. In "Le Minotaure" and in "L'Été à Alger," Camus describes with humor or with gravity his fellow countrymen, who, like himself, are so ready to burn up their lives for fear of losing them. Algerians are capable of patient resignation, but they also have a capacity for revolt which sometimes reaches a pitch of insane fury. Caligula, who is Roman and who personifies an evil which spread over the banks of the Weser and the Moskva, is kin to the men of Algeria who, passive for many years, become suddenly armed for their misfortune by the frenetic desire to live, combined with the sudden despair of dying. From that moment the Plague draws nearer; it hovers nearby, watching Oran, the city that turns its back to the sea.

Undoubtedly, the Plague of which Camus speaks symbolically came
to us from the East. It swept over Europe, and it seemed to Camus that
Africa would be spared, protected by the equilibrium inherent in "La
Pensée de Midi," the classical thought of Greece, the Mediterranean
moderation which he found exemplified in the balance between the
ancient Greek gods of light and darkness, between Apollo and Dionysus,
between Socrates and Callicles. He had confidence in the fierce individualism and earthiness which had once motivated the Spanish anarchists in
their struggle against the "right" of the Falangist state and the "right"
of the Stalinists. Yet Camus knew better than anyone that Cadiz still
lived in a state of siege; neither the sea nor the sun serves as protection
against the implacable laws of the Plague. They only render the triumph
of evil more overwhelming, more tragic, as in Oran encircled by barbed
wire. Beauty outlawed, men living amid fear and hate, observation towers
and barbed wire, the compounds for the pest-ridden victims—no doubt
that at the moment he wrote his novel, Camus rejected them for Algeria,
his homeland. He knew it was capable of bloody uprisings, massacres, the
basest passions, and the worst acts of violence. But he could not imagine
that it might give way to a reign of systematic terror and cold violence, to
the spirit of the Inquisition. The conclusion of *L'Homme révolté* (the
chapter on "La Pensée de Midi") makes this clear. Moderation!

From Casablanca to Beirut, from Damascus to Seville, the Mediterranean world is shaken by convulsions; Socrates drinks hemlock everywhere along its shores. And in the faces intoxicated by pain and blood
which his fellow countrymen turned toward him Camus no longer recognized Algeria, but only the Absurd, and the temptation of annihilation.
The gentle lines of the Chenoua, the caressing bite of the sea, the tea roses
of Tipasa, smooth as cream—these are the deadly nuptials which Algeria
celebrated from 1955 to 1962. And those who were astonished by
Camus's silence were very shallow indeed.

It had been some time since he had seen the first rats die in the
stairways, the rats of colonialism, an old sickness that was dragging on in
Algeria. Camus did not consider the presence in Algeria of people of
French origin as illegitimate or even contestable. His father's family had

fled the German occupation of 1870, seeking a new Alsace on Algerian soil. But no justice was being rendered the mass of Arabs, most often condemned to a life of misery for which even the difficulties of Camus's own childhood provided little basis for comparison. As did the leftists at the time, Camus dreamed of substituting, for these two Algerias that were juxtaposed rather than intermingled, an Algeria without fault, without discrimination, borrowing from official language, peopled by Frenchmen —each entirely equal to all others. For practical reasons, he thought it well to turn to a rat-exterminating enterprise in vogue at that time: the Algerian Communist Party. But he discovered in less than a year that the struggle against the Plague in Algeria furnished a social pretext to a branch office more intent upon rationally exploiting suffering for the profit of the home office than upon progressively abolishing it. Since a certain preference for the living human being inclined him toward the living Arab of today rather than toward the Arabs of the century to come, he decided that the Communist method was not the most desirable one.

A short time later the Popular Front brought him new hope: "In 1936, the Blum-Violette Project made the first step, after seventeen years of stagnation, toward a policy of assimilation. It proposed nothing revolutionary. It took up once again the proposal to grant civil rights and electoral status to 60,000 Moslems. The relatively modest project raised an immense hope among the Arab population . . . The powerful *colons,* grouped in financial committees and in the Association of Algerian Mayors, set in movement such a counteroffensive that the project was not even presented before the Chamber of Deputies."

Three years of inertia: Algeria sank back into oblivion. In the midst of the Nazi vociferations, who was to take notice of colonial problems? Who even among the European settlers or the rich Moslems was to concern himself over the misery of the Arab mountaineers or the Kabylian peasants? In 1939, a famine devastated Kabylia. To this famine Albert Camus, one of the reporters for the Socialist-leaning *Alger– Républicain,* devoted a lengthy news report, hoping to move, if not the administration, at least the mass of his fellow countrymen. I think that I was the first to draw attention to that series of articles, remarkable already for their style, their restrained feeling, and their humane sentiment. As he follows the "itinerary of a famine," it is in human beings that

Camus takes an interest. He continually cites actual incidents which he had witnessed with his own eyes, using statistics only to support and give generality to the facts.

He noted the failings and the needs; he was careful not to make of this level-headed indictment of generalized negligence a polemic weapon against any particular administrator. Camus wished to be of service to the Kabylians rather than to damn those responsible for their difficulties. As he repeated again and again, what he proposed were reparations for the former, not expiation on the part of the latter. In the realm of justice, he had no desire to appeal to the tribunals that punish; he appealed rather to the courts of arbitration which order that amends be made.

His findings remained, in the main, sadly up-to-date in 1955: "Kabylia is an overpopulated area; it consumes more than it produces." Few cereal grains, but some figs and olives. Now, the Grain Control Office (a creation of the Popular Front government in 1936) supported wheat prices, "but the price of neither figs nor olives has been revaluated." Emigration had long countered this imbalance; but the French internal crisis had driven back the Kabylian workers. Consequently there was famine, and one can almost hear La Bruyère's or Bossuet's words of indignation over the lot of the seventeenth-century peasant when Camus writes: "I think I can state that at least fifty percent of the population sustains itself on herbs and roots while waiting for assistance from administrative charity in the form of grain distributions . . . At dawn in Tizi-Ouzou, I saw children in rags fight with Kabylian dogs over the contents of a garbage can. To my questions people replied, "It's like that every morning." Nonetheless, the imperturbable administration continued to enforce the customary regulations: "The forest rangers forbid the consumption of pine seeds and impound the donkeys and charcoal of peddlers without licenses—and with good reason. As for the back-taxes of the poor, they are deducted from their already meager wages; these withholdings are sometimes equal to the whole amount of their wages."

"What remedies have been found for such suffering? I answer at once, 'Only one: charity.' " Politically oriented charity, moreover, the administration of which was left to the discretion of the caïds, local Moslem chieftains. In the same way, nothing had been done about the unemployment that affected one-half of the population. Nothing had been done about the "insulting wages" that made of working conditions in the Kabylia "a regime of slavery." The settlers objected that the output of the Kabylian worker was inadequate. Here Camus takes a firm stand "against that abject line of reasoning which deprives a man of strength because he does not have enough to eat, and then wants to pay him less because he lacks strength." They also invoked the Kabylian's mentality and his minimum needs: "I know of nothing more despicable than these arguments. It is despicable to say that those people adapt themselves to any condition . . . In the attachment of a man to his life there is something stronger than all the suffering in the world. It is despicable to say that these people do not have the same needs as we have. If they had no needs such as these before, we would certainly have created them a long time since. It is strange to see how the very nature of a people can be used to justify the debasement in which one holds them, and how the proverbial reticence of the Kabylian peasant can legitimize the hunger which gnaws his stomach. No, it is not in this way that things must be viewed . . . The truth is that we rub elbows daily with a people who live three centuries behind the times, and we are the only ones who are insensitive to this incredible discrepancy."

At least, some will say, France made a huge effort in the area of education. She responded to the Kabylians' "thirst for knowledge" by constructing numerous schools. Indeed, in 1939, "only one-tenth of school-age Kabylian children [could] benefit from that instruction." The Joly-Jean Marie school construction project had never gotten off the ground. To the number of small schools it planned for, people preferred the construction of a few educational palaces "for tourists and investigating teams," sacrificing "to the prejudices of prestige the elementary needs of the indigenous people." The egalitarian prejudice—the same kind of buildings for everybody—amounted to a form of *de facto* discrimination. In truth, the walls made little difference; the education dispensed within them alone counted for anything: "The Kabylians will have more schools the day we will have suppressed the artificial barrier which separates European instruction from indigenous instruction; the day when, on the benches of the same school, two peoples made to understand one another will begin to know each other."

At the conclusion of his investigation, Camus recommended the suppression of dual-governed communes (townships governed by two administrations, a European one for Europeans, and a Moslem one for

Moslems) and immediate experimentation with local democracy, a first
stage toward administrative emancipation; a vast public-works program
and massive investments of money: "We have found the necessary credits
to give the nations of Europe four hundred million francs, now gone
forever. It seems unlikely that we cannot manage to give one-hundredth
of this sum for the improvement of the well-being of men whom, no
doubt, we have not made Frenchmen, but of whom we ask Frenchmen's
sacrifices." He further suggested that colonization of areas in southern
France which were suffering declining population be turned over to the
Kabylians.

To those who expressed surprise at this cry of revolt, this protest
against a cancer that gnawed at the French body politic, Camus concluded
by replying: "They say to us, 'Take care, foreign powers are going to take
advantage of this.' But those who in fact could take advantage of it are
already judged before the whole world for their cruelty and cynicism.
And if France can be defended against them, it is no more so by cannons
than by that freedom we have still to speak our thoughts and to contribute, each one in his modest way, to repairing injustice." A statement for
which he was nonetheless not to be forgiven. The *Gouvernement Général* of Algeria, which did not believe in the plague, held that it was
defeatist and subversive. We continued to throw a prudish veil over the
Kabylia's atrocious nudity and to content ourselves with soothing promises. And for Camus, there was exile to Metropolitan France.

The rats continued to die nevertheless, invading the gutters and the
mouths of sewers. In 1945, the Arabs rebelled at Sétif—a bloody popular
uprising, followed by pitiless repression. At that time Camus was direct-
ing *Combat*. He left at once for a three-week trip with the intention of
informing the indifferent mother country. As the years of World War II
were coming to a close, who else was concerned with the "incident" at
Sétif? While Hiroshima was being wiped off the map, how unimportant
these individual massacres seemed. At the source of the drama, Camus
found the ever-present suffering of the people: "Algeria, in 1945, is
plunged into a political and economic crisis which has always been
endemic there but which has never been so acute." Because of the lack of
rain, the harvest was extremely poor; for lack of reserve provisions,
famine ravaged the entire country. The little wheat in Algeria was being
sold on the black market or unequally allocated. Theoretically the Arabs'

ration was five-sixths that of the European settlers; in reality it was one-third or one-half. Hunger and injustice were painfully awakening the political consciousness of a people who had remained resigned until that time.

Most certainly France had chosen the way of assimilation of the Arab populations, and the ordinance of March 7, 1944, continued, on the whole, along the lines of the Blum-Violette Project—but ten years behind schedule. Now, Camus noted, "France's defeat and her loss of prestige have intervened, as also has the Allied landing of 1942, which put the Arabs in contact with other nations and awakened their capacity for comparison. Finally there is the Pan-Arab Federation, which is a constant temptation for the North-African populations." Thus, he affirmed with bitterness, the policy of assimilation did not correspond to the realities of the situation. In 1945, he wrote: "I have just read in a morning paper that eighty percent of the Arabs want French citizenship. But I can sum up the present state of Algerian politics by saying that they indeed *wanted* it, but that they no longer want it . . . Arab opinion, if I am to believe the results of my investigation, is indifferent to the policy of assimilation."

Ferhat Abbas and the Socialist Aziz Kessouz symbolized this evolution. They had once demanded assimilation; they now insisted upon "the recognition of an Algerian nation tied to France by bonds of federalism." Not for a moment does it occur to Camus to reproach Ferhat Abbas, "that product of French culture," with his earlier statements on the non-existence of the Algerian nation. Instead he seeks to understand the Arab leader's evolution, and an analysis of Ferhat Abbas' "Manifesto" proves eloquently that the French had missed an opportunity some time earlier. General Catroux, in 1943, had accepted this text as a basis for discussion. The French administration, however, had taken the uprising at Sétif as a pretext for the imprisonment of the "Friends of the Manifesto." "Pure and simple stupidity," Camus responded. If Ferhat Abbas were mistaken in considering assimilation as an unattainable reality, "it would have sufficed to make that reality attainable in order to deprive the Friends of the Manifesto of any tenable argument."

Ten years passed, in which a new status for Algeria was conceived and allowed to abort in trumped-up elections—ten years, in the course of which Camus had to bear witness for his Moslem friends who were imprisoned and dragged before the courts;[1] ten years of hope and disappointment, during which the insane war in Indo-China, the contradictions of French policy in Morocco and in Tunisia succeeded in awakening despair among the Arab masses and hope among the most intransigent Nationalists. The former could expect nothing more from the will of the French nation; the latter based their hopes on the incoherence of its decisions. It was then that rebellion broke out.

A savage rebellion, as excessive in its objectives as in its means. Camus could understand a terrorism like that of the Just, which recoils from murdering children and strikes only at the guilty, which offers life for life, as Kaliayev or Sophia Peroskaya once did. But he could not understand a blind terrorism which struck preferably at the innocent or the enlightened; nor a reactionary terrorism which attacked schools and all symbols of modern life; nor the mutilations that resulted from barbaric instincts, superstition, and religious fanaticism. The form of revolt that Camus advocated must find its limits within its own structure. Standing firmly against oppression, the rebel affirms his right to live, but his rebellion begins to decay at the moment when, in its turn, it gives way to organized oppression and terror. Typically, Camus takes this occasion to recall the rebel to a respect for life. Though he may deplore the fact that these "forgotten men," the Arabs, have taken arms against "the dream of a power that thinks itself everlasting and forgets that history always marches forward," he can still excuse them. But when they in their turn come to dream of eradicating the existence of the French in Algeria, to deny the presence of a million Frenchmen, in Camus's eyes, they exceed the limits of justifiable rebellion and bring down suffering upon everyone.

French elections were drawing near. French policy could be made flexible. Therefore, Camus, in *L'Express,*[2] launched toward both sides the

---

[1] In 1951, at Blida for a group of nationalist militants. In 1953, when a group of North-African demonstrators were attacked and struck down by the Parisian police. In 1954, in favor of a group of Tunisian Nationalists who had been condemned to death.

[2] He gave to Jean Daniel, who questioned him concerning his return to journalism, three reasons for doing so: "The first is that I am part of my times . . . The second is that journalism has always seemed to me like the most agreeable form of commitment, on condition that one say everything. The third, finally, is that I want to help Pierre Mendès-France return to power. . . ."

appeal of Socrates to the Athenians. Like Montaigne refusing to choose between Guelphs and Ghibelines, like Romain Rolland combating both French and German lies, Camus wanted "to place himself in the no man's land between two armies and preach, in the midst of bullets, that war is a deception and that bloodshed, if it sometimes carries history forward, carries it forward to further cruelty and suffering." Since Parliament was procrastinating, he would himself undertake to explain to both sides that life is of prime value and that power and justice lose all meaning in the middle of a cemetery. He was aware of the chasm which separated the Metropolitan Frenchman and the Algerian settler. Therefore he reminded the former that they had also benefited from colonization and that they had closed their ears to the cries of suffering of the Arabs. Rather than cause the settlers to band together from "a bitter sense of solitude," and so force them to unite in "dreams of criminal repression or of spectacular secession," Camus suggested that it would be better to arouse and sustain in them a liberal state of mind which would prepare them for reasonable compromise. Of the French settlers he asked that they loyally recognize the defeat of the policy of assimilation, "first of all because it has never been implemented, and secondly because the Arab people have retained their individuality, which is not compatible with ours." A national Arab individuality did exist, and the dream of reconquest would lead straight to abandonment. Finally he asked the militant Nationalists to renounce their intransigent position as well as the temptation of Pan-Arabism. To all he issued an appeal for the protection of civilians so that the hellish cycle of hatred might be broken.

He personally took us this appeal for a civil truce in Algiers on January 22, 1956. He meant by this gesture to facilitate the task of his liberal friends, Maisonseul, Poncet, and Miquel, who maintained contacts with Moslem groups in the framework of "L'Association des amis du théâtre d'expression arabe" [Association of Friends of the Arabic-Language Theatre]. The liberals, who called for the suppression of Algeria's colonial status, elimination of the "gros colons"—the powerful, wealthy minority among the French settlers—opposed to any change, and a "round table" of the various Algerian movements, were in contact with Nationalists like Amar Ouzegane, Mohammed Lebjaoui, and Boualem Moussaoui. Arriving in Algeria on January 19, Camus became fully aware of the gravity of the situation: "In no time, all this can turn into a

fearful civil war, an ethnic war. The Europeans themselves will wind up
slaughtering one another." The meeting of the twenty-second was almost
sabotaged both by the Algiers municipal government, which denied use
of a public hall, and by the European "ultras" who attempted to assault
Camus.

Three Nationalist leaders attended that meeting: Ferhat Abbas,
Ahmed Francis, and Tewfik el Madani. The F.L.N. was not opposed to
this effort; at least they wisely left it alone. Two weeks later came the
events of February 6, during which the newly elected Premier, Guy
Mollet, was greeted by the Algiers populace with jeers and overripe fruit.
Paris had lost the last shred of its authority in Algeria, and with that
Camus's hopes were dashed. I had the occasion to see Camus twice during
the days that followed. He had decided to end his collaboration with
L'Express; the Government, according to him, had lost the Arabs' confidence by virtue of not having been able to resist by every means the
pressure of the European settlers. The "Maisonseul Affair" confirmed this
in his mind.[3] Every alternative had been closed. When the "Algerian
Community" plan proposed by Aziz Kessouz had to be abandoned, there
was nothing left for the liberals but silence. Each day the powerlessness
of the civil authorities became more apparent, and the pacification program took on the twisted face of war.

What could he do at that point? He did not approve of the total
condemnation of the *Français d'Algérie;* he did not accept the idea of one
day becoming a foreigner in his own country; he condemned blind
terrorism. "My position has not varied on this point [since *Les Justes*] and
if I can understand and approve of the liberation fighter, I have nothing
but disgust for the killer of women and children. On the contrary, I
continue not only to reject but to condemn absolutely, today as yesterday,
the murder of innocent civilians," he wrote in the draft of a letter,
intended for Jean Senac, in February, 1957. On the other hand, repression
nauseated him and he found the settlers' position unrealistic and hypocrit-
ical. "I have decided to keep quiet concerning Algeria," the manuscript of
the letter continues, "in order to add neither to her misfortune nor to the
stupidities that have been written with respect to the subject."

In April, 1958, Mouloud Feraoun summed up in these few lines a

[3] Jean de Maisonseul, an old friend of Camus and a liberal, was arrested for
having acted as a "post office" for the Nationalists.

long conversation he had had with Camus: "There was in him that fraternal warmth which makes devastating fun of forms and effects. His position concerning events was what I supposed it to be: nothing but the most human. His pity for those who suffer is immense, but he knows, alas, that pity and love have no power whatsoever over the evil which kills, demolishes, which would seek to destroy everything and create a new world from which the timorous, the skeptics, and all the weak enemies of the new or the old truth would be banished by means of machine-guns, scorn, and hatred."

He was only to break the silence in which he shut himself up, in order to make brief remarks and to publish *Actuelles III*, subtitled *Chroniques algériennes*. This time it was the French press that remained silent concerning the book, for political reasons. And we were to witness an extraordinary phenomenon, often noted by every Camus specialist: the public was to remain unaware of this book of nearly three hundred pages, written by a Nobel Prize author, on a problem of burning current interest, because it had displeased a majority of the publicists. It is true that certain of Camus's remarks in the book were intended to displease: "Thus, there are certain people who move without transition from speeches on the principles of honor or brotherhood to the adoration of the fait accompli or the cruelest party. I continue meanwhile to believe, with regard to Algeria and all the rest, that such aberrations, on the right as well as on the left, only make clear the nihilism of our age." Faithful to himself, Camus refused to condone fanaticism. In his eyes the revolt of the Arabs posed the problem of their oppression, which demanded reparations; it did not resolve it any more than fear on the part of the French justified blind repression. Terrorism and torture reinforced and complemented one another to the supreme satisfaction of totalitarians of whatever breed they might be. Both attitudes—the events proved it —were as ineffective as they were immoral. To render passions calm and sober: such was the object of Camus's remarks. "But," he added, "its effects have been nil up to now; this book is also the story of a failure."

It is true that the proposals that he made there already appeared outmoded to many observers. "An Algeria made up of a federated people and bound to France seems to me to be preferable, in terms of plain justice, to an Algeria bound to the Islamic Empire, which would accomplish nothing, so far as the Arab people are concerned, except to increase their poverty and suffering, and which would uproot the Frenchmen of Algeria from their native land." In a final note he gave an outline of what this new Algeria should be. First he defined basic principles: condemnation of colonialism, of the repeated lie of assimilation, of the unjust allocation of tax revenues, of scornful attitudes; he also condemned the claim to total independence and asserted the right of indigenous French settlers to remain in Algeria. A federal structure, which Camus borrowed from the Lauriol Plan,[4] would have to be worked out. The Algerian Federation would only exist on an individual basis because of overlapping of different ethnic groups in the same areas. Therefore, in the early stage, the French Parliament would include a Metropolitan section (approximately five hundred deputies, of which fifteen would represent the French settlers) and a Moslem section of about one hundred members. The latter would legislate separately on problems pertaining to the Arab population, the former on problems pertaining to the settlers, and Parliament, in a joint session, would legislate on common problems. The administration would be responsible to each of the sections or to the combined legislative body, depending upon the problems involved.

In the second stage, when the French Commonwealth would have been set up, the Algerian Regional Assembly would express Algeria's local autonomy and be integrated through the channels of the Federal Senate and the Federal Government into the whole Commonwealth—this requiring a constitutional revision.[5] But now, of course, all of this has hardly anything more than an anecdotal value.

For the rest, Camus limited himself to numerous interventions in favor of condemned Moslems.[6] "After long reflection, I am persuaded," he wrote to President René Coty, "that your indulgence will finally help to preserve a little of the future that we all wish for Algeria." I had the opportunity to sort the mail he received at the time, and I noted with surprise that even certain of those who gladly accused him of having

---

[4] Marc Lauriol, *Le Fédéralisme et l'Algérie* (Published in Paris by *La Fédération*).

[5] Camus was writing before de Gaulle came to power in May, 1958.

[6] I have given a summary of these in *Essais*, pp. 1844–45.

adopted a "Boy Scout moral attitude" were the first to run to him as a mediator.

All this went long unnoticed. By contrast, the utmost possible was made of his Stockholm declarations. During a public speech, a young Algerian had vehemently questioned Camus and continually interrupted him. The *Association des Algériens en Suède,* moreover, was to ask Camus's pardon, in a letter, for the young man's behavior, which it regretted, and emphasize that he had not spoken in the name of any nationalist organization whatever. To his heckler, Camus replied:

> I have kept silent for a year and eight months, which does not mean that I have ceased to act. I have been and am still a partisan in favor of a just Algeria in which the two populations must live in peace and equality. I have said and repeated that it was necessary to do justice to the Algerian people and to grant them a completely democratic regime, until it came to the point where hatred on both sides became such that it was no longer proper for an intellectual to intervene, his declarations running the risk of worsening the terror. It has seemed to me better to wait until the propitious moment came when one could unite instead of dividing. Meanwhile, I can assure you that you have comrades who are alive today thanks to actions you know nothing about. It is with a certain repugnance that I give my reasons this way in public. I have always condemned terror. I must also condemn a terrorism which is practiced blindly, for example, in the streets of Algiers, and which could one day strike my mother or my family. I believe in justice, but I would defend my mother before I would justice.[7]

Proceeding to make a few minor rectifications, Camus added, speaking of his interlocutor: "I feel closer to him than I do to many Frenchmen who speak of Algeria without knowing anything about it. He knew of what he spoke and his face was not that of hatred, but that of despair and suffering. I share this suffering; his face is the face of my country."

People have dwelt long on that famous sentence: "I believe in justice, but I would defend my mother before I would justice." The sentence, incisively tossed off, could be taken in its literal as well as its symbolic sense. It reaffirmed quite simply a preference for the concrete, the carnal, the living being rather than for the abstraction. Once again

[7] *Le Monde* (December 14, 1957).

Camus appeared for what he had always been: a man of limits rather than a man of uncompromising principles.

Overall, the Algerian tragedy only emphasized a few of the constants of Camus's thought with their grandeur and their weakness: the horror of a world of violence, disgust for uselessly spilled blood, spilled for want of timely reforms; instinctive repulsion in face of intolerance and fanaticism, all of which amounts to an old background of liberal pacifism, poorly adapted, doubtless, to these times of nationalisms, to these cycles of revolt and repression to which the modern world seems to be condemned. Camus was henceforth an exile not only in his own country, but in his own century, and all the more painfully so in that he shared its passions.

13

An Ambiguous World

> "I look upon myself and
> question myself: am I a monster
> more twisted than Typhon
> and more fuming with pride?"
> —SOCRATES (*The Phaedo*)

"All my work lies before me."[1] What a mocking use the hero of *La Chute* might have made of this brief sentence! Well, then! Camus thus denies his work and holds it to be abortive? One imagines the famous laughter of the *Pont des Arts* erupting and then diminishing behind him. False modesty, Camus! . . . Unless it is true, you have never said anything of value and . . . unless again you were dreaming of the impossible, like Jonas before a virgin canvas. Well? But no one laughs any longer, neither the lovers of scandal nor the professional slur-slingers. "Forty-seven years old and a rather astonishing vitality."[2]

Did anyone ever laugh, moreover? He had a stubborn way of saying things that shook the most skeptical. To be sure, between *L'Homme révolté* and *La Chute* five long years went by, almost imperceptibly interrupted by the brief *L'Été*, and many were able to wonder about his relative silence and the drying up of his inspiration. But anyone who knew his obstinacy never doubted that his work was coming to fruition. In 1952, still smarting from the polemical exchange surrounding *L'Homme révolté*, and as though in reaction to it, he prepared for a new departure: he planned to adapt Dostoevski's *The Possessed* and to create a Don Juan crossed with Faust, to try his hand at a novella on the theme of exile, and to bring "the first man" back to life in a novel.

Simple notes, no doubt, over which he was to dream for years

[1] Preface to *L'Envers et l'endroit*.
[2] Jean-Claude Brisville, *Camus* (Paris, 1959), p. 257.

running. "One day the idea comes, the conception which coagulates all the scattered particles. Then begins the long and difficult work of putting it all in order. And it takes all the longer in that my profound anarchy is boundless."[3] In November, 1954, *La Femme adultère* appeared, published in Algiers in a limited edition illustrated by Clairin. The other novellas were still in draft form. *La Chute* was not to be long in conquering its autonomy. "There is a plan which circumstances on the one hand, execution on the other, modify."[4] A whole corpus of manuscripts and typescripts show us how the work was enriched little by little, until it formed a novel of one hundred and seventy pages.

At this moment, Camus realized that his fortieth year might mark, if not a rupture, at least "a kind of turning point in my work and in my life."[5] It was then that he drafted that preface to *L'Envers et l'endroit* in which, as in "Jonas," his determination to begin anew is affirmed. He speaks openly of going back all the way to the first work which, in spite of its imperfections, contained all the contradictions, the fecund ambiguity with which he intended to live and to create: "the right side and the wrong side" of the world, its surface of light and its surface of darkness, innocence and a vague sense of guilt.

At that time, I ended my earlier study with these lines: "The subjective and confidential nature of his work could very well find itself in the way of being indicted. Let us prepare, then, forewarned as we are by the publication of *L'Été,* for an 'opportunistic' reaction against moralism and abstraction, to which the necessities of the past struggle constrained him. The virtuous explosion of the Resistance and its aftermath has had its time. Camus means to elude the Manichaeism in which people have sought to imprison him and rediscover existence in all its living complexity." Some time later, Camus sent me a copy of *La Chute* with the following dedication: "To Roger Quilliot, to prove his prophecy right."

That torment to which success gave birth and which the ever watchful critics rendered more keen is evidenced in the character of Jonas

[3] Brisville, pp. 257–58.
[4] Brisville, p. 257.
[5] Letter to R. Q. (January 21, 1956).

in the story of the same name from *L'Exil et le royaume*. "Don't you see, he's painting his own picture and he will hang it on the wall." From Classicism to *Académisme*[6] there is but one step, easily taken. Therefore, Jonas, devoured by the whale, "Glory," and the whale, "Envy," demands to be reassured, loved: "A little love is an enormous thing." And Clamence echoes him: "how we admire those of our masters who no longer speak, their mouths being full of earth. Homage comes quite naturally, that homage which, perhaps, they had waited for all their lives."

But even those among his friends and disciples who reassure him are so many whales that swallow up his free time. It seems to Jonas that he is indebted to them, that he must give them a few minutes more, a small fragment of space and time. And if the obligations in which he is lost were only a means of masking his impotence? If, one day, withdrawn into an obscure corner of his house, in its ceiling as it were—"up in the air," Jeanson called it—in order to reconquer a kingdom in the depths of exile, there was nothing left to him but to write the word "solitaire"—although it might be "solidaire." Tragic and necessary solitude, Spanish solitude, as Camus liked to say;[7] unhappiness lies in being alone and in not being able to be so.

If he fled, he was accused of being boorish; if he showed himself, he was self-satisfied. Doubtless he had a tendency toward self-effacement as well as toward conquest, tendencies that were alternating and sometimes concurrent. If he spoke up, he was accused of complicity; if he kept silent, he was also accused of complicity. Was his style of writing at least spared such criticism? Not at all. Its aristocratic tone, its disdain, its "rhetorical orderliness,"[8] were denounced; it was based on a disorder of the spirit. And Camus questioned himself with a sense of humor charged with bitterness: "I know very well that the fondness for fine linen does not necessarily suppose one's having dirty feet. Makes no difference. Style, like fine poplin, too often covers up eczema" (*LC*). Was he not rather threatened by dryness of style? "My dikes, still today, are perhaps too high. From this comes that occasional rigidity."[9] Had he not, out of

[6] A reference to membership or association in *L'Acadmie française,* a stronghold of conservative and traditional values [trans. note].

[7] "My solitude disgorges shadows and works that belong only to me" (from an unpublished document).

[8] Sartre, *Les Temps modernes* (August, 1952), pp. 334–53.

[9] Preface to *L'Envers et l'endroit.*

mistrust of that romanticism and that unrestrained passion which dwelt within him, come to the point of killing all spontaneity, all love? He noted sadly that landscapes disappeared from his work. Listening to himself on the radio in 1951, he discovered in himself "a frigid tone." "When one is a man of passion, to dream of morality is to give oneself up to injustice at the very moment when one is speaking of justice," he wrote in the preface to *L'Envers et l'endroit,* "Man sometimes seems to me to be injustice on the march: I am thinking of myself."

Stiffness of style could indeed reflect a profound aridity. It could be asked if *La Peste* did not owe its grey-toned militancy to the struggle it describes, to the morality it secretes. Shut up behind the barbed-wire barriers of suffering, Oran, in order to defend itself, had recourse to isolation camps. Similarly, *L'Homme révolté,* taking a stand opposed to the philosophers of abstraction and the fetishism of history, borrowed its weapons from abstraction.

From out of Camus's fear of being misrepresented—sometimes decked out in the raiment of the Absurd, at others clothed in the disguise of a lay saint—came the discovery that he was partially responsible for that betrayal of his true nature. Only what lends itself to deformation can be caricatured. "When one is a man of passion, to dream of morality is to give oneself up to injustice at the very moment when one is speaking of justice." All of *La Chute* is already summed up there in that short sentence from *L'Envers et l'endroit.*

That sentence was not tossed off haphazardly. Camus knew what blows he received and which ones he returned. At each wound, he stiffened, wounding in return. Because he was accused, he made himself a judge in the name of tolerance. An infernal cycle of verbal violence, from which he sought to escape—neither victim nor executioner! But is not to fight for justice and freedom to accept injustice in some form or another? Is there not some inevitable intolerance in the struggle against fanaticism and totalitarianism? The dilemma of all democrats and of all pacifists who are insulted and slapped in the face—in the name of their principles —until they are driven out of themselves or out of this world. The dilemma of all Pyrrhonians who admit, "I know that I know nothing." The response: "You do know, then; you said so. Therefore, you judge, you who contested the right of judgment."

From this point on, that right side and wrong side of things upon which Camus founded his equilibrium is nothing more than the double visage of Janus. The worm is in the fruit; ambiguity takes on the countenance of duplicity, complexity that of complicity. The areas of light and shadow become Pharisaic or Sadducean camouflage.[10] Camus looked at himself and was astonished. He had not thought he looked like that. From *L'Étranger* to *L'Homme révolté*, he had done nothing but explore within his consciousness the questions of suffering and guilt. But Meursault, the accused, *denounced* legal crime;[11] but the plauge victims, Tarrou as well as the Othan child, *denounced* totalitarianism and even God; but *Les Justes,* at the foot of the scaffold, *denounced* tyrants as well as conscienceless terrorists. *L'Homme révolté* does likewise for fanaticism, power, and socialized revolutions. Well then! Always denouncing? At a certain level, it is no longer any more possible to write innocently than it is to reign innocently.

Rieux's discretion and the Just's purity suddenly appeared suspect. Everything was lies, including the litotes, that rejection of the lie so dear to Meursault, which had become through some kind of devilish trick the art of saying the most by saying the least, and, to use Clamence's expression, "a shattering discretion." Sartre took it upon himself to enlighten Camus concerning himself in a fierce letter to which Camus replied in a tone of bitter derision. According to Sartre, "solemnity," "intellectual disorder," "somber self-sufficiency," were the least of Camus's faults. There was a still more serious one: "You are a lawyer who says: 'These are my brothers,' because it is the word that has the greatest chance of making the jury weep. And not only a lawyer, like Clamence, but a policeman. We are on the Quai des Orfèvres, the cop is walking and his shoes squeak as in the movies." Lawyer, cop, the one complementing the other, as in one of the manuscript versions of the novel in which the mute interlocutor is a policeman. Camus had become involved in the mortal game of judgment and his plea smacked of the prosecutor's indictment: "A violent and ceremonious dictatorship has taken root in you, which rests upon an abstract bureaucracy and seeks to assure the reign of moral law . . . Has the Republic of Belles-Lettres named you its

---

[10] Hellenists, aristocrats, and Sadducees did not believe in a future life.

[11] Thus René Girard sees in *L'Étranger* a work of resentment "exacerbated by romantic pride" and in *La Chute*, the re-trial of *L'Étranger* (See "Camus's Stranger Retried," *PMLA,* LXXXIX (1964), pp. 519–33.

public prosecutor? . . . But what surpasses all measure, is that you should have had recourse to this practice which was denounced quite recently, again in the name, I believe, of unity, at a meeting in which you took part . . . Where is Meursault, Camus, where is Sisyphus, where are those courageous Trotskyites who advocated permanent revolution? Assassinated, doubtless, and in exile."

Assassinated! Suddenly, everything collapsed. "Since I was bleeding a little, I would be gobbled up entirely: they were going to devour me . . . From the day that I became alerted, lucidity came to me, I received all the wounds at once and I lost all my strength at a single stroke." Camus discovered with discomfort the hardened countenance that his work had composed for him even in its hesitations. "I understood, then, by virtue of living in my memories, that modesty helped me to shine, humility to conquer, and virtue to oppress." Virtues are changed into vices; everything is a betrayal. "Alas! I hardly speak than my words are already/Turned into poison in every parable,"[12] says Vigny's Christ. Nothing is pure any longer. The devil is hidden everywhere, in sensual pleasure as well as in the taste for justice, in chastity as well as in the beds of whores.

"In our society, every man who does not weep at his mother's funeral risks being condemned to death," Camus had paradoxically written with respect to *L'Étranger*. In the aftermath of the publication of *L'Homme révolté*, all the tears he had not shed, all the outcries he had not uttered, all the manifestos he had not signed were suddenly thrown up to him as so many denials. It was the same with his love of the world and of sensation, his desire for happiness and his personal longings. "Weigh that well, dear sir; I lived unpunished. I was not concerned in any judgment, I did not find myself on the floor of the courtroom, but somewhere high up amid the arches . . . well above the human ants." And if, in spite of what might actually have been, things were as Jeanson would have it? If Camus, like Meursault, was responsible for his entire past, guilty of too much insolent innocence? If judges and critics had been right to impose total unity on disconnected instants and to recompose them into a case history with its own tendencies and currents? Then,

[12] *Le Mont des oliviers,* 11. 67–78: "Hélas! je parle encore que déjà ma parole/Est tournée en poison dans chaque parabole . . ."

everything was simple. As at any given Moscow trial, Camus would never have been what he thought he was. Within his very being, eternity was changing him: "Far from my having lied, Camus, is it not you who have *cheated?* Is the liar in this case really the one who undertakes to strip bare? . . . Your bright outlook turned to black without my having had to insert any malice into the matter." As in an algebraic universe, each word, each book changes meaning according to whether one endows them with a plus or a minus sign.

La Chute is first of all the end of an illusion. Camus falls from the clouds. He had thought himself well liked—and who would not want to be?—or at least esteemed. Suddenly writers, critics, some of them friends, from Sartre to Jeanson, from Patri to Breton, from Hervé to Lebar, unleash upon him anger, rancor, and sometimes hatred. He became indignant, he protested, and the reproaches multiplied. To protest further, to pursue these dialogues between Trissotin and Vadius?[13] What ridicule and what suffering for a writer of Camus's reserve. He was to shout his cry of pain, the cry of a man skinned alive, in one of those ambiguous works of which he had the secret.

His disarray explodes in a number of notes. He was haunted at night by nightmares: execution and marching to torture, Meursault begun all over again. There was the awareness of a desire for harmony, for equilibrium for which he had to reach through the upheavals and struggles. Again, there was his own ambiguity: the rejection of the failures in which our epoch abounds and his desire to assume his place in it. And the sense of having lived an unintentional lie. "Each time someone tells me they admire the man within me, I have the impression of having lied during my whole lifetime . . . Each time someone takes it upon himself to speak of my honesty, there is something deep within me that shudders." He plunged into Tolstoï's correspondence; he drew from it a few sentences: "I have learned after thirty-two years of experience that the truth of our situation is terrifying . . . Arrived at his highest degree of development, man perceives very clearly that everything is nothing but a lie and

[13] The two argumenative pedants in Molière's *Les Femmes savantes.*

stupidity, and that the truth he nevertheless loves more than anything else in the world is terrible."[14]

He conceived a novel; one about a coward who believed himself courageous. "One incident is enough for him to become aware of the contrary—and he has to change his way of life." Is this not what Clamence does, when he falls victim to an aggressive motorcyclist, even before having yielded to his fear of water?

The evidence is undeniable that the author is present in his work in the form of a distorted, falsified presence. What we have is a detective novel, as all novels are. And the number one suspect is the author himself, proof of which lies in that "I" with which he hooks us. We recognize his bearing, that of a "rugby player," an "indefatigable dancer,"[15] his charm;[16] "do you know what charm is? a way of seeming to hear a reply of 'yes,' without having asked any precise question." Then, too, there was his fondness for sports and for the stage: "Still today, the Sunday games in a stadium full to overflowing, and the theatre that I loved with an unequalled passion, are the only places in the world where I feel innocent."[17] Clamence, like Camus, loves the sun, islands. Paris, that *trompe-l'oeil*, irritates him with "its four million silhouettes," exactly as the voracious social cells exasperated Camus (profession, organized leisures, family). Both have a fondness for beautiful style, for feminine friendships; both like to be of service; both refused the *Légion d'Honneur*. One like the other is easily given over to "disorder, to violence,"[18] to cynicism, "the most constant temptation" (*CN, II*); they waver between chastity and fondness for pleasure, possessed by the same sexual jealousy treated in *La Mort heureuse* and *L'Homme révolté*. Is this a case, as Simone de Beauvoir thinks, of filling a fissure that she considers "deeper than in most authors, between their life and their work"?[19] Perhaps. At any rate, it was an effort

---

[14] "Those who have been fecundated by Dostoevski and Tolstoi both, who understand one as well as the other, with the same facility, those people are natures who are fearful, for themselves as for others" (from an unpublished document).

[15] Jean Bloch-Michel: "How can one not recall the happiness, the amusement, the simple and open pleasure with which he danced."

[16] Simone de Beauvoir: "He spent a few triumphant years: he pleased, he was liked."

[17] *Racing Universitaire d'Alger.*

[18] Preface to *L'Envers et l'endroit.*

[19] *La Force des choses.*

to free that nocturnal side of his personality, that famished ardor with which he was capable of giving himself over to life and its pleasures.

La Chute takes up anew, like an echo, a certain number of obsessive themes that run through Camus's work: the haunting preoccupation with age, with judgment which one finds in the first chapter of *L'Étranger*. In this sense, Clamence would be a sort of pardoned Meursault, but caught in the trap of good intentions and language, or more simply the lawyer himself and that entire world of the trial in which he evolves. Like Caligula—"a Caligula who no longer accuses the world, but himself" (*CN*)—he wanted the moon, innocence. One wants "to be the equal of the gods," the other "to feel like God the Father and distribute irrevocable certificates of bad character and conduct." Caligula denounced lies and intended that men live in truth; Clamence dreamed of confessing his lies, aware that a fondness for the truth at any price is a passion that spares nothing and against which nothing can resist." For both, guilt will be universal; the two of them abandon themselves to nihilism and total freedom; both brightly illuminate a certain kind of mind's inclination for servitude—for servitude or for tyranny, one the wrong side to the other's right side. Still more, both are pedagogues of the Absurd. Who does not recall, finally, that "incalculable fall in face of the image of what we are" which *Le Mythe de Sisyphe* analyzed, the fear that Tarrou experienced of being himself a bearer of the plague's contagious germs, and Cottard ensconced in the plague and complicity as Clamence is in his fog, both cozily installed in "that very narrow little universe" of which they are "the king, the pope, and the judge"?

With *La Chute,* Camus renewed profound ties with the works of his youth. In it he returns to the problems of scandal, to alienation. He calls upon that fund of indifference that had once constituted his strength and his weakness. One might do well to compare this sentence: "the same infirmity that made me indifferent or ungrateful, then made me magnanimous," with the two following ones: "with me, the mercy of which I speak is rather called indifference" and "this indifference which is within me like an infirmity of nature." Is it not obvious that the first statement, taken from *La Chute,* extends and condenses the reflections from the *Carnets* and the preface to *L'Envers et l'endroit?*

But the tone, one senses, is different. Yes, the author presents us the shadowy side of his face, but it is made up, smeared with grease paint.

This confession is a mockery: you call me a cheater; I am one from within my soul, you had no idea how right you were. Now it is his turn to burst out laughing! *La Chute* could have been only one of three things: a humorous work, a long complaint, or an appeal to pity. Camus chose humor. He had been called a Pharisee, scornful, uncommitted. All right, so be it! He accepted it. And he consented to unmasking himself, to sinking his teeth into his own flesh with a somber pleasure. These gentlemen wished to knock the statue off its pedestal? He was their man. And here he is, pushing harder than anyone who is trampling on the idol. Full of pride? Well, what of it: "In truth, by virtue of being a man in such fullness, I found I was something of a superman." Vainglorious even, and stuffed to the gills with self-importance, carrying with him his "portable pedestal."[20] "Half Cerdan, half de Gaulle," if you like . . . "Yes, I never felt more at ease than in elevated situations . . . I preferred buses to subways, câleches to taxis, terraces to mezzanines." Generous? Sartre said to him, if self-sacrifice "is a sometimes thing, we are very close to Madame Boucicaut[21] and alms-giving." Camus counter-bids, "I loved also, ah, this is more difficult to say, I loved to give alms." Did they accuse him of playing "the cops"? He adds: "I began to write an *Ode to the Police* and an apotheosis of the guillotine." They suspected him of practicing political mergers; he confesses: "I began suddenly to advise the merger as a method of defense." "It may be," Sartre told him, "that you were once poor, but you are no longer; you are a bourgeois, as Jeanson and I are." He agrees to whatever one wants and to more: "Yes, I was rich; no, I did not share anything with others." "I greatly fear," they hurled at him, "that you have joined the camp of the stranglers and that you are abandoning forever your former friends, the strangled." So be it. "In philosophy as in politics, I am therefore for any theory which withholds innocence from man, and for any practice which treats him as a guilty party . . . All together, then, but on our knees and with heads bent." In this game of slaughter in which his head was the prize, Camus intended to take first place, as if from bravado. He was thus able to burst into a half heart-rending, half triumphant laughter, dominating the sneers or the murmurs of pity with which one sought to accompany his fall.

[20] Sartre, "Réponse à Albert Camus."
[21] The wife of a nineteenth-century department store tycoon and a well known philanthropist [trans. note].

But suffering is not put far aside: the same suffering that tears long moans from Temple Drake in *Réquiem pour une nonne* and that makes Stavrogin cry out: "I want to erase one act from my life, and I cannot do it."[22] The scream of a drowned woman never ceases to echo in *La Chute* and to disturb Clamence's rhetoric. This scream—at the two extremities of language, there is little else but the scream and silence—sums up all the little cowardices of which a man is capable, all the failures, all the uncompassionate moments. Who has not sometimes lied, at least by omission? Who has not let an outstretched hand slip away? Who has not turned away, out of indifference or weariness, from someone in despair who wanted to die?

Here is where Camus is waiting for us. His confession is ours: "Let him who has never sinned cast the first stone at me." All those who had reproached him for having played at being judge and public prosecutor, who were they themselves if not so many other Fouquier-Tinvilles? So many manifestos, so many signatures collected for the entire world's victims. And to what end? To assure the signers of an easy conscience, these professional humanists! All guilty! And all miserable for being so. Everybody into the cramped little cell beneath the spit of the passers-by.

Camus holds up his mirror to his detractors, to everybody. Sartre, who had promised himself one day to settle his own account, recognized himself in it. "I took the beast by surprise," he wrote in *Les Séquestrés d'Altona,* "I struck, a man fell. In his dying eyes, I saw the beast still living, me. One and one make one; what a misunderstanding! This rank and insipid taste in my throat? Mankind? Myself? It is the taste of the times. Happy centuries, you know nothing of our hatreds. How would you comprehend the atrocious power of our mortal loves? Love, hatred, one and one . . . acquit us." Listen again to him confess to Madeleine Chapal: "to tell the truth is the dream of every aging writer. He thinks he has never told it, and he has never done otherwise, he is naked . . . Formerly, when I published a book, I possessed innocence; I no longer have it . . . In our youth we were gentle and bothered by the problem of violence . . . the result is that the young have retained violence and thrown its problems overboard . . . Responsible and accomplices . . .

[22] *The Possessed.*

And there we are all together, caught in the midst of violence, always a little more. That is what I wanted to say, among other things, in *Les Séquestrés*. Frantz, when he dies, that executioner, he is us, he is me."

Let us turn to Sartre's autobiographical *Les Mots:* "I can no longer ignore my double imposture: I feigned being an actor feigning to be a hero . . . We were two people, however." Poulou has the same pride as Clamence, the same passion for domination: "I made myself a tyrant; I knew all the temptations of power." The fog into which Clamence penetrates, Poulou carries within himself: "Hardly was I seated when my head was filled with fog . . . I had lost innocence, scorn corrupted my generosity." He, too, is a penitent: "I am gifted in self-criticism," and he is no less a judge: "dogmatic, I doubted everything except being doubt's chosen one." Clamence admits: "I know what you're thinking; it is very difficult to unravel the true from the false in what I tell you. I confess that you are right. Myself . . ." And Sartre writes in the same vein: "I was influenced only by those [his childhood heroes] who were influenced by God, and I do not believe in God. See if you can see yourself in that. For my part, I cannot see myself there."

It is not necessary to say more. In their respective solitudes, Sartre and Camus had reached a point where they could better understand one another without any longer being able to bear one another: "an argument is nothing . . . no more than just a way of living together."[23] One and one make one. There is no salvation either in this world or out of it. One and one . . . this world is a lie and yet the only truth. The man who betrays and kills dreams of innocence, but this dream itself is deceptive. "My image was smiling in the mirror, but it seemed to me that this smile was double" (*ET*).

La Chute hence figures as a descent into Hell. "Do you know Dante," Clamence asks. Holland[24] and its people (I love this people . . . for they are double") symbolize the modern hell of bad faith: merchants and puritans, the Dutch dream of gold and wisps of smoke. With "its musty waters, the odor of dead leaves that soaked in the canal," with its aura of rot, it is the heart of universal ambiguity. Everything here is

[23] Sartre, "Albert Camus," *France-Observateur* (January 7, 1960).

[24] Let us recall, for the sake of the anecdote, that Camus went to Amsterdam in 1954. The Mexico City Bar was located at 91, Warmoe-Straat; it has since changed its name.

equivocal: the "primate" with his "deafening mutism," in which certain ones[25] have sought to see a divine avatar, rough-hewn, simple and yet mistrustful. The prostitutes, dream-women, the opium of the lonely: "The gods descend upon nude bodies and the isles are set adrift, demented, crowned with a ruffled head of hair like palm trees in the wind." The Isle of Marken offers us the most beautiful of negative landscapes, the "wrong side" par excellence. The Zuyder Zee is a dead sea: "you don't know where it begins and where it ends," an absurd sea. Amsterdam, finally, rises beyond its canals like Pluto's kingdom beyond the Styx of the "three times triple turn."[26] There one finds oneself encircled as in plague-stricken Oran. Dripping skies, murky sunlight; we are at the antipodes of Algiers, in complete exile.

Who lacks ambiguity? Each of us pretends to innocence, but we all yield to the irresistible vocation of judgment. "We are all exceptional cases. We all want to make an appeal from something. Each of us demands to be declared innocent, even if for that we have to accuse men and the whole human race."

Deceitful powers, self-love, imagination, all these falsify: "I have brought to light the profound duplicity of the human creature." A few sentences suffice to close to us all recourse. Equilibrium is only a longing, "the order of the world is also ambiguous." Beneath its grave exterior, humanism is frivolous: "Of wherein seriousness lay, I knew nothing." Nietzschean power ends up in delirium. Even faith is equivocal, in the way of Peter, thrice a renegade, "upon whom the Church is built." As for Christ, is he not the symbol of innocent culpability, he who profited from the massacre of the children of Judea? If religion were at one time "a great laundering enterprise," it hardly lasted any longer than the three years which preceded the crucifixion. Since then, "judges swarm in profusion, judges from all races, those of Christ and of the Antichrist, who are, moreover, all the same."

Tribunals are everywhere; the innocent indict themselves publicly: "There are no more friends, there are only accomplices," victims and executioners, masters and slaves. Through the power of money[27] we turn away from, we distract ourselves less from the threat of boredom than the

[25] Kurt Weinberg.
[26] Du Bellay.
[27] "Wealth, dear friend, is still not acquittal, but it is a welcome reprieve."

threat of judgment. Now, this judgment is henceforth without foundation. The modern world has the sense of the sacred without faith in future life. It would be well to suppose the relativity of sentences since "a day comes when the guilty party, too quickly executed, no longer seems so black," and since our civilization "has lost the only values which, in a certain manner, can justify the suppression [of human life]."[28]

The human animal, the one who accuses, tortures, and kills, the very one who erupted in Caligula or Martha, who rose up in Oran over the rats' corpses, which *L'Homme révolté* unmasked, that human beast has insinuated himself into the doctrines created to fight against him. Christianity secreted the Inquisition, Marxism went astray into Stalinism, existential freedom has bowed before the necessities of history. Every liberating idea ends by justifying the fait accompli and arming itself with the sword of justice. Is this perhaps owing to man's natural impotence?

Is evil perhaps to blame? Not only the evil of our age, which makes of Clamence "a hero of our time . . . the agglomeration of the defects of our generation in all the fullness of their development,"[29] but eternal evil: "You know the Scriptures; decidedly, you interest me." Clamence's first name is Jean-Baptiste, *vox clamans in deserto,* "an empty prophet for a mediocre age." Like his namesake he wears a camel's skin, made into an overcoat. Clamence, "Christ after our own paltry fashion," is the inverse of Meursault, "the only Christ we deserved."

People have rightly pointed out all the Christian vocabulary with which *La Chute* seems stuffed. The doves,[30] which are grace itself, vainly await a head on which to alight. Ever since the theme on Bergson, from his student days, Camus had sought for that which, along with Jan, he called the answer. Clamence confesses in his turn: "I had to answer or at least to seek the answer." The scream which gives birth to remorse or to his obsession, "I understood that it would continue to wait for me on the seas and rivers, everywhere, finally, that the bitter water of my baptism could be found . . . We will not find our way out of this immense holy-water fount. Listen! Do you not hear the cries of the invisible sea gulls? If they cry out toward us, to what are they calling us? Is it love that awaits us? Who, dear sir, will lie down on the hard earth for us?

[28] *Réflexions sur la guillotine.*
[29] A quotation from Lermontov, used as an epigraph for the fourth version of *La Chute.*
[30] "Let us hope that they are bringing the good word."

Would I be capable of it myself? Listen, I should like to be, I will be. Yes, we will all be capable of it one day."

The universe of *La Chute* is an evangelical universe turned upside down, caricatured. The light that glows in the darkness is gin (p. 1479); the Cro-Magnon man is a boarder in the Tower of Babel (p. 1475). If Rachel's voice rings out (p. 1531), it is to call Christ to a sense of guilt. As for Peter, he is "the little coward" (p. 1532). The burning bush (p. 1488), the beginning and the end, is Clamence in person, "Elias sans messiah, crammed full of fever and alcohol, my back pasted up against this moldy door, my finger raised toward the low sky" (p. 1533).[31] Mockingly, he imagines himself carried away by a chariot come down from Heaven (p. 1548), or decapitated (p. 1549) as was John the Baptist . . . and Meursault.

Yes, the language is Christian, but as provoking as anyone could wish: "Our father who art temporarily here . . . ," Clamence prays, addressing himself to the masters of the world, "more roguish" than he himself. And if he covers his head with ashes, if he tears out his hair in the best ancient Jewish traditions, it is for effect, in order better to turn his confession to his own advantage. The confession is finished; in the glass that he holds before his interlocutor, Clamence finds his own image, that of a lawyer—he was to have been a policeman in the manuscript version. But what does it matter, since lawyers and policemen are both auxiliaries in the process of judgment. The mute interlocutor has said nothing, but he has avowed everything from one ellipsis to another . . . By turns, lyrical, bantering, insinuating, sententious, the judge-penitent imposes his gasping and his caprices on everyone—the critic as well as everyone else. Feigned friendliness, grating sarcasm, off-handedness, the tragic poetry of his mysterious aims, the passion for domination, whisperings and sudden outbursts, everything is calculated to lead us astray dramatically.

L'Étranger owed its rhythm to indirect style, to techniques of isolation, to deliberate difficulties of language. *La Chute* is nothing but direct style, facility of elocution, twists and turns of language to the point of vertigo. Meursault was simplicity and innocence incarnate; Clamence is duplicity, grimaces and masks. The former is reduced to a transparent thickness; the latter plays tricks with mirrors, finding a face for himself in the

[31] In Catholic iconography, John the Baptist is generally represented with his finger raised toward Heaven.

faces of all his readers. He chatters, sheltered behind words as though behind thick dark glasses, a ham actor like the liar in Cocteau's *Le Men-
teur,*[32] forever slipping away from us.

There is not a one of his sentences that is not an interrogation, a
challenge—and what is irony if not an interrogation without response?
Everything that will accentuate the dynamic and provocative character of
the work is used: incantatory and polemical repetitions, ellipses, interrup-
tions, breaks in sentence structure. Clamence has thrown himself into the
general mockery. His ferocious laughter wounds him and wounds us. This
chatterbox has something in him of the man possessed, the paranoid, the
terrorist who would devote himself to experimental explosions to see
what would happen. Resuming within himself centuries of Manichaeism,
of confession, of Christian or revolutionary inquisition, he breathes his
fetid breath over everything. He corrupts, he blows things apart with
precision and destruction. A veritable bomb!

Through different means, the shock effect is analogous to that which
L'Étranger produced. The reader is bewildered and fascinated at the same
time. But Meursault's ambiguity was not fully discernible until the end of
the book when his life appeared, falsely reconstructed through the social
lie, and truly assumed by himself. Clamence's ambiguity, by contrast,
appears from the opening lines; from there it goes on swelling like a
wave endlessly re-formed. Finally, Meursault, while using the first person
"I," excluded us from his intimacy; Clamence, under color of a confidential revelation, draws us into the wildest of strip teases in which the
personality is no longer anything but swirling confusion. In the earlier
work, a man was born; in the later one, a man's humanity
disintegrates.

Only an elusive character could smile out of suffering, be modest
with brilliance, fraternally domineering, and courteously cruel. He alone
could sum up all sorrows, all doubts, and make of failure not only a
revenge but a victory.

An attentive study proves that *La Chute* was born from rancor and
pain that had to be exorcised. It is also evident that Camus charged it

---

[32] "Am I lying when I say that I am lying? Or do I not not lie?"

with his hostility toward "our philosophers," as the manuscript indicates. A plethora of texts prove that he sought to settle accounts with a certain intellectual attitude: "The hero of *La Chute* gets himself shut up in a final impasse with his 'solution.' but I only wished to eliminate a certain kind of prophet who runs rampant in our intellectual society. And I would entirely share the opinions of Lacroix and Malebranche concerning the remedy he needs: a little self-esteem."[33]

But to so limit this great book would be to diminish it. Camus did not forget his own temptations—of nihilism and cynicism—and he himself leads this derisive merry-go-round. Who is Clamence? Camus? Yes and no. Sartre? Yes and no.[34] An aging man, a forty-year-old who "is acquainted with some troubles of poor health" (p. 1495), insomnia (p. 1528)? "After a certain age, every man is responsible for his face. Mine . . ." (p. 1502). "I measured the years that separated me from my final end" (p. 1521). Françoise Taque in an excellent study was able to point out pertinently that the novel sets forth the problems of the forty-year "climacteric," marked by depressive states and the threat of nervous collapse. The fall could also be the discovery that one will never be what one might have dreamed of being. "One has gotten out of one's youth what one can, and that is very little."[35]

Let us go a bit further. Camus brings into question a certain modern civilization; his and ours with its eroticism and its intellectualism: "They fornicated and read newspapers." A society which we today call a society of consumption, the one depicted in *The Red Desert* and *Tati's Play-Time*. Especially it takes up in a different mode the analysis of human duplicity that runs from antiquity to our own times, and which has since provided us with Sartre's *Saint Genêt, comédien et martyre* or Aragon's *Mise à mort*.

It seems that, finally, evil, that part of inhumanity that dwells within us, has invaded everything. A Christian book, then? Faulkner would have

[33] From an unpublished text.

[34] Simone de Beauvoir has clearly sensed this ambiguity, but she appreciates only one of its aspects: "I found it heart-rending, the way in which he, ordinarily so withdrawn, revealed himself. Suddenly his severity turned abruptly . . . from a penitent he became a judge; he deprived his confession of all sharpness in putting it too explicitly at the service of his resentments." De Beauvoir accepts the disguised confessions but rejects the mirror held out to her.

[35] Aragon.

had it so, even in face of this work which smells of sulphur and hell. However, Camus said to him: "I do not like to believe that death opens a door on another life. For me it is a door that closes."[36] An anti-Christian undertaking then, in which we must pardon the pope and pity that Christ "perched up on a judge's bench"? It is not so simple. It could be, in one sense, the story of a Javanese—which Clamence claims spiritually to be—and yet this book could have been born only in Christian Europe.

It is the adventure of a world gone mad, in which Van Eyck's "Just Judges" are shut up in a cupboard, the Mystical Lamb in a false prophet's room, and the insane in the house of Descartes; a world jolted into movement, shaken by convulsions and incapable of finding a firm base. A universe which is deprived or freed of God, but not resigned to this fact, and which is looking for the moon in a thousand places. We sail by dead reckoning, without a compass, eaten up by fever and doubt and ready to tear each other apart, like Christopher Columbus' crew. But there is no America to discover.

An unfamiliar technique was needed to tell of this shipwreck. Dostoevski had used a similar one in *Notes from the Underground,* as had others before him. Some wanted to see in *La Chute* a new novel, plotless, characterless. All this is true enough; but Clamence is no more a pure field of conscience than the novel itself is the universe of logorrhea. "I used the dramatic technique (the dramatic monologue and the implicit dialogue) to describe a tragic comedian."[37] Clamence is a myth, the temptation to despair carried to the point where there is nothing left to do but laugh at it. "When a writer," Camus said in 1943, "gives evidence of an admirable mastery of expression, it is then that his failure becomes instructive."[38] Could one not say that the cramped torture cell endowed upon the author an increased ease in the use of his pen? As though suffering, awakening in him long absent cruelty, rendered him alert and already as if delivered.

For he did deliver a part of himself. He proved that neither Meursault nor Sisyphe had been assassinated. He reawakened and brought to light all the inquietude formerly repressed in order to seek a cure, and which he had been accused of having stifled. *La Chute* is an act of

[36] *La Nouvelle Revue française* (May, 1960).
[37] "Camus's Last Interview," *Venture* (December, 1959).
[38] Letter to Francis Ponge.

purification. The supposed narrator, like Temple Drake or Stavrogin, let himself slip into confession and disgust with life. He drained the abscess, in order better to be born again. His pleasantries are the rictus of the patient who unburdens himself of his pain. At the depths of despair, he is sure, he will succeed in unleashing the kick that directs one back to the surface and to the right side of things. He accepts his share of responsibility in order to reconquer his share of innocence. He puts an end to "the fear of not being sincere and of lying in the face of death,"[39] in order to rediscover the multiplicity dear to the actor as well as to the absurd Don Juan, the fragile equilibrium between the intoxication of Dionysus and the light of Appollo.

This is the end, then, of the master of philosophy and life! "In order to teach, one has to know. In order to direct others, one must control oneself." Once more Camus took to task that "longing for the profound unity of the universe . . . that fondness for ontology" which never ceased to haunt him. He, and we along with him, comes back to relativity. "We come into the world burdened with an infinite necessity . . . total responsibility never exists nor, consequently, does absolute punishment or reward."[40] At one moment we must defend the individual against the collectivity and, at another, the collectivity against the individual. Relativity of method, moral opportunism, everything is a question of proportions. We are forever running from one extreme to the other, from the scourge of exact balance, toward greater solitude or greater solidarity.

Camus himself presents us his art in no other guise. In Stockholm, dealing with the artist and his times, he rejected the evasions and flighty diversions typical of *La Parisienne* equally well as the black and white viewpoint of social realism. "The highest form of art will always be, as in the Greek tragedians, in Melville, Tolstoi, or Molière, the one which achieves a balance between the real and the denial that man opposes to the real . . . The world is nothing and the world is everything: there is the double and tireless cry of every true artist . . ."[41] Ambiguous by vocation, the artist "absolves instead of condemning. He is not judge but

---

[39] From an unpublished document.
[40] *Réflexions sur la guillotine.*
[41] *Discours à Stockholm.*

justifier . . . The great work of art ends by confounding all the judges."
Camus no longer wanted to see black and white superimposed, the one
hiding the other to the greater joy of every species of prosecutor, but set
side by side and somewhat blended together. No wrong side without a
right side, no exile without a kingdom, and vice-versa. No realism
without its part of dreams.

Discharged of the burden of Manichaeism with which many had
sought to weigh him down, Camus breathed freely. Nothing is pure, to be
sure. Nothing nor anyone is innocent; but no one is any longer completely guilty. Innocent *and* guilty, that is man. The conjunction re-estab-
lishes equilibrium and reconciles us with ourselves. What matters those
multiple faces that so many lend us and discover in us; ambiguity is no
longer a lie, complexity is no longer complicity. The adulteress of *L'Exil
et le royaume* was not guilty of betrayal: she is double, she is bound to
her traveling-salesman husband by all the strength of habit, and the
desert calls out seductively to her. Pressed up against her sleeping husband, she is alone; but face to face with the desert, would she be less
alone? Who will talk to us of adultery when hers is a case of long exile
and a kingdom barely glimpsed? With this bourgeois housewife, who is
grown a little heavy and yet who is a daughter of spaciousness and a
nomad in the depths of her heart, we are perhaps quite far from the
abstract and anonymous judge-penitent reduced to nothing but his sneer-
ing laughter. Could the sobs of a somewhat middle-aged woman deliver
us finally from judgment?

Janine, forty years old, is without children or future. The loneliness
and cold of the coming winter stalk her.

"She was dreaming of the straight and flexible palm trees and of the
young girl she had been" (*ER*). Janine has put on weight, slowly
degenerated with the years: "She could not stoop over, in fact, without
gasping for breath somewhat . . . She stayed upright, heavy, her arms
hanging, a little bent . . ." Too thick and too white . . . What do we
know of Marie Cardona, of Rieux's wife, of Rambert's mistress? A
beautiful body, a silhouette glimpsed through a train window, a head
pressed into the hollow of a shoulder. Janine, on the other hand,
"breathes with difficulty . . . is fearful of the heat, swarms of flies, dirty
hotels filled with the odor of anise." She carries a purse, wine fogs her
mind. Camus's characters are no longer seen from the back, as with

Rieux, or as projected shadows as with Tarrou. They have a body; or rather, the body's and the senses' place is constantly noted in the narrative. The symbol—previously prepared for in the details of observation and brought out by incidents and commentaries—is worked deeply into the mass of details, and only appears at the very end of the novella. These characters' very weight protects them against abstraction.

The same kind of implantation, which carries with it a certain deliberateness of the narrative, characterizes those two robust novellas, *L'Hôte* and *Les Muets.* If Camus wanted to prove that he, too, was capable of sticking to his narrative and, as he said jokingly one day, of writing "socialist realism," he certainly won his wager. There is nothing to say about *Les Muets* except that the novella can be read at a sitting, and that the characters impose themselves upon us through their presence, their shabby happiness, their artisans' pride, their bursts of anger and their impotence. Theirs is a virile world, hard and rough, in which each word makes its weight felt. In *L'Hôte,* Daru, the schoolteacher, the gendarme, the Arab murderer are hardly any more talkative—as though to throw *Le Renégat*'s logorrhea into greater relief. Beneath each of these silences, as in *L'Envers et l'endroit,* we come smack up against the panicky fear of death, poverty, and so many unexpressed sorrows. All of Algeria's wretchedness, that of the Aurès region and of Kabylia, is suggested by a notation, a detail: "A cruel country to live in, even without men who, however, do not make anything any better. But Daru had been born there. Everywhere else he felt himself in exile." Daru, Balducci, Janine, Marcel, the coopers, Ballester, Esposito, Marcou, Yvars, are Algerian *petits blancs,* like those Camus had known during his youth. His uncle, the cooper, is still forty, but the comrades of Belcourt have aged. They have become grade-school teachers, policemen, shopkeepers, workers, hardly any more well off than before. Modest men, gnarled like grapevines, like Céleste, the bistro-keeper of *L'Étranger.* They have their troubles, a cramped existence, without any hope as they grow older. Like them, Yvars "had nothing to do except to wait, quietly, without knowing too well what for." But in them something rebels and echoes that call of the desert which, earlier, had set their ancestors in motion: "You are from here, you are a man." A man, Céleste had already said of Meursault, not a condensed product "of honesty, of conscience, of humanity, oh, you know, all that modern mouthwash," but a certain sense of honor, physical courage, boredom, dreams. A prince on the beach and an exile in the city.

All of Camus's adolescence came back in gusts, all his present status as an Algerian torn apart. As if he feared that people might have misunderstood him and that the luxuriance of *Noces* might have stifled in our memories the cold Algeria of the Aurès and Kabylia, he brings to life, as a counterpoint, a whole meager and soundless world, worn down by the wind like the stones of Djemila. Greeted by the raucous shout of the shepherds, confronted with the gnarled, disturbing and proud faces of the Arabs, among the red and black carpets, the odor of wool, mint, and spices, our *Algérois* feel they are both strangers and kinsmen. Poor princes, reduced to indignation—"they think they can do anything they want"—to petty consolations—" 'They act as though they were God himself,' Marcel said, 'but they sell, too.' " Here, we are far removed from the proud adolescence of "L'Été à Alger," far from the tea roses of Tipasa. Algeria is as much a land of exile as it is a kingdom. And, as though by contrast, the desert, eternally virgin and sterile like the sea, glows red beneath the fiery rays of the setting sun. "A few men, who possessed nothing and served no one, made their way without surcease . . . Wretched and free overlords of a strange kingdom." Absurd beings par excellence, belonging to space and not to time, knights of adventure and endless renewal of experiences in the midst of emptiness, the nomads live on the margins of our civilization, like the last embodiments of our longing, like a reproach and a temptation. Janine, their sister and their secret wife, facing the desert finally breathed again, "forgot the cold, the weight of other beings, frantic or stagnant life, the long anguish of living or dying . . . The last stars of the constellations let their clusters fall a little lower over the desert's horizon and became immobilized. Then, accompanied by an unbearable pain, the sea of night began to fill Janine, submerged the cold, mounted little by little to the obscure center of her being and rose in uninterrupted waves to her mouth filled with deep moaning."

For a moment, Daru yields to the same wonderment above the barren South Algerian plateaus. He "drank in, in deep breaths, the cool light. A kind of excitement rose in him before the vast familiar space, almost entirely yellow now under its skullcap of blue sky." And the renegade priest himself, for whom faith was a beacon of sunlight: what did he come seeking in the city of salt, if not the sun's burning rays? "Savage sun! It is rising, the desert is changing, it no longer has the color of the mountain cyclamen; oh, my mountain, and the snow, the gentle snow; no, it's a little yellow, a little grey, the wretched hour before the great bedazzlement. Nothing, nothing still, all the way to the horizon, in front of me, out there where the plateau disappears in a circle of slightly soft color . . . I feel the sun on the stone above me, it strikes, it strikes like a hammer on all the stones and makes the music of noontime, the vibration of air and stones over hundreds of kilometers." A strange poetry that celebrates only sterility or delirium, and whose barbaric accents echo all the way to the heart of South America, in that thick, hot night when the black girls in a trance celebrate the feast of Saint George: "The redoubled rhythm of the drums alone gave her a sort of invisible stake around which she unfurled her sinuous arabesques until, coming once more to a stop at the same time as the music, rocking on the verge of lost equilibrium, she uttered a strange bird-cry, piercing and yet melodious."

Fascinating black Diana, grimacing fetishes, haunting images of a barbarism in the process of being obliterated, you were floating about in Camus's memory like a shadowy Greece. Innocence was there too, in those "long collective and toneless outcries, without perceptible breathing, without modulations," of bodies abandoned to convulsions, in the interminable march of nomads without problems and without illusions. But our heroes, like the author, are similar to Janine, "too heavy, too white for the world into which she had just entered." The color of their skin, the weight of their limbs which proclaim a superabundance of worldly goods, excludes them from the community of simple peoples. "D'Arrast, fascinated by that slackened dance, was contemplating the black Diana when Le Coq suddenly surged up before his eyes, his smooth face now drawn. The kindness had disappeared from his eyes, which reflected only a kind of unknown greed. Without any warmth, as though he were speaking to a stranger, he said, 'It's late, Captain. They are going to dance all night, but they don't want you to stay now.' " Too late for d'Arrast, for Janine, for Daru; too late for a mechanized, mercantile Europe, plunged entirely into Promethean conquest. "They don't want you to stay . . ." Neither Janine nor Daru will henceforth be at home in the desert borderlands. Tourists and ethnologists, perhaps. But never again hosts. Janine's giving of herself, the loyalty of the schoolmaster, the servility of the renegade priest do not prevent their being suspect. A sunrise over the plateaus, a glimpse of the desert's immensity, the hallucinatory memory of a black city of lights and ritual dance, is all they will be permitted to take away with them. "It's too late, Captain." It is midnight in our century. They will bury their kingdoms deep in the secret depths of their hearts until the hour when they go to sleep at the bottom of a valley of olive trees.

To be sure, d'Arrast had carried the stone as far as the man's hut, and there he heard himself told, "sit down with us," by the previous day's mistrustful native. But to gain the confidence of a few, he has had to disappoint the expectation of the crowd which was shouting "To the church, to the church." Will the friendship of a chosen few console him for not being loved by everyone?

The misunderstanding is universal. It resides in Jonas, torn between the necessities of art and the obligations of fame; in Janine, called by dreams and love, and whom habit and the need to be two people holds back; in Daru, a prisoner of his double fidelity, crushed between nascent fanaticisms; in the silent men, caught between the logic of the workers' struggle and the emotion inspired by a child's suffering; in d'Arrast, momentarily tempted by the mystique of community and soon brought back down to the human level; it even resides in Le Coq, torn between pleasure and his given word. Innocents? Guilty parties? Would no one any longer be guilty? Neither husband nor wife, boss nor worker, artist nor disciples, murderer nor policeman, and especially not the schoolteacher with clean hands?

If it were to go thus, if each of these characters, endowed with a life of his own, but embodying one of Camus's temptations, escaped judgment, we would be returned to the point of *L'Envers et l'endroit* in which nothing, certainly, is justified, but in which everything is explicable. An "adulterous" woman, a renegade missionary, workers reduced to silence, a suspect host, a perjured Creole: "What difference does it make if we accept everything? . . . After all, the sun warms our bones anyway" (*EE*). Camus shrugs his shoulders. And yet, did he not inflect into his work, introduce forcefully the kingdom in the *Nouvelles de l'exil* [News from Exile],[42] bet on life, on men? A single stone in the middle of the

[42] The title which, from 1952 to 1955, he had envisioned giving to his collection.

hearth, but a stone that grows and which d'Arrast has cast there through extreme effort before parting. Was this a gesture of consolation, or the stone around which "the first man"[43] would reconstruct his hut? By crowding themselves a bit, all our exiles could come there to warm their old age.

All? Not quite. The "Confused Spirit" will not obtain his grace. It is too evident that Camus does not pardon that missionary whose passion for the absolute bends before fetishes, whose eagerness to serve plunges him into slavery; he is no more forgiving of him than he is of those judge-penitents who strike their *mea culpas* "on the breasts of others" (*A, III*). Between its publication in the *Nouvelle Revue française* and the final version, the story changed titles: *L'Esprit confus* [The Confused Spirit] became *Le Renégat* [The Renegade]. To live, alas, is to judge. But this remaining scrap of guilt, like an unforeseeable ricochet, hits the mountain schoolteacher, too: "You have handed over our brother; you will pay." An anonymous hand has made a traitor of the innocent and turned the host into a stranger in the only land he has ever loved. The Algerian housewife, guilty of dreaming, is an adulteress; Le Coq is a perjurer. From equilibrium to the equivocal there is but a single step quickly taken. With the exception of the renegade, strangled by a handful of salt, all our heroes are destined for the torture cell, condemned to live in both love and despair. The renegade betrayed, doubtless, out of a desire to evangelize. Having come to smash idols, he adores them. He is subjugated when he thought he was subjugating. But did he think so? Did he not yield to some profound masochism? Is there not an apostate within the missionary as there is a whore in the heart of the "lady," Temple Drake? Clamence's insinuating voice has not finished murmuring and whispering over the vast holy water fount in which our century is steeped. The fogs of the Zuyder Zee float over Mount Chenoua as well as the Forests of the Amazon. There is no longer any land virgin of sin. Oh, Greek heart, where is your innocence? Your serenity? But, were they ever?

L'Envers et l'endroit, L'Exil et le royaume: twenty years of an artist's life, at the end as at the beginning, the nakedness of Algeria, the acrid odor of humble lives, a few quickly repressed lyrical flights, irony. The

---

[43] The title planned for Camus's last novel, which he had begun work on before his death.

brilliant chatter of *Le Renégat,* the modest reserve of *La Femme adultère,* the realism of *Les Muets* and *L'Hôte,* everything that ceaselessly revitalizes form is good. But the artist says no less the same things, haunted by "these two or three simple and great images" willed him by his childhood.

"All my work lies ahead of me." In saying this, Camus denied nothing of his past. He was speaking in the manner of Sisyphus, determined to smile at his doubts and to pursue his way, always the same way. After Oedipus, after Montaigne, he obstinately repeated: all is well, everything is in order, failures as well as hatreds, triumphs as well as weaknesses. Only he no longer went along with the same assured step. From *La Chute* he had retained a less assured bearing, a bitter fold at the corner of his lips and a kind of quiver in his voice.

"We aren't sure of anything, do you see." Neither of what we do nor of what we write. *Verba volant, scripta manent.* Two means of being betrayed. "To cease being doubtful, it is necessary to cease being all together." Supreme irony! We have not finished with questioning his work and with answering his questions. Today as yesterday, Camus remains doubtful. Unquestionably, because he never stopped being so.

Conclusion

Why deny it? Camus's last years were darkened by a physical and moral crisis bordering sometimes on depression. While in the
seven years from 1936 to 1943 he had written three essays in varying
modes: *L'Envers et l'endroit, Noces,* and *Le Mythe de Sisyphe;* two
novels: *La Mort heureuse* and *L'Étranger;* two plays: *Caligula* and *Le
Malentendu;* while from 1943 to 1953 he produced *L'État de siège* and
Les Justes for the stage, a thick novel—*La Peste,* a weighty essay—
L'Homme révolté, a lyrical essay—*L'Été,* and two collections of *Actuelles;* in the six years that followed, only *La Chute* and *L'Exil et le royaume*
appeared.

To be sure, the collection of a whole series of literary articles would
have provided us with a critical essay. Certainly, *Actuelles III* could have
been quickly followed by an *Actuelles IV.* As for *Le Premier Homme,*
whose conception dated back precisely to around 1952, Camus had just
begun to work on it when death surprised him. One might all the more
easily assume a drying up of inspiration in that Camus noted in October,
1953, after the publication of *Actuelles II:* "The inventory is finished—
commentary and polemics. Henceforth, creation."

He was not lacking in projects for plays and novels, but in strength
and faith. The days following the aftermath of *L'Homme révolté* had
been painful ones: friendships had been broken, moorings cut in two. A
sort of malaise seized the author who, if he did not doubt his way,
doubted his ability to follow it. Add to that an always precarious state of
health and one can better understand in what solitude, in spite of the
notoriety, he found himself imprisoned. "The essential for the writer," he
said following Chekov, "is not fame; it is the patience to endure."

And what did he not have to endure? "I do not have," he wrote to
Pierre Berger, "the actual time or the interior leisure to see my friends as
I would like. Ask Char, whom I love like a brother, how many times we

see each other in a month . . . I have neither the time nor the interior leisure to be sick . . . But the most serious thing is that I have neither the time nor the interior leisure to write my books and I devote four years to writing what, with freedom, would have cost me one or two years. Moreover, for several years now my work has not liberated me, it has enslaved me. And if I pursue it, it is because I can do nothing else and because I prefer it to everything else, even to freedom, even to wisdom or true fecundity and even, yes, even to friendships . . . Life goes on and I, on certain mornings, weary of all the uproar, discouraged in face of the interminable work to be done, sick, too, of the world's madness which assails us, upon awakening, in the morning newspaper; finally, certain that I will not suffice and that I will disappoint everyone, I only want to sit down and wait for evening to arrive. I feel that urge, and sometimes I yield to it."

La Chute, like *L'Exil et le royaume,* is the outcry of a man in exile. However, with the theatre Camus found some sense of fraternity. For him, the stage had always been both a passion and a vacation. Unable to create the *Faust* of which he dreamed, it was still possible for him to adapt and make known unknown masterpieces, to contribute indirectly to the renewal of modern tragedy. While waiting for a new springtime, he kept his hand in as in his early days.

La Dévotion à la croix and *Le Chevalier d'Olmedo* attest to a never-denied predilection for the Spanish Golden Age with its subjects borrowed from national history, its popular characters, its legends. In a certain sense, Calderón and Lope de Vega indirectly avenged the failure of *L'État de siège.*[1]

Circumstances played a decisive role in the adaptation of Faulkner's *Requiem for a Nun* and Dino Buzatti's *Un Cas intéressant* [*Un Caso Clinico*]. Without doubt, the two plays corresponded to Camus's personal preoccupations. Already sensitive to the qualities of Buzatti's *Désert du Tartare,* he discovered in *Un Cas intéressant* the invalid's solitude and the loneliness of man in the clutches of the exhausting logic of modern life. This kind of symbolic and ironic nightmare rooted in daily experience, which owes much to Kafka and Dostoevski, was just the thing to attract his attention.

Camus scarcely knew of Buzatti. On the other hand, he admired

[1] We leave aside Pierre de Larivey's *Les Esprits,* the adaptation of which dated from 1940 and which Camus merely polished up a bit.

Faulkner. The sudden death of Marcel Herrand led him to take over the adaptation of *Requiem for a Nun.* He saw in it one of the most effective attempts at renewing tragedy. "Here there is nothing, nothing except an interior ascent . . . We begin with the improbable in order to arrive at tragedy. And there is a 'public' element: the progressive unveiling of the truth, as in a detective novel . . . A great tragic language and a modern play. Who has succeeded in creating this?"[2] But something else fascinated him in this work. Faulkner's world, like that of *La Chute,* is memory of crime committed and the passionate quest for this crime. "What Faulkner sees is that suffering is a hole."

Did not Faulkner, just like Dostoevski, say of his heroine, Temple Drake: "We have come here and we have awakened you in order to give Temple an honest chance to suffer, you understand, only to suffer for the sake of suffering, as *that Russian* or whoever it was said, who wrote an entire book on suffering." Camus always admired and frequented Dostoevski. *The Possessed* presented him with a world shaken to its foundations and which sought its salvation in violence, hatred, blood, or frivolity. The superficial agitation of intellectual circles with Stépan and Varvara, the temptation of cynical revolution with Pierre, obsession with suicide in Kirillov and with God in Shatov, and on top of it all, that explosive mixture of pride and contrition, of humanity and bestiality. *The Possessed,* in his eyes, expressed "our historical destiny," announced "our nihilism," and put before us "torn or dead souls, incapable of loving and suffering from not being able to do so, wanting and not being able to believe." The fondness he had for this novel, the obsessions he found in it, perhaps explain why Camus erred on the side of abundance in his adaptation. Wishing faithfully to translate the frenetic whirlwind which sweeps away men, things, and events, he condemned himself to saying too much.

"It is at least a vice which I can satisfy without offering myself up to censure."[3] Dramatic creation, even indirect, gave him back an innocence which neither his work nor his life any longer obtained for him.

The Nobel Prize, which consecrated his fame, found him thus in full disarray. "We are very much alike," he wrote to René Char, "and I know

2 *Le Figaro littéraire* (September 22, 1956).
3 *Figaro littéraire* (September 22, 1956).

that it happens that one is struck with the desire to disappear, to be
nothing, in sum . . . In the end, one could die of chagrin, literally. And
we have to live, to find the words, the flights, the reflection which found a
joy, the joy."[4] Unfortunately he felt himself struck down by sterility,
suddenly insensitive. "I die of thirst, deprived of light," he wrote to Char.

The Nobel Prize did not give him back his courage. The Swedish
ambassador set forth the reasons for his having been chosen: "Like the
Corneillian hero, you are a man who belongs to the Resistance, a rebel
who was able to give a meaning to the Absurd and to sustain from the
depths of the abyss the necessity for hope, even if it meant a difficult
hope, by giving back to creation, action, and human nobility their rightful
place in this senseless world." It seemed to him he was playing a role,
listening to remarks which applied only very imperfectly to his uncertainties. The welcome given by the French press to this distinction pained
him. The king is naked, they cried from the right; the crowning is a
burial beneath flowers; the Nobel prize crowns a gasping, academic body
of work. The rebel is nothing but a bourgeois, a Red Cross sermonizer,
replied some on the left. And as if to justify both of them, the most
favorable comments attempted to annex him, some of them to the
middle-of-the-road position, some of them to a spiritual position. And
finally, some sought to see a political choice in the decision: Camus,
under the circumstances, was the government's spokesman, whether for
one it meant honoring French Algeria or, for another, championing
liberal solutions.

Such quarrels could only exasperate him. He turned back toward his
childhood, paying the homage of his distinction to his mother, who had
never read his books, and to his schoolteacher, M. Germain. Received by
the Swedish ambassador, he had himself accompanied by several of his
comrades from his youth. He celebrated the prize among printers and
typographers, Spanish Republican exiles, and resistance comrades.[5] He
did everything as if to transfer to others, his friends, a part of the glory

[4] Letter to René Char (September 17, 1957).

[5] "I saw him again when we celebrated his Nobel Prize, in the midst of
Spanish Republicans, nobly exiled, poor, deprived in their material lives, de-
prived of their country, but rich in their convictions . . . That evening in
January, 1958, Camus, with that simplicity of language that was his strength,
explained himself: He wanted to be neither 'prince nor street-sweeper' " (Jacques
Piette, *Démocratie,* No. 60 [January 7, 1960]).

that weighed upon him: "The excessive honor that has been done me and which embarrasses me a little, I owe also to those who have taught me the rules and conduct of honest thought. *Nothing* for me is changed."[6] It was this permanency of youth, in spite of the years and the vicissitudes of existence, that he was determined to preserve.

At least, the Nobel Prize would give him the opportunity to clarify his own conception of his art. Never, in the course of his existence, had he wished to separate beauty from the fight for justice. "Why create if not to give a meaning to suffering, if it only be in seeing that it is unacceptable? If the artist cannot reject reality, it is because it is his responsibility to give it a higher justification. How justify it if one decides to ignore it? But how transfigure it if one consents to be subjugated by it?"[7] Having so said, he was opposed both to pure estheticism, to a return to art for art's sake whose adherents are increasing, as well as to "commitment" pure and simple or to "socialist realism."

Camus never hid the fact that literary techniques in themselves did not interest him. "The error of modern art is nearly always putting the means before the end, the form before the content, the technique before the subject matter."[8] Limited by his imagination, he did not intend to be limited either by an esthetic or by any style whatsoever. Style and esthetics, in his eyes, remained simple matters of procedure.

By contrast, his concern was with situation and meaning. The writer, placed in the world, caught in its backwash "must not be unaware of any of the dramas of his times . . . But he must also keep and take up again from time to time a certain distance with regard to our history. Every work of art presupposes a content of reality and a creator who fashions the container. Thus the artist, if he must share in the misfortunes of his age, must also tear himself away from them in order to consider them and give them form. This perpetual going back and forth, this tension which, to tell the truth, becomes more and more dangerous, is the task of today's artist."[9]

The Stockholm speeches say exactly the same thing. They transform

[5] Letter to M. Mathieu, who had been one of his lycée professors.
[7] Preface to the French edition of *The Ballad of Reading Gaol* (*La Ballade de la geôle de Reading*).
[8] *Venture* (December 20, 1960).
[9] *Demain* (October 24–30, 1952).

into theoretical terms, into categorical positions what was elaborated in doubtfulness: "The artist today walks in the night, groping, with the same footsteps as the man in the streets, incapable of separating himself from the world's suffering and passionately desirous of solitude and silence, dreaming of justice and a source of injustice himself, dragged along, when he thought to lead, behind a chariot larger than he is. In this exhausting adventure, the artist can only seek the help of others, and, like the others, he will seek help in pleasure, forgetfulness, and also in friendship and admiration. And like the others, he will seek help in hope."[10] All art consists in making of vice a virtue and of weakness a strength, in nourishing itself on its own suffering, in finding through words the unity of a disparate world, and in translating anguish into terms of equilibrium and tension.

The conflict between doubts, interior hesitations, and the search for a clear and forceful form of expression, explain a number of critical misunderstandings. It is true that commentators and readers have often underestimated Camus's mental reservations, his irony, that blind and instinctive part of himself which forms the substratum of an author's work. It is equally true that the concern for avoiding the mixing of genres often causes us to misconstrue. Reading an essay, we over-value its intellectual pretensions to the detriment of its elements of confession and protest. With a novel, we strive to find psychological insights which evade us. And yet, all "these different books . . . say the same thing."

Approach them as one will, one always finds in them the Absurd, revolt, and love.

The Absurd is the décor, human limits, the heavens' silence, the "hell" to which the entire human race is condemned. "By reason of my incapacity to reason beyond a lived experience, I place more confidence in a form of thought which leaves its future in uncertainty at the risk even of remaining a bit this side of the limits of its own intuition."[11] Lack of imagination? Algerian heritage? It does not really matter. But Camus's agnosticism, for all that, is not a source of comfort; it rarely stands without an accompanying obsession with the sacred or, if one prefers, the

[10] *Demain.*
[11] Letter to M. Nicolas (1955).

tragic. It is "passionate disbelief,"[12] which transforms itself into an intransigent relativism on the political level out of fear of some secret frenzy.

For revolt, which is action in this absurd décor, bursts forth first in delirium, in hatred of the self and the world, in desire for destruction, before being converted into creation. The "no" precedes the "yes," denial comes before acquiescence, even if one of the two terms never goes without the other. Little by little equilibrium is established; little by little the will to build prevails over the inclination to draw back, until the day when everything has to start over again. The rock that Sisyphus wished to raise on to the summit of the hill: does he let it roll back down out of fatigue, carelessness, or a kind of horror of ultimate achievement? That carefully woven canvas, that slowly conquered equilibrium, it seems sometimes that Camus casts them from himself, suddenly attracted by misfortune like Meursault at the moment of the murder. There are few works which are more luminous, more lucid, and which sometimes seem to be obscured by their own light, to thicken and become fixed like a blood-red sun sinking on the horizon.

Then love surges to the fore. The stubborn, animal-like love of the son for his mother, the obstinate love the foot bears the earth and the sky bears the waves, the desire of man for woman, or the heart-breaking tenderness of those who are going to die. Then, from the depths of misfortune, like an attack of nausea at the foot of the scaffold, there rises the solidarity of the defeated, the suffering, the humble, the victims, that solidarity which drew him to the events of his time when his indifference or his nostalgia drew him away from them.[13] This century, what a looking-glass! In it one finds barely restrained passions, barely stifled hatreds, but also dreams, ambitions, a face that grows wrinkled from year to year and that bitter fold at the corner of the mouth.

Everything is ambivalent, will-o'-the-wisp, fleeting. What is Meursault? A drifter or an Algerian full of life? A murderer or a victim? Is he indifferent by nature or by choice? A lover of life incapable of loving a woman? A quiet man who hates bombast and fiction?

---

[12] See the article with this title by Paul Viallaneix, *Revue des lettres modernes* (1968).

[13] He never ceased to express his revolt: against the invasion of Hungary by the Soviet Union, against the Falangist and South American dictatorships, against the repression in Greece or Iran, and, finally, to "take the side of freedom."

Who is Caligula? A Nazi, a Stalinist, a raving madman, a fancy talker, or a sorrowful comedian? What is the plague itself if not life—and therefore humanity—but also the inhumanity that each of us carries within him; all simultaneously, the ordinary and the days of wine and roses, the everyday and the exception. Everything is double, everything comes in couples: the right side and the wrong side, exile and the kingdom, solitude and solidarity, indifference and passion.

How can one seek to draw some lesson out of all that? "When someone spoke of me as a 'director' (someone, in sum, who teaches the right direction) a part of me, of course, swelled up with imbecilic vanity. But another part of me, during all those years, never ceased dying from shame."[14] What message can be found there? "I speak for no one; I have too much to do to find my own form of expression. I guide no one; I do not know, or I barely know, where I am going. I do not live on a tripod; I walk in the streets of our times with the same steps as everyone else."[15] How did one not see what uncertainties were hidden in that assurance in his voice, in that tension of his whole body bearing down on each word? And that he too had to judge despite his inclinations, to affirm in order to affirm himself, and to take positions because events or men required him to do so?

Moreover, he loved the fight, challenges; at the heart of detachment even, he created duties for himself. He raised his dikes; and, one day, the dikes gave way. Then he was seized with the desire to curse everything and to take on everything. "To love life, after all, is not only to enjoy its face of light, but to love also its face of darkness, to wish that it be, to bless the enemy, to look misfortune straight in the face."[16] To the lukewarm, the temperate, the lazy, it is necessary tirelessly to oppose revolt, which smashes comforts and privileges. To often salutary—but sometimes murderous—intransigence, one must in turn oppose moderation and acquiescence. Life lies in this tension and this delicate balancing act.

Shall we speak then of an evolution in his work? Yes and no. The lighting, the ingredients often changed; it was a matter of accentuation. "Far from there having been evolution in any one case, there was, on the

---

[14] October, 1953.
[15] *Venture* (December 20, 1959).
[16] Letter to M. Mathieu (December, 1958).

contrary, an obstinacy in presenting, within different genres, the individual aspects of a single work or a single undertaking."[17] The themes and the obsessions are indeed the same: innocence and judgment, life and death, happiness and misfortune, murder and its retribution, the sea and prisons. However, nothing is simple. "It is both true and false that there is nothing more in the notion of revolt and in the notion of the Absurd, and your proposition can be defended only on condition of taking for granted that no change in a body of thought is possible outside an ultimate broadening of it which opens it to the absolute."[18] Relativity and the Absurd always constitute the frame for life and reflection; its movement occurs in the form of a spiral within an unchanged landscape whose perspectives alone are modified. Through a seeming opportunism, conscious or instinctive, Camus wavers between Nietzsche and Socrates, between paganism and Christianity, between solitude and solidarity, without ever holding fast to any of them; he doubles himself within a moving existence, always dreaming of a unity which death alone could bring him.

It is now nearly ten years since he found that peace. His work has made its way. His theatre? It is played now and then, in France as well as abroad. Audiences are pleased with it and at the same time put off by it, by the interplay of symbols, but a certain cerebrality. Through his rejection of psychology, he takes his place in the modern current which turns away from states of soul to deal with the eternal tragic: the murderous logic at work in history, revolt and its scruples, misunderstandings, a certain human condition composed of face-to-face fraternity and inhumanity. Passions, yes, but collective passions in a pure state. And if *Caligula* remains the most haunting of these plays, it is because it echoes with the painful cry of a dissatisfied youth, driven to murder or suicide by the very excess of their generous ambitions.

One senses the same impatience quivering in the early essays: an awkward and distressed tenderness for what will perish in *L'Envers et l'endroit,* the hymn of love and death in *Noces,* haughty defiance of the forces of destiny in *Le Mythe de Sisyphe.* We pass from deliberate greyness to exploding lyricism to reach a culmination in a kind of

[17] From a manuscript note.
[18] Letter to M. Nicolas.

shimmering lucidity. But Camus is less at ease in acceptance than he is in refusal. We feel the effort, the constraint, the stiff smile of him who is determined to convince during the very moment in which he doubts. For him, nothing equals indignation, that reaction of one's whole physical being against injustice, those explosions of a profound anarchy. *L'Homme révolté,* which without any doubt will take its place in the history of thought in our times, appears no less stiff, awkwardly decked out in moderation as in a Sunday suit. This paving stone tossed into the stagnant pool of our times comes wrapped with precautions, as if Camus, in this delirious universe, was showing us the quiet disarray to which the drama of Algeria would reduce him.

But it will be enough to toss this paving stone back at him for him to unleash, grimacing, a fund of restrained vehemence. Prosecutors to the pillory! And all those who wanted to be reassured for anxiously standing beyond the fray. No more father confessor, no more guide. True morality makes light of morality; it comes into being by way of a preliminary demoralization, through irony or derision.

Camus is never so much at ease, literarily speaking, as when he disturbs. *L'Étranger* and *La Chute,* indeed, *La Peste,* when it takes upon itself the whole of the world's inhumanity, plunge us into an invigorating distress. Negative works, to be sure, in that they dispel comfort, self-satisfaction, and conformism—even when it is the comfort of anti-conformism—shock-pieces whose effects recreate themselves in successive waves, like a stone let go into placid waters. Then an entire secret world reawakens, our image is muddled, and facts are wiped out. But this skillfully exploited confusion is expressed in a clear and measured language, by way of myths strongly rooted as in *L'Étranger,* or volatile to the point of dizziness as in *La Chute.*

In a certain sense, Camus's entire work is only a dialectic between fixity and movement. On the one hand, the deep implantation in the soil, the native land, the attachment to the mother, to the past, the fidelity to oneself as a prime virtue. On the other a mobile world, fluid, like the sea itself, a perpetual mutation and the vertigo which clutches us. On the one hand, the myth of Greece; on the other, the myth of modernity. Like each of us, but more so than each of us, Camus had lived this division. How many times did he not reaffirm his solidarity with our age? How many times did he not let his nostalgia and his hesitations show through? "After so many months, I know nothing about New York, and whether one walks about here among madmen or among the most reasonable people in the world; whether life is as easy as all America says it is, or if it is as empty as it sometimes appears to be there . . . whether New Yorkers are liberals or conformists, modest souls or dead souls." Replace New York with our universe and carry on: "yes, I am losing my footing. I am finding out that it is with cities as with certain women who irritate you, who push you about, who flay your soul, the precious scar of which you bear on your entire body, scandal and delectation all at the same time . . . It is thus that I bear New York within me, as one carries about a foreign body in one's eye, unbearable and delightful, with tears of compassion and mad urges to deny everything."[19]

Nothing is simple: irritation has its delights and exile its charm. Everything is contradiction: solitude is a refuge as much as a torment; one can simultaneously do battle and dream of peace, strike without hatred and extend a helping hand. One can press every being in the world close to oneself and be defended against nothing; on the other hand, there is a beauty in the world which gives you the courage to brave prisons.

No, Camus is not a modern, since he likes neither the mechanical nor efficiency. And yet he is more modern than anyone else, since he lived and represented our heartbreaks, our disarrays, our dreams, and our longings; since he held off despair unendingly without sinking into hope, he held off ugliness without succumbing to estheticism; since he felt intuitively that transition is henceforth our lot; since he created without ever forgetting that works of art, like civilizations, are mortal.

A humanist? Yes, insofar as he limits his outlook to the earth on which men live and die, without ignoring any of those things that haunt them, the relative or the sacred, honor or abandon, happiness or torment, without refusing any of their battles. An anxious humanism, which leaves us no repose, embarked as we are upon a shoreless sea of history. And a moralist, too, if one likes, without a defined morality, painting men and himself, their ambitions, their anxieties and their passions, reaffirming "in

[19] *Pluies de New York.*

the heart of our age, counter to the Machiavellians, counter to the golden calf of realism, the existence of the moral fact."[20] But he was completely an artist, who mimed the universe and raised up therein a few reference points in the form of myths. "To deny that creation may in itself be a source of values comes down to hindering history from ever being creative and art from ever being truly revolutionary."[21] And these values which he illustrated, he kept fast in his closed fist. But, as he never ceased to repeat, everything remained to be done. Haunted by his youth, even by his childhood, he set out in search of a father with the hope of discovering himself. "He sees the father take a vague form. Then everything fades. Finally, there is nothing. Thus it was always on this earth . . ."[22] But no. Sartre rightly said: "Every life that is stopped—even that of so young a man—is both a record that ceases playing and a complete life."[23] This work, which we have followed in its living movement, now mutilated, we have to see as a totality. So many questions that remain in the air! And yet, in this irrevocable silence, Albert Camus's books have not finished questioning us.

[20] Sartre, "Albert Camus, 1960."
[21] "Présentation," in *Valeurs.*
[22] Note for *Le Premier Homme.*
[23] "Albert Camus, 1960."

Bibliographical Note

All of Camus's published writings, except for his note-books (*Carnets,* vols. I and II) and a few articles, have been reprinted in a two-volume critical edition edited by Roger Quilliot:

Théâtre, récits, nouvelles. Paris: Editions de la Pléiade, 1963.

Essais. Paris: Editions de la Pléiade, 1965. The Pléiade edition also includes useful supplementary documentation in the form of letters, articles, previously unpublished notes and fragments, etc.

CAMUS'S MAJOR WORKS IN ENGLISH TRANSLATION

Caligula and Three Other Plays. Translated by Stuart Gilbert. New York: Alfred A. Knopf, 1958.

Exile and the Kingdom. Translated by Justin O'Brien. New York: Alfred A. Knopf, 1957. (Also available, along with *The Fall,* in a Modern Library edition.)

Lyrical and Critical Essays. Translated by Ellen Conroy Kennedy. New York: Alfred A. Knopf, 1968.

The Myth of Sisyphus. Translated by Justin O'Brien. New York: Alfred A. Knopf, 1955. (Also in a Vintage paperback edition.)

Notebooks: 1935–42. Translated by Philip Thody. New York: Alfred A. Knopf, 1963. (Also in a Modern Library edition.)

Notebooks: 1942–51. Translated by Philip Thody. New York: Alfred A. Knopf, 1965.

The Plague. Translated by Stuart Gilbert. New York: Alfred A. Knopf, 1948. (Also in a Vintage paperback edition.)

The Possessed. Translated by Justin O'Brien. New York: Alfred A. Knopf, 1960.

The Rebel. Translated by Anthony Bower. New York: Alfred A. Knopf, 1954. (Also in a Vintage paperback edition.)

Resistance, Rebellion and Death. Translated by Justin O'Brien. New York: Alfred A. Knopf, 1960. (Also in a Modern Library edition.)

The Stranger. Translated by *Stuart Gilbert.* New York: Alfred A. Knopf,
    1946. (Also in a Vintage paperback edition.)
Speech of Acceptance upon the Award of the Nobel Prize for Literature.
    Translated by Justin O'Brien. New York: Alfred A. Knopf, 1958.
    (Also printed in *The Atlantic Monthly* [May, 1958], pp. 33–34.)

BIBLIOGRAPHICAL STUDIES

Bollinger, Renate. Albert Camus: *Eine Bibliographie der Literatur über
    ihn und sein Werk.* Köln: Greven Verlag, 1957.
Crépin, Simone. *Albert Camus: Essai de Bibliographie.* Bruxelles: Com-
    mission Belge de Bibliographie, 1960.
Fitch, Brian T. *Calepins de bibliographie, Albert Camus, 1937–1962.*
    Paris: Minard, Lettres Modernes, 1965.
Roeming, Robert F. *Camus: A Bibliography.* Madison: The University
    of Wisconsin Press, 1968.

BOOKS ON CAMUS AND HIS WORK IN ENGLISH

Brée, Germaine. *Camus.* Rev. ed. New Brunswick: Rutgers University
    Press, 1961.
Burnier, Michel-Antoine. *Choice of Action: The French Existentialists
    on the Political Front Line.* Translated by Bernard Murchland,
    with an additional chapter by the translator: "Sartre and Camus—
    The Anatomy of a Quarrel." New York: Random House, 1968.
    Vintage Books edition 1969.
Cruickshank, John. *Albert Camus and the Literature of Revolt.* New
    York: Oxford University Press, 1960.
Hanna, Thomas. *The Thought and Art of Albert Camus.* Chicago: Henry
    Regnery Co., 1958.
Maquet, Albert. *Albert Camus: The Invincible Summer.* Translated by
    Herma Brissault. New York: George Braziller, 1958.
Onimus, Jean. *Albert Camus and Christianity.* Tuscaloosa: The University
    of Alabama Press, 1970.
Parker, Emmett. *Albert Camus: The Artist in the Arena.* Madison: The
    University of Wisconsin Press, 1965.
Thody, Philip. *Albert Camus: 1913–1960.* London: Hamish Hamilton,
    1961. (This is a revised and augmented edition of *Albert Camus:
    A Study of His Work* [New York: Grove Press, 1959].)

Index

126834